The Unique and Universal Christ

The Unique and Universal Christ

Refiguring the Theology of Religions

Drew Collins

BAYLOR UNIVERSITY PRESS

Cover and book design by Kasey McBeath
Cover art: Shutterstock/pluie_r

The Library of Congress has cataloged this book under ISBN 978-1-4813-1549-4.
Library of Congress Control Number: 2021939823

Printed in the United States of America on acid-free paper with a minimum of thirty percent recycled content.

For my mother, Andrea Shaffer Collins

Contents

Preface

Who is Jesus to those who do not know him? Who are those who do not know him to those who do? Can "we" who follow Jesus meet him in "those" who do not? Can we grow in understanding of and faith in Jesus through our encounters with those who do not profess to understand him, much less have faith in him? Does the particularity of God's self-revelation in Jesus of Nazareth preclude the possibility of God's revelatory presence in communities and traditions in which Jesus is a stranger?

This book is about these questions, because these questions nearly cost me my faith.

Throughout my childhood, my Jewish mother took me and my brother to a Lutheran church on Sundays while my Presbyterian father either worked or enjoyed a precious few moments of sleep. When I was eleven, my mother, my brother, and I were baptized together with water from the River Jordan that our pastor had brought back with him from a trip to the Holy Land. We still have the baptismal water in little plastic bottles. There was much rejoicing over this in our church and our nuclear family. Even my mother's Jewish family were not too bothered by it.

I too rejoiced. Being baptized alongside my mother, being reborn alongside the woman who had born me was an indescribably powerful experience. But it also filled me, for the first time, with a sense of dread. My mother's conversion made clear the religious divide within my family in ways it had not been clear before. Her newfound faith in Jesus underscored her parents' and extended family's lack of faith in him.

Four years later, I stopped calling myself a Christian and would refrain from doing so for almost five years. The problem was not the reality of religious pluralism itself. Despite what many books on the "theology of religions" would have us believe, neither the sheer fact of religious plural-ism nor Christians' firsthand experience of living in contexts character-ized by it are new. They are as old as the faith itself. Many of the questions that orient the theology of religions are particularly salient questions for our time and place, but they have been the questions of times before ours and of places far from where I write today. Many hands have been wrung over the apparent tensions that arise from the dual affirmation of Jesus' historical particularity alongside his universal import.

What plagued me was not the question of what it means for Chris-tians to have faith in a historically particular yet universal savior. The problem, I came to see only much later, was *why and how* the question was being asked. Time and again, books exploring the Christian theol-ogy of religions insist we find ourselves today in uncharted theological territory. And indeed, there is some truth to this. For while the reality of religious pluralism is not new to Christian faith, *other concerns* that it gives rise to are. These concerns have to do not with pluralism but with plausibility. Put bluntly, the Christian theology of religions is a discourse dedicated above all else to exploring questions concerning the philosoph-ical (broadly construed) plausibility of Christian faith, a pursuit in which other faiths and their adherents have become mere pawns. Other religions and their adherents are treated not as ends, not as the subjects of the theol-ogy of religion itself, but simply as opportunities for exploring *truly* press-ing questions concerning the philosophy of history, epistemology, and biblical hermeneutics. Such questions in and of themselves have no direct bearing on the issue of religious pluralism itself, but are instead oriented around those aspects or articles of Christian faith that might seem the most outlandish to current sensibilities, such as the metaphysical cogency of the Chalcedonian definition of Jesus' full humanity and full divinity, the epistemological warrant of faith in the transcendent, and the status of scripture and scriptural interpretation in the light of such questions.

Is the incarnation itself, not to mention the miracles and resurrection of Jesus, a legitimate belief by today's standards? Relatedly, what con-stitutes a legitimate source for religious belief? And what do the "rea-sonable" answers to these questions, which appear to be at odds with the scriptural narrative of the New Testament, mean for the way we can read scripture such that its meaningfulness is protected even as its plain syntactical sense is rejected?

These questions lie at the heart of the theology of religions discourse as we find it today. Yet they are not questions that emerge from the fact or experience of religious pluralism itself, but from the Enlightenment. Certainly, they were not my questions, at least insofar as religious pluralism was concerned. My concerns about religious pluralism did not arise from a preceding worry about the philosophical plausibility of Christian faith, but from a realization that I did not understand how Jesus could be utterly particular as a human and yet be said to have an abiding universal presence. My question was not "In light of the reality of religious pluralism and the philosophical difficulties with certain related aspects of Christian faith, is my faith in Jesus as the incarnate Son of God, crucified, died, resurrected, and ascended, philosophically reasonable?" But more simply, "How is the uniqueness of Jesus' identity connected to his continuing presence to creation?"

To the extent that religious pluralism provides us with an opportunity to reflect on certain philosophical issues, one can see how the two matters might have become intertwined. But there is a world of difference between pursuing an explicitly philosophical exploration of Christian faith wherein religious pluralism bears consideration, and the pursuit of an implicitly philosophical apologetic for faith in the transcendent masquerading as a Christian theological account of religious pluralism. And for me, the overwhelming orientation of the theology of religions around philosophical apologetics, and the seemingly unavoidable implication that to affirm Christian orthodoxy, such as a Chalcedonian Christology, is equivalent to relegating the non-Christian world to a realm outside the purview of God's love and presence, led me, for a time, to abandon my faith in Jesus altogether.

Ironically, the price of affirming the very possibility of God's presence in the lives of non-Christians was supposedly to do away with the Jesus I had encountered in the Gospels all over again, rendering him not as divine but as enlightened, as an exemplar of profound moral and/or spiritual significance. It took me years to move past that question insofar as it had been a roadblock to my own Christian faith. It took writing this book to see that the generosity of Christian orthodoxy, the generosity of Jesus Christ's particular identity, is itself the foundation on which our hope for Christ's surprising and abiding presence in the world, to Christians and non-Christians alike, rests.

Acknowledgments

I am deeply indebted to Professor David F. Ford for his initial confidence both in the significance of this topic for contemporary Christianity and in the possibility of discerning new and important horizons for Christian theological engagement with individuals, communities, and traditions beyond the Christian faith. Many thanks also to Professor Emma Wild-Wood, who was instrumental in helping me to recognize the significance of the ecumenical movement in the twentieth century both in making the question of the "theology of religions" of central concern for Christian theology and in advancing a surplus of models and theories in answer to it. Without their joint influence and guidance, this work would not have been possible.

I am particularly grateful to Mike Higton, Ian McFarland, Ben Fulford, and Paul Weston for the invaluable feedback they gave on this project at various stages in its development. It is a different, and undoubtedly a greatly improved piece of work, thanks to their input.

Profound thanks also to Professor Miroslav Volf, who as my undergraduate advisor, friend, boss, and the first Christian theologian I ever read, has influenced my theological interests and sensibilities in so many ways. I discover areas of his influence on my thinking anew nearly every day. I am thankful for the advice and support of my colleagues, past and present, at the Yale Center for Faith & Culture—Matt Croasmun, Sarah Farmer, Angela Gorrell, Justin Crisp, and Ryan McAnnally-Linz. Deepest thanks also to another colleague at Yale, Willie James Jennings, whose work transformed both my understanding of the nature of the problem(s) with which I had been concerned and my hopes for the future of the Christian theology of religions.

Thank you to my parents, Tim and Andrea, for their unwavering encouragement and support. There are no words to express the depth of gratitude I owe my wife, Mary. Her selfless love has been a source of constant encouragement, even as it is something I all too often take for granted. To my parents, my wife, and our wonderful children—Agatha, Archie, and Wilfred—I love you all. Thank you for everything.

1

Introduction

What Is the Christian Theology of Religions?

The questions raised by religious pluralism themselves are as old as Christian faith: Who is the unique figure of Jesus, identified as the Son of God in Christian communities of faith, to those who live outside of those contexts? How is the comprehensiveness of God's concern for creation to be understood in light of the variety of apparent limitations imposed on humanity's awareness of it, stemming from this account of God's self-revelation in Jesus? These are questions Jesus fields and even raises himself (cf. Matt 7:13-23, 25:34-46; Luke 10:21-37; John 2:11-21). Yet the Christian theology of religions is a discourse that was acknowledged only in the late twentieth century as a theological subdiscipline in its own right. From the start of the century up to the 1960s–1970s, this as yet unnamed discourse was mainly explored as a matter of missiology. While these conversations were diverse and admitted a wide range of contrasting perspectives, the (anachronistically titled) Christian theology of religions of the first half of the twentieth century is broadly characterized by its focus on exploring the relationship between Jesus Christ's theological and historical particularity and the universality of his significance; how, if at all, Christian missionaries might discern Jesus' presence beyond Christian tradition and community, and what is at stake in such discernment.

This last aspect regarding the stakes of Christological discernment has been phrased carefully so as to include but not limit the stakes to the question of salvation. Indeed, while soteriology was never far from the fray, it appears generally to be the case that it was not the primary question. The theology of religions in this period had recognized and perhaps unavoidable soteriological implications, but was not itself primarily construed soteriologically. It was, rather, missiological and therefore concerned with the relationship between Christianity and other religions in a more comprehensive or wholistic way, as one concerning not just the afterlife but our life together, here and now. *Who is Jesus to Christians? Who is Jesus to those who are not Christians? And, in light of these answers, who are we to each other?* Willie Jennings writes that, within Christianity, there is "a breathtakingly powerful way to imagine and enact the social, to imagine and enact connection and belonging."[1] The question of belonging, of the identity of the God revealed in Jesus to whom humanity belongs and how the answer to that shapes how we imagine and enact belonging with and to each other, was at the heart of the matter.

Yet as the missiological context for the question receded, and as the threat of secularism came ever closer into view, the question became increasingly oriented around the notion of religious truth and its soteriological implications. No longer was the question asked by and for particular people in particular places, seeking to understand how to imagine and enact their lives together. Indeed, while the ecumenical movement continued to pursue questions concerning the theology of religions, the center of gravity has shifted away from missiology.

Instead, it became an abstract and academic matter. Jacques Dupuis points to the 1960s as the period in which "the possibility of a positive role played by the other religions for the salvation of their members became an object of theological reflection in its own right," identifying 1973 as the year in which the first "synthetic treatment" of the theology of religions was produced by V. Boublik. Paul Hedges cites Owen Thomas as an earlier example (1969) of "the first formal distinction of theologies of religions into different types."[2]

At the same time, worries about advancing secularism and the plausibility of Christian faith, particularly in light of trenchant historical and epistemological criticisms, were beginning to dominate these very same contexts, ecumenical and academic. So, it is perhaps not surprising that concerns over salvation and apologetics appear to have coalesced into one, framed in terms

---

[1]   Willie James Jennings, *The Christian Imagination: Theology and the Origins of Race* (New Haven, Conn.: Yale University Press, 2010), 4.

[2]   Jacques Dupuis, *Toward a Christian Theology of Religious Pluralism* (Maryknoll, N.Y.: Orbis, 1997), 2–3; V. Boublik, *Teologia delle religioni* (Rome: Studium, 1973); Paul Hedges, "A Reflection on Typologies," in *Christian Approaches to Other Faiths*, ed. Alan Race and Paul M. Hedges (London: SCM Press, 2008), 25; Owen C. Thomas, ed., *Attitudes toward Other Religions: Some Christian Interpretations* (London: SCM Press, 1969).

of the *experience* of salvation. This approach, at least in ecumenical circles, became most closely associated with liberation theology and its concern for social justice, thereby preserving the concern for imagining and enacting connection and belonging within and between peoples.[3] But, in its most influential and well-known form today, the question of salvation construed in terms of religious experience has been pursued not politically, but philosophically by academics such as John Hick and Wilfred Cantwell Smith.

Then, in the early 1980s, Alan Race put forward a threefold typological overview of the Christian theology of religions in *Christians and Religious Pluralism*.[4] Significantly, Race describes the question behind the theology of religions rather differently from the World Council of Churches (WCC). Maintaining the tension between the particular and the universal, Race omits reference to Jesus Christ and instead casts the issue as one concerning transcendent religious experience: "How then should Christians respond theologically to the experience of . . . the 'transcendent vision of human transformation' ('salvation,' to use the Christian term) at the heart of the religiously other?"

To map out the possible answers, Race suggests the categories of "exclusivism," "inclusivism," and "pluralism." Other typologies or maps have subsequently been put forward, and Race's original typology has also been amended by making each type plural, in a nod to the variety within each type.[5] The so-called postmodern fourth type of "particularism" has also been added.[6] Some have taken issue with the very notion of

---

[3]   E.g., the WCC's Commission of World Mission and Evangelism Bangkok Assembly in 1972–1973, "Salvation Today," in *Bangkok Assembly, 1973: Minutes and Report of the Assembly of the Commission on World Mission and Evangelism of the World Council of Churches, December 31, 1972 and January 9–12, 1973* (Geneva: WCC, 1973).

[4]   Alan Race, *Christians and Religious Pluralism: Patterns in the Christian Theology of Religions* (London: SCM Press, 1993).

[5]   Hedges, "Reflection on Typologies," 27.

[6]   Alan Race, *Making Sense of Religious Pluralism: Shaping Theology of Religions for Our Times* (London: SPCK, 2013), 44–54; cf. Paul M. Hedges, "The Interrelationship of Religions: A Critical Examination of the Concept of Particularity," *World Faiths Encounter* 32 (2002): 3–13; Paul Hedges, "Particularities: Tradition-Specific Postmodern Perspectives," in Race and Hedges, *Christian Approaches*, 112–35.

For different approaches to the organization of different Christian theologies of religions, see David Bosch, *Transforming Mission: Paradigm Shifts in Theology of Mission* (Maryknoll, N.Y.: Orbis, 2011), 185–94; Veli-Matti Kärkkäinen, *An Introduction to the Theology of Religions: Biblical, Historical, and Contemporary Perspectives* (Downers Grove, Ill.: IVP, 2003); Paul Knitter, *Introducing Theologies of Religions* (Maryknoll, N.Y.: Orbis, 2002).

a theology of religions, suggesting that the entire project is itself perhaps overburdened with a priori commitments which renders even pluralism incapable of supporting actual interfaith engagement, and that the path forward involves disciplines such as Comparative Theology.[7]

In what follows, I will argue that the familiar typology of exclusivism, inclusivism, and pluralism is not simply incomplete, as if more categories are needed, and not simply defective, as if it merely fails to describe its objects, but that it only arises in light of and attends to concerns about the philosophical legitimacy of religious faith. As David Kelsey notes at the start of *Eccentric Existence*, a reader is "entitled to know at the outset whether a book addresses questions you—or anyone else—really ask . . . framing the question correctly lies at the heart of the matter."[8] In a sense, it is this task, raised in the context of Race's typology, that motivates what follows. *The question concerning Christianity's relationship to other traditions—in terms of both what the possibilities are and their relative merits—is too important to be framed as simply subsidiary to Christian theology's philosophical plausibility.* This is not to say that questions concerning the philosophical legitimacy of various Christian doctrines and beliefs are insignificant, much less illegitimate. But what is unwarranted is the quiet transposition of this set of questions onto those more directly pertaining to and arising from the empirical fact of religious pluralism.

Yet a vast quantity of theology of religions scholarship has taken Race's tripartite typology as in some way constitutive of the discipline as a whole.[9] Those who propose alternatives do so in reference to it, and even those who develop alternative approaches often end up falling back upon the three-

---

[7]   Cf. John Berthrong and Francis X. Clooney, editors' introduction to "European Perspectives on the New Comparative Theology," *Religions* 3, no. 4 (2012): 1196–97. See also Marianne Moyaert, "Recent Developments in the Theology of Interreligious Dialogue: From Soteriological Openness to Hermeneutical Openness," *Modern Theology* 28, no. 1 (2012): 45–47.

[8]   David Kelsey, *Eccentric Existence: A Theological Anthropology* (Louisville, Ky.: Westminster John Knox, 2009), 1.

[9]   See Perry Schmidt-Leukal, "Exclusivism, Inclusivism, Pluralism," in *The Myth of Religious Superiority*, ed. Paul. F. Knitter (Maryknoll, N.Y.: Orbis, 2003), 13–27; John Hick, "The Non-absoluteness of Christianity," in *The Myth of Christian Uniqueness*, ed. John Hick and Paul Knitter (Eugene, Ore.: Wipf & Stock, 1987), 16–36; Stanley J. Samartha, "The Cross and the Rainbow," in Hick and Knitter, *Myth of Christian Uniqueness*, 69–88; Raimondo Panikkar, "The Jordan, the Tiber, and the Ganges," in Hick and Knitter, *Myth of Christian Uniqueness*, 103; Tom F. Driver, "The Case for Pluralism," in Hick and Knitter, *Myth of Christian Uniqueness*, 203–18.

fold typology.[10] Terry Muck refers to Race's typology simply as "The Paradigm" in view of its astounding prevalence.[11] Muck asserts elsewhere that Race's typology has been employed, whether approvingly or critically, by the majority of scholars in the field of theology of religions, thanks to its having been taken up (with slight shifts in terminology) in the work of John Hick and Paul Knitter, who "set the agenda for the burgeoning field [of theology of religions] during this second wave of interest in the eighties and nineties."[12] Other prominent theologians who have used the typology or have advocated for one of its types over the others include Gavin D'Costa, Francis Clooney, S. Mark Heim, Alvin Plantinga, and Schubert Ogden.[13]

This book is about the Christian theology of religions in general and how it is shaped by accounts of the relationship between Jesus' particularity and God's universal presence. But any analysis of the current state of the Christian theology of religions, especially along these lines, must pay special attention to Race's typology. As a theoretical apparatus intended not just to

[10]   See Moyaert, "Recent Developments," 46; David Pitman, *Twentieth Century Christian Responses to Religious Pluralism* (Farnham, UK: Ashgate, 2014); S. Mark Heim, *Salvations: Truth and Difference in Religion* (Maryknoll, N.Y.: Orbis, 1995); idem, *The Depth of Riches: A Trinitarian Theology of Religious Ends* (Grand Rapids: Eerdmans, 2001); Schubert M. Ogden, *Is There Only One True Religion or Are There Many?* (Dallas: Southern Methodist University Press, 1992); Joseph A. DiNoia, *The Diversity of Religions: A Christian Perspective* (Washington, D.C.: Catholic University of America Press, 1992); Dupuis, *Toward a Christian Theology*, 305–16; Terry C. Muck, "Instrumentality, Complexity, and Reason: A Christian Approach to Religions," *Buddhist-Christian Studies* 22 (2002): 115–21; Bosch, *Transforming Mission*, 489–94; Gavin D'Costa, "Christ, the Trinity, and Religious Plurality," in *Christian Uniqueness Reconsidered: The Myth of a Pluralistic Theology of Religions*, ed. Gavin D'Costa (Maryknoll, N.Y.: Orbis, 1990), 16–29; Christoph Schwöbel, "Particularity, Universality, and the Religions," in D'Costa, *Christian Uniqueness Reconsidered*, 30–46; Francis X. Clooney, S.J., "Reading the World in Christ," in D'Costa, *Christian Uniqueness Reconsidered*, 63–80; John B. Cobb Jr., "Beyond 'Pluralism,'" in D'Costa, *Christian Uniqueness Reconsidered*, 81–95; Alvin Plantinga, "Pluralism: A Defense of Religious Exclusivism," in *The Rationality of Belief and the Plurality of Faith*, ed. Thomas D. Senor (Ithaca, N.Y.: Cornell University Press, 1995), 191–215. Even Paul Knitter, who suggests a typology drawn up around denominational and ethical lines, affirms that "Race's 'types' . . . and my models evince an amazing and confirming similarity. Our studies will complement each other." Paul Knitter, *No Other Name? A Critical Survey of Christian Attitudes toward the World Religions* (London: SCM Press, 1977), xiv.

[11]   Muck, "Instrumentality, Complexity, and Reason," 115.

[12]   Terry C. Muck, "Theology of Religions after Knitter and Hick: Beyond the Paradigm," *Interpretation* 61, no. 1 (2001): 7.

[13]   Cf. D'Costa, "Christ, the Trinity, and Religious Plurality," 16–29; Clooney, "Reading the World in Christ," 63–80; Joseph A. DiNoia, "Pluralist Theology of Religions," in D'Costa, *Christian Uniqueness Reconsidered*, 119–34; Heim, *Depth of Riches*, 8; Plantinga, "Pluralism," 191–215; Ogden, *Only One True Religion*, x.

describe the possibilities for the theology of religions but also to affirm the preeminence of pluralism as the best type—the only type that is in accord with the dictates of contemporary intellectual credibility, or what Race calls "critical thought"—the typology's theological priorities and philosophical assumptions are of particular interest for such an interrogation.[14]

It is tempting either to designate Race's typology as an outworking of his own brand of theological liberalism, or to point out the exclusivist undertones of pluralism itself. Indeed, this has often been the basic criticism of theological pluralism.[15] But to limit this criticism to the pluralistic type alone is not enough. Indeed, others have pointed out the limitations of Race's typology, sometimes also offering alternative typologies that present a range of additional or alternative positions within the Christian theology of religions.[16] Some of these criticisms have acknowledged the apologetic objectives of Race's entire typology, noting that Race's affirmation of pluralism's preeminence is tied to his response to criticisms against religious belief in general.

Accepting its apologetic emphasis vis-à-vis pluralism, Race's outlining of exclusivism and inclusivism is therein revealed to also be inherently polemical, as it is these kinds of religious faith which Race believes undermine the reasonableness of all religious faith. Mystifyingly, this has not dissuaded theologians from aligning themselves with exclusivism or inclusivism. A large part of what follows will therefore be devoted to demonstrating that the typology is fundamentally an apologetic polemic in favor of pluralism rather than an attempt at sensitive description. Implicit in this critique is that the alternative types of exclusivism and inclusivism are themselves innately inadequate and fatally flawed. Perhaps more importantly, the analysis of Race's typology will focus on something that has been largely absent from this conversation: a consideration of how Race's approach to the theology

---

[14]   Race, *Christians and Religious Pluralism*, viii.

[15]   E.g., Gavin D'Costa, "The Impossibility of a Pluralist View of Religions," *Religious Studies* 32, no. 2 (1996): 223–32; Heim, *Salvations*, 99ff.; Joseph A. DiNoia, "Varieties of Religious Aims: Beyond Exclusivism, Inclusivism and Pluralism," in *Theology and Dialogue*, ed. Bruce D. Marshall (Notre Dame, Ind.: University of Notre Dame Press, 1990), 252f.

[16]   Ian Markham, "Creating Options: Shattering the 'Exclusivist, Inclusivist, and Pluralist' Paradigm," *New Blackfriars* 74, no. 867 (1993): 33–41; E. L. Copeland, "Christian Theology and World Religions," *Review and Expositor* 94 (1997): 423–35; Paul Varo Martinson, *A Theology of World Religions: Interpreting God, Self, and World in Semitic, Indian and Chinese Thought* (Minneapolis: Augsburg, 1987), 200–11; Ted Peters, *God—The World's Future: Systematic Theology for a Postmodern Era* (Minneapolis: Fortress, 1992), 339–49; DiNoia, "Varieties of Religious Aims," 249–74.

of religions as presented in his typology reflects a very specific, and controversial, understanding of the nature of Christian theology itself. In what follows, it will be suggested that in the context of the theology of religions, it is not the conclusions of any one type but *the construal of Christian theology itself* that merits typological consideration.

Nonetheless, to dismiss Race's typology without first attempting to understand its premises and logic inevitably also means talking past those who uphold (wittingly or not) its descriptive power. Moreover, a thorough interrogation of his theological rationale, priorities, and assumptions will aid us in an attempt to resituate the theology of religions within a typology better suited to the task of sensitively describing the possibilities for Christian theology's account of different faiths—possibilities that are not just theoretical, but which have already emerged over the course of history. In so doing, this book will suggest that the theology of religions discourse would be greatly aided by a typology that did not posit an immutable, inverse relationship between a theology's hospitality to Jesus Christ—as the unique and unsubstitutable person at the center of Christian faith—and its capacity to generally affirm and particularly discern the presence of God outside Christian tradition and community.

Race's typology and its three categories—themselves formed in light of the work of thinkers like the philosopher of history Ernst Troeltsch, the philosopher of religion John Hick, and the comparative religious scholar and hermeneutician Wilfred Cantwell Smith—have become the framework against which all other theology of religions accounts must contend. But this is only the first step.

The problems with Race's philosophically prioritized approach to theology, and the typology he creates in this light, will be shown first in relation to the account of Christian theology provided by Hans Frei, and second in relation to the actual history of Protestant ecumenical discussion on the relationship between Christianity and world religions. The Protestant ecumenical movement, first through the International Missionary Council (IMC) and later through the WCC, was an unwavering, and often pioneering, advocate for the significance of theological engagement between Christians and non-Christians for almost the entirety of the twentieth century. Its ecumenical councils served as forums for working out the basis and objectives of interfaith engagement in ways acceptable for large swathes of Western Christianity and provided enormous resources for creating and supporting opportunities for such engagement between Christian and non-Christian communities. It is a basic assumption of this book that any typology of Christian theology and the relationship between it and other traditions must strive to be descriptively attuned to the variety manifested in the ecumenical movement, as a real, sizable, and theologically diverse Christian community whose statements and positions therefore merit consideration as theologically legitimate possibilities. Not only will engagement with Frei's theology and methodological analyses show Race's approach to be symptomatic of a particular and problematic trend in modern theology, but the survey of the ecumenical history will show Race's typology to have very little descriptive use in relation to Protestant ecumenical history. In other words, it will be argued that Race's typology is neither theologically sound nor historically illuminating.

We will turn instead to Frei's fivefold typology as an indispensable means of discerning the differences across Christian theologies of religions vis-à-vis their different construals of Christian theology between the poles of theology as *Wissenschaft* and theology as self-description.[17] It will be demonstrated that Frei's typology provides a better means of discerning the different commitments at the root of various Christian theologies in general and theologies of religions in particular. Moreover, it will also be suggested that in delineating the diversity of approaches in this way, Frei is able to helpfully and productively demonstrate the ineradicable, and fruitful, tension which exists for Christian theology as it is pulled between these poles.

Constructively, we will consider Frei's theological work on the nature of Christian interpretation of the Bible (the synoptic Gospels in particular) and his analysis of the critical and constructive interplay between Christian theology as philosophy and as self-description. Unlike Race's prioritizing of philosophical concerns related to the nature of history and knowledge, Frei will foreground hermeneutical, or more accurately *exegetical*, considerations. Frei's construal of Christian theology is primarily rooted in a reading of the Gospels emphasizing the *sensus literalis*, conceived as a unity between the apparent syntactical sense of the Gospel narratives and their ecclesial interpretation. This, in turn, grounds a vision of a *figural* Christology which provides Christians with a versatile and nuanced vision of the unique identity of Christ in relation to the universality of Christ's presence, pointing to the theological fruits inherent in Christian engagement with non-Christians. Following Frei, it will be argued that such theological fruit is born not out of one's philosophically

---

[17]   Hans Frei, *Types of Christian Theology*, ed. George Hunsinger and William C. Placher (New Haven, Conn.: Yale University Press, 1992), 2.

motivated inclination to place Christology on the theological chopping block, as Race would have it, but rather precisely by virtue of the figural implications of a robust affirmation of something like a Chalcedonian Christology, which with all doctrine might be viewed as a fragmentary, potentially revisable, but presently adequate "statement that renders a true description" of Jesus Christ.[18] As Frei sees it, the Chalcedonian definition is therefore *not* applied to an interpretation of the Gospels by virtue of its status as doctrine, but emerges from the primacy the Christian church across the ages has afforded to the *sensus literalis*.

Following this, Frei's typology will be applied to the twentieth-century ecumenical discussion concerning the theology of religions in the IMC, in the WCC, and in groups that splintered from them, such as the Laymen's Foreign Missions Inquiry and the Lausanne Movement. Here it will be demonstrated that Frei's typology is not only a far better heuristic tool for discerning what undergirds the vastly different visions offered across the various councils and congregations over the course of the ecumenical movement's history, but also that for all the variety evident therein, the Christological struggle behind these efforts was the same as the one most central to Frei's own work. For Frei, alongside most of the ecumenical movement, is concerned above all with discerning not *whether* Christians are warranted in affirming the irreducible uniqueness and universal significance of the death and resurrection of Jesus Christ, but *how* such an affirmation might also open Christian theology to a "secular" sensitivity to the everyday happenings in the world and the myriad of lives lived outside the confines of "the church." Unlike Race and those in the "pluralist" camp, the Christological question which sets Frei's typology into motion is not only the tension that undergirds not only his own theological deliberations but also those of the ecumenical movement at large. Within the ecumenical movement, it is a tension which most prominently emerges as part of the discussion surrounding the relationship between interfaith dialogue and evangelism, i.e., the relationship between Jesus Christ, those who seek to follow him as God's Son, crucified, dead, and resurrected for them and for the whole world, and those who do not know him as God's incarnate Son. Following Frei, we see that how this Christological tension is conceived and addressed is inextricably bound up with questions concerning theology's relationship to philosophy or external discourses; questions concerning the very nature of Christian theology itself.

---

[18]   Frei, *Types of Christian Theology*, 4, 25.

2

Alan Race's Threefold Typology

Introduction

Race's typology is not so much a *typology* of the theological subdiscipline now known as "theologies of religion" as it is an *argument* for an approach to Christian theology, writ large, as a philosophical or *wissenschaftlich* discourse—an argument in which the fashioning of the three types of exclusivism, inclusivism, and pluralism serves the project of designating pluralism as the only viable option. No doubt every typology is to some degree freighted with normative commitments that shape its organizational and descriptive logics. But given the broad influence of Race's typology, and the fact that many have taken his rejection of exclusivism and inclusivism as somehow separate from his description of the types themselves, embarking upon a quixotic attempt at defending positions which were *designed to be indefensible*, Race's typology demands greater scrutiny. The strangeness of this situation might in part be explained by the fact that Race himself offers shifting accounts of the typology's guiding logic and of the basis for each type. Sometimes the types are described in soteriological terms, other times they are differentiated in terms of their supposed logical coherence.[1] But, at its core, Race's case for the viability of pluralism, and the inadequacy of exclusivism and inclusivism, is rooted in apologetic concerns for the rational plausibility of religious faith—concerns which dictate both Race's formulation of all three types and his designation of

---

[1]   Cf. Alan Race, *Christians and Religious Pluralism: Patterns in the Christian Theology of Religions* (London: SCM Press, 1993), viii.

pluralism as the only credible approach to Christian theology. Broadly speaking, Race depicts them as follows:

Exclusivism "counts the revelation in Jesus Christ as the sole criterion by which all religions, including Christianity, can be understood and evaluated."[2] Inclusivism "accepts the spiritual power and depth manifest in" other faiths, "so that they can properly be called a locus of divine presence . . . [yet] it rejects them as not being sufficient for salvation apart from Christ, for Christ alone is savior."[3] He finds pluralism somewhat harder to define succinctly, perhaps because its very existence depends on the suggestion of inadequacies in the preceding types, but after Race argues for the inability of exclusivism and inclusivism to deal with what might be loosely described as philosophical criticisms—logical, historical, epistemological—it emerges as the only viable type of Christian theology in light of its superior capacity to accommodates itself to such criticisms. In so doing, pluralism points to the experience of "personal faith" as "the creative factor over the 'cumulative traditions'" and "the uniting factor between people of different traditions because it is the real locus of religious truth." Pluralism, in brief, is the view that faith as "[t]he one 'global human quality' is manifest in diverse forms."[4]

Race's formulation of the pluralist type is key to understanding the other two types and the purpose of the typology itself. At their root, *all three types are defined by their compatibility or incompatibility with philosophy* (as Race understands it). Loosely defined as a discourse that embraces a *wissenschaftlich* methodology, Race's view of philosophy is that it is an indispensable partner for theology, as it is a discourse focused on identifying general and universal truths, guided by insights and commitments supposedly derived independently of any particular community or tradition.[5] This view, it should be noted, appears not to result from any particular philosophical commitments but is rather motivated by apologetic concerns. The contemporary world has, in Race's view, adopted a *wissenschaftlich* approach to the accumulation of knowledge, and it is left to Christian theology to either adapt or descend into irrelevance.[6]

As the polemical tone of Race's accounts of exclusivism and inclusivism implies, and as is underscored in even a cursory survey of the twentieth-

---

2   Race, *Christians and Religious Pluralism*, 11.
3   Race, *Christians and Religious Pluralism*, 38.
4   Race, *Christians and Religious Pluralism*, 101.
5   Race, *Christians and Religious Pluralism*, vii, 30, 127.
6   Race, *Christians and Religious Pluralism*, 92.

century Protestant ecumenical movement's assembly statements and the like, Race's insistence on Christian theology's dependence on philosophy is far from a representative position. Among other things, this suggests that not only is his typology of limited use in describing the historical and contemporary ecclesial and ecumenical positions on the nature of Christian theology itself and its relation to other traditions, but for similar reasons it is also unhelpful in analyzing the majority of positions *actually* advanced. For it is set up to discount the very possibility of holding traditional or orthodox Christian interpretations of scripture and the related doctrinal beliefs alongside an enduring commitment to a continuous theological engagement with non-Christians, capable of both surprising and mutually informative points of theological discovery.[7] The twentieth-century ecumenical movement has rejected such a binary approach, with only a few exceptions. That these exceptions appear particularly close to Race's types is, therefore, not a sign of the typology's descriptive or analytical capacity but a crucial indication of typology's limitations.

Race's typology presents Christians with an unnecessarily stark choice: either establish the possibility for theologically affirmative, mutually informative, ethically constructive relationships with non-Christians by denying the literal sense of Jesus' description in scripture and his celebration in the church as the incarnate Son of God, or affirm this and forsake the possibility of loving, respectful, and theologically constructive relationships with non-Christians. He writes:

> No matter what form of words may have been used, the central meaning of the belief has been thought to be constant. Augustine has been judged to have been correct in singling out the Incarnation as the distinctive core of Christian belief, and in drawing the conclusion that this is where Christianity claims finality *vis-à-vis* other faiths. It would seem, therefore, that in the doctrine of the uniqueness of Christ, Christianity has been furnished with a criterion which renders the theological evaluation of the relationship between Christianity and the other faiths a relatively straightforward matter.[8]

For Race, to affirm the incarnation of Jesus is to deny the presence of God in the lives of non-Christians. Jesus Christ is framed, first and foremost,

---

[7]   Cf. Hans Frei, "The 'Literal Reading' of Biblical Narrative," in *Theology and Narrative: Selected Essays*, ed. George Hunsinger and William C. Placher (Oxford: Oxford University Press, 1993), 142.

[8]   Race, *Christians and Religious Pluralism*, 106.

as a *philosophical* problem—for the theology of religions, but by extension, for Christian faith in general. Race's typology pits an affirmation of
a Chalcedonian account of Jesus Christ's particular and unsubstitutable
identity against an affirmation of God's universal presence. Significantly,
as Frei shows, this is not unique to Race but is in fact a dichotomy that has
beset modern theology more widely. Its appeal, Frei suggests, is a symptom of the prioritizing of general philosophical cogency over sensitive
and detailed self-description in Christian theology, characteristic of the
modern period and the academic context in which Christian theology has
largely been pursued.[9]

Pluralism, Philosophical Apologetics, and the Incarnation

The prioritization of philosophical apologetics justifying a universal faith
in the transcendent, and the related unsuitability of Race's typology for
describing the historical range of positions on the theology of religions,
emerges as its premises are clarified and considered. While Race makes
clear his devotion to thinkers such as Ernst Troeltsch, John Hick, and
W. C. Smith in his construction of the type of "pluralism," he is not always
explicit in delineating the suppositions he draws from them upon which
he constructs the broader typology.[10]

This tendency toward ambiguity is found in Race's delineation of the
types themselves, which variously appear to hinge on questions concerning salvation, incarnation, religious knowledge, historicism (i.e., the critical philosophy of history), theological anthropology, and the limitations of
language in describing the infinite nature of God. On the one hand, Race's
typology is perhaps most frequently referred to as a "soteriological typology."[11] In the preface to *Christians and Religious Pluralism*, Race describes
theology of religions as an exploration of questions concerning salvation:

---

[9]   Cf. Hans Frei, *Types of Christian Theology*, ed. George Hunsinger and William C. Placher (New Haven, Conn.: Yale University Press, 1992), 92–116.
[10]   Brian Hebblethwaite, review of *Christians and Religious Pluralism: Patterns
in the Christian Theology of Religions* by Alan Race, *Religious Studies* 20, no. 3 (1984)
515–16. Cf. Race, *Christians and Religious Pluralism*, 7.
[11]   E.g., Marianne Moyaert, "Recent Developments in the Theology of Interreligious Dialogue: From Soteriological Openness to Hermeneutical Openness," *Modern
Theology* 28, no. 1 (2012): 25–52; Gavin D'Costa, "Theology of Religions," in *The Modern
Theologians*, ed. David Ford (Oxford: Wiley-Blackwell, 1998), 627; Amos Yong, "'Not
Knowing Where The Wind Blows . . .': On Envisioning A Pentecostal-Charismatic Theology of Religions," *Journal of Pentecostal Theology* 14 (1999): 82–83; Harold Netland,
Dissonant Voices (Vancouver: Regent, 1991), ix–xi; Paul Knitter, preface to *The Myth
of Christian Uniqueness*, ed. John Hick and Paul Knitter (Eugene, Ore.: Wipf & Stock,

How then should Christians respond theologically to the experience of what I have come to call the "transcendent vision of human transformation" ("salvation," to use the Christian term) at the heart of the religiously other? That is the task of the Christian theology of religions, which is now beginning in earnest.[12]

Elsewhere, however, Race indicates that the real issue facing the Christian theology of religions is the doctrine of the incarnation in relation to the possibility of religious knowledge:

> The Christian faith's dependence on the uniqueness of Christ has often been called "the scandal of particularity," and it is possible to elevate this particularity to the extent that it excludes or denies all confessions of the knowledge of God other than that deriving from the event of Jesus Christ.[13]

But even on the question of the incarnation Race is unclear, suggesting at other points in his typology that the problem with the incarnation is not so much the possibility of its restricting non-Christian knowledge of God, as described in the quote above, but rather that it is a scientific and historical impossibility.[14] Undoubtedly, salvation has something to do with Race's concern over the "scandal of particularity." But if salvation itself were his sole, or even primary, concern, inclusivism would suffice for him as a legitimate option. That it does not suggests that his insistence upon the superiority of pluralism, with its mythological interpretation of scripture and the related rejection of Chalcedonian Christology, has more to do with inclusivism's affronts to philosophical clarity and the dictates of "critical thought."[15]

Indeed, Race's most constant refrain throughout his typology is: "Christian theology cannot remain indifferent to changes in historical knowledge."[16] This is not so much an affirmation that concrete evidence casting doubt upon the incarnation (or more likely, the resurrection) would have devastating implications for Christianity—an affirmation, it

---

1987), viii; Gerald R. McDermott and Harold A. Netland, *A Trinitarian Theology of Religions: An Evangelical Proposal* (Oxford: Oxford University Press, 2014), 12–13.

[12] Race, *Christians and Religious Pluralism*, viii.

[13] Race, *Christians and Religious Pluralism*, 107–8; cf. 7, 35, 89, 98–99, 106–37.

[14] Race, *Christians and Religious Pluralism*, 118.

[15] Race, *Christians and Religious Pluralism*, viii.

[16] Race, *Christians and Religious Pluralism*, 138; cf. 2, 7f., 28–37, 41f., 53, 56, 62, 68, 78–83, 104, 108, 112f., 122–25, 136, 140, 159f.

should be noted, that would be shared by Hans Frei. Rather, Race here is referring to changes in the *philosophy* of history and the establishment of what Race calls the "new historical consciousness."[17]

This is simply to say that Race's focus on the incarnation and its basic relation to his typology is primarily in service of the unstated but unambiguous objective of making Christian faith less of a philosophical embarrassment, at least as he sees it. In Race's view, Christian faith is at an existential crossroads, and its survival is dependent on whether it can be brought in line with contemporary critical philosophical insight so as to present an account of faith in the transcendent that conforms to such "critical thought," rendering it historically feasible (by historicist standards), epistemologically valid (by neo-Kantian standards), and phenomenologically verifiable (in line with W. C. Smith's distinction between authentic interior "faith" and distorted exterior "tradition").

To describe this typology as soteriological in any precise sense, then, is to miss the point. It is instead best conceived as an argument for Race's belief that philosophy is the final arbiter of theological discourse. To make this case, Race fashions exclusivism and inclusivism not to depict deficiencies in their perspective on other religions but to suggest that it is only in pluralism's philosophical sophistication that we find an intellectually credible approach to religious faith and therefore (and *only therefore*) an acceptable position on the relationship between Christian faith and other religions. So, the bulk of Race's interrogation of the incarnation, from which his typological distinctions stem, is focused not on its implications for non-Christians but on the historical criticism of scripture surrounding the Gospel accounts, historicism's undermining of the very possibility of an event such as the incarnation, and straightforward attacks on the incarnation's logical coherence.[18]

In other words, for Race, theological validity is a function of philosophy. This prioritization of philosophy should not be viewed as the result of any particular philosophical commitment in Race's thought, but rather as the result of Race's concern for theology's popular credibility. He is not *imposing* a particular philosophical scheme onto Christian theology but *responding* to those philosophical criticisms he thinks have the widest purchase in contemporary society.

His constant emphasis on popular opinion, under the guise of "critical thought," as the decisive factor in adjudicating issues of intellectual

[17]   Race, *Christians and Religious Pluralism*, 53.
[18]   Race, *Christians and Religious Pluralism*, 106–48.

legitimacy suggests that, were he to live in another society with vastly different "philosophical" commitments, Race would take these as normative instead. Race believes the world outside Christianity has adopted critical historicism, certain epistemological positions, and an acceptance of the primacy of interior religious faith over exterior religious tradition and that Christianity's continued viability therefore depends on it doing the same. As such, he views the philosophical chastening of theology as the best means of making faith plausible in the modern world.

Race's invocation of philosophy to justify religious pluralism (and to criticize exclusivism and inclusivism) is in service of an apologetic argument for the rationality of faith in the transcendent. To this end, Race focuses the force of his philosophical critiques on Chalcedonian Christology both to differentiate between each type and to demonstrate their philosophical viability, or lack thereof. This is most conspicuous in his treatment of Christology in relation to historicism, epistemology, and phenomenological hermeneutics, foci which he uses both to distinguish between exclusivism, inclusivism, and pluralism, and to champion pluralism as the best approach to Christian theology. Again, this is all to say that Race's typology is *not* a typology of the Christian theology of religions but an argument for a particular, philosophy-first approach to Christian theology itself. With this in mind, we turn now to Race's treatment of historicism and his view of the limitations it imposes upon Christian theology.

Ernst Troeltsch and the Historical Method

Race takes the influence of historicism, particularly as expressed by Ernst Troeltsch, to have underscored a complex of metaphysical, epistemological, and methodological problems for traditional Christian theology.[19] Race references the work of Maurice Wiles, Arnold Toynbee, and David Friedrich Strauss (who, with Troeltsch, was a significant interlocutor for Frei) as having contributed to the debate about the impact of historical understanding on contemporary theology.[20] But it is the work of Ernst Troeltsch which has evidently had the biggest impact on Race's view of history in relation to theology.

Race sees Troeltsch as playing a pivotal role in drawing theology into contact with the modern paradigm of historical inquiry. From there, Race

---

[19]   Cf. Sarah Coakley, *Christ without Absolutes: A Study of the Christology of Ernst Troeltsch* (Oxford: Clarendon, 1988), 6–8.
[20]   Race, *Christians and Religious Pluralism*, 56, 76, 120ff., 155, 171f., 175, 177; 71ff., 76, 172; 117.

traces a direct line to John Hick and pluralism: "In the Christian theology of religions the full-scale pluralism first enunciated by Troeltsch is finally endorsed by Hick."[21] And while historicism itself had previously been supported by Gotthold Ephraim Lessing, David Friedrich Strauss, and others, Race singles out Troeltsch as making the best *apologetic* case for theology's ability to accommodate its critiques.[22] Such an accommodation is, for Race, a crucial feature of Christian theology and is both a defining characteristic of the pluralist type and one of the key differences between it and exclusivism/ inclusivism. As Race writes in a 1993 book review, Troeltsch "became a hero who opened a narrow door to theological intelligibility in a secularizing world and set an agenda which is as binding now, if also more complex, as it was in his lifetime."[23] A theology's failure to follow Troeltsch is therefore a failure of its credibility: "not to go through the door that Troeltsch opened is likely to be at the cost of an honest reckoning with historical consciousness."[24]

The impact of the new historical consciousness, for Race as for Troeltsch, is far-reaching and presents serious questions for Christian theology, including those that might lead us to question its claim of superiority over all other faiths. While it might be tempting to designate both as relativists, the reality is more complex.[25] Indeed, as both make clear,

---

[21]   Race, *Christians and Religious Pluralism*, 90; cf. 78ff. For a pluralist critique of Hick's role in supporting pluralist theology, see David Ray Griffin, "John Cobb's Whiteheadian Complementary Pluralism," in *Deep Religious Pluralism*, ed. David Ray Griffin (Louisville, Ky.: Westminster John Knox, 2005), 58–66.

[22]   Cf. Gotthold Ephraim Lessing, "On the Proof of the Spirit and of Power," in *Lessing: Philosophical and Theological Writings*, ed. and trans. H. B. Nisbet (Cambridge: Cambridge University Press, 2005), 87; David Friedrich Strauss, *The Life of Jesus, Critically Examined*, trans. George Eliot (London: Continuum International, 2005); idem, *The Christ of Faith and the Jesus of History*, trans. Leander E. Keck (Philadelphia: Fortress, 1977).

[23]   Alan Race, "An Original Mind in Religious History," *Times Literary Supplement* 4707 (1993): 31.

[24]   Race, "Original Mind," 31. Frei too thinks that grappling with historical consciousness is morally imperative for Christian faith today. Frei differentiates between asking the *question* of "the continuity between Jesus and faith" and arriving at the *answer* appropriate to Christian faith. For Frei, the historical and Christological question posed by Troeltsch and Strauss is "binding," to use Race's term—Frei even says that *not* asking the question is "a disservice to the morality of belief"—but the historicist *answer* is anything but obligatory for Christians. Cf. Frei, "Letter to Van Harvey," in *Reading Faithfully: Writings from the Archives*, ed. Mike Higton and Mark Alan Bowald, 2 vols. (Eugene, Ore.: Cascade Books, 2015), 1:26.

[25]   Cf. Coakley, *Christ without Absolutes*, 5–44. Coakley maintains Troeltsch's commitment to relativism, but in a circumscribed and very specific way. Race too makes ambiguous claims about relativism. Sometimes he advances a limited, historical, or epistemological relativism, disavowing metaphysical relativism; see Race,

a "debilitating relativism" was something to be shunned and avoided.[26] Here, and in the wider analysis of Troeltsch's thought, Sarah Coakley's book *Christ without Absolutes* serves as a helpful guide, though for our purposes here, a full account of Troeltsch's thought is less important than an accurate description of Race's interpretation of Troeltsch.

Coakley lays out three principles in her account of Troeltsch's view on the nature of history and the historical method: criticism, analogy, and correlation. The "principle of criticism" dictates that "historical work yields only judgements of varying degrees of probability, not of absolute certainty." The "principle of analogy" is the idea that "historical events are not radically dissimilar from one another." And third, the "principle of correlation" is the belief that "historical events take place in contexts, which condition them, and which they themselves in turn affect."[27]

Coakley suggests that Troeltsch's metaphysics change over time, shifting from a position influenced by David Friedrich Strauss to one more teleologically focused and drawn from Hegel, such that "the claim to a final or exclusive revelation in Christ . . . becomes just vastly 'improbable' rather than logically or metaphysically impossible."[28] Yet this earlier view, clearly stated by Troeltsch in *The Absoluteness of Christianity* ("Strauss . . . has shown clearly and irrefutably . . . that no absolutely perfect principle can be realized in history at any single point"), is the one that Race focuses on.[29] The shift Coakley observes in Troeltsch's thought is not reflected in Race's discussion of Troeltsch, and he interprets Troeltsch as consistently advocating the logical and metaphysical impossibility of the incarnation, which Coakley cites as his earlier and

---

Christians and Religious Pluralism, 20, 81, 132, 154. Other times, he veers into a more extensive metaphysical relativism, as when asserting that just as all religious truth claims cannot escape cultural relatedness, the same "is true for *any* claim to truth or knowledge." Race, *Christians and Religious Pluralism*, 76, emphasis added.

[26]   Race, *Christians and Religious Pluralism*, 78, 90, 97; Ernst Troeltsch, "Historical and Dogmatic Method in Theology," in *Religion in History*, ed. and trans. James Luther Adams and Walter F. Bense (Edinburgh: T&T Clark, 1991), 27.

[27]   Coakley, *Christ without Absolutes*, 25.

[28]   Coakley, *Christ without Absolutes*, 25, 111, 132. Cf. Ernst Troeltsch, *The Absoluteness of Christianity and the History of Religions* (Richmond, Va.: John Knox, 1971) 78; idem, "The Significance of the Historical Existence of Jesus for Faith," in idem, *Writings on Theology and Religion*, ed. and trans. Robert Morgan and Michael Pye (London: Duckworth, 1977), 189.

[29]   Troeltsch, *Absoluteness of Christianity*, 78; cf. Coakley, *Christ without Absolutes*, 111.

abandoned view.[30] It will be to this earlier and more metaphysically doctrinaire Troeltsch to which we refer.

"The Principle of Criticism"

On one level, the "principle of criticism," as Coakley notes, is "a noncontroversial point about the method and procedure of historians."[31] Simply put, it says that as and when new evidence emerges that has implications on prior interpretations of historical events, those events can and must be reconsidered in the light of the new evidence. But it is important to note the way in which this seemingly simple methodological statement has, for Race, wider ramifications. As he states in the second sentence of *Christians and Religious Pluralism*, Race sees the "increasing awareness" of religious pluralism as new evidence with which Christian theology must deal.[32] He claims that this awareness calls into question all preceding historical judgments made within or on behalf of Christian faith, and especially those which have influenced the interpretation of scripture relating to Jesus' resurrection and the formation of Christian Christological doctrine. So, while religious pluralism was not entirely foreign to the early church,

> the present experience transcends any earlier sense Christians may have had of its significance . . . The so-called "history of religions" school has amassed an enormous store of detail concerning the beliefs and practices of the world's faiths. In this light, ignorance [today] about the world's religions can only be regarded as culpable ignorance, a state of affairs which cannot be condoned when one comes to the theological problem of the relationship between the faiths.[33]

The beliefs and practices of other religions are cast as new empirical data against which any prior Christian theological or doctrinal hypotheses must be tested. The more evidence that is gathered, Race's thinking goes, the greater the demand is for Christianity to reformulate itself in a philosophically sound manner that is appropriate to the new historical consciousness.[34]

[30]   Cf. Race, *Christians and Religious Pluralism*, 78ff. For the later view, see Troeltsch, "Historical Existence of Jesus," 189.
[31]   Coakley, *Christ without Absolutes*, 25.
[32]   Race, *Christians and Religious Pluralism*, 1.
[33]   Race, *Christians and Religious Pluralism*, 1–2.
[34]   We will see later that Race turns to W. C. Smith's phenomenological approach as the most reliable means of interpreting this data and accomplishing this task.

For Race, the weight of this empirical evidence comes to rest most directly on the doctrine of the incarnation:

> The acknowledgement of other faiths as forms of communion with God is part of the evidence from which a Christology must be constructed. Methodologically, the question of the Incarnation must proceed in tension with the search for a Christian theology of religions.[35]

So, the principle of criticism leads Race to focus on the incarnation in light of a growing body of empirical data concerning the tenets and practices of the world religions. Those types—exclusivism and inclusivism—which do not take such empirical data into account *before* reaffirming their commitment to Christian doctrines like the incarnation are in Race's opinion bound to arrive at an empirically and philosophically untenable theology: ". . . the exclusivist theory functions independently of the knowledge of other faiths. In point of fact it is the product of a particular view of the notion of revelation. If Christianity rests on true revelation, it argues, then by logical inference the other faiths of mankind must be false or illusory. The empirical facts are irrelevant to the argument."[36]

That said, Race's argument against the contemporary plausibility of Chalcedonian Christology seems not to be anchored in an appeal to the empirical body of evidence of religious diversity, but in his recasting of Christian faith as subject to the methodological constraints of historical research. The new evidence that Race really seems to have in mind is not discrete information about other religious traditions but *historicism itself.* What is most significant and distinct about our context today is not simply that we have more evidence about other religions, but that the historicism of Troeltsch and others has changed the very rules to which Christian faith, indeed religious faith in general, is accountable:

---

[35]   Race, *Christians and Religious Pluralism*, 112.
[36]   Race, *Christians and Religious Pluralism*, 25. Race's use of the word "fact" in apparent reference to the veracity of some indeterminate range of religious beliefs in various traditions reveals the ambiguity of his argument. In the sense that other faiths maintain beliefs in different sources and means of divine revelation, the word "fact" would be appropriate. But, perhaps implicitly invoking the phenomenological hermeneutic he adopts from Smith later in the book, Race appears to suggest that by virtue of their very existence, such beliefs should be viewed as verifiably true and deemed *fact*, even while he also insists that the events such beliefs refer to are themselves *myths*. Frei, in comparison, displays reluctance in even using the word "fact" to refer to those aspects of *Christian* tradition that he affirms, including the resurrection of Jesus, arguing that to use such language risks undermining the extra-theological integrity of the word.

The reconstruction of christology [sic] today begins with historical observation. For our sharpened historical consciousness has taught us how the human response to Jesus has differed markedly through history, and this is a legacy to which any survey of the history of christological reflection will testify. At one level these present a sobering picture of how cultural epochs and settings have created their own version of "Christ" in their own image . . . On the other hand, surveying the pluriform fortunes of christological reflection grants a kind of permission to develop a view of Jesus that is suitable for our own age and circumstances . . . the multifaith context of today's global environment represents simply one latest context in a history of contexts.[37]

Significantly, while he appears to acknowledge that this new historicist outlook, abiding by Troeltsch's principle of criticism, asserts the limited contextuality of all Christological descriptions (and any other belief in Christianity or another religion that violates Troeltsch's historicist principles), it is hard to imagine how any subsequent developments would impinge upon or alter the view Race sees as forced upon us today. For the key insight provided by our particular, globalized world is that all beliefs or aspects of tradition (only in the religious realm apparently) that claim both historical uniqueness and universal meaning across time are myths.

While Race's case is here concerned with the figure of Jesus, the force of this new historicist approach cannot be limited to Christianity and will be experienced in different ways in different traditions. For Christians, the implications of a contemporary perspective and experience of religious pluralism are felt most forcefully in the area of Christology. Race's apparent embrace of religious relativism is the premise of his case against all nonmythological Christologies—and all nonmythological claims of all religions vis-à-vis their historical claims—yesterday, today, and tomorrow. The fruit of our current context is that we can now see through all past contexts. And while the experience (or at least awareness) of today's religious pluralism constitutes a body of supporting empirical evidence, the key piece in Race's case is the historicist outlook itself. Not only is it no longer satisfactory for Christians to consider Christology primarily from within a context of Christian scripture or tradition, but the Christological

---

[37]   Alan Race, *Interfaith Encounter: The Twin Tracks of Theology and Dialogue* (London: SCM Press, 2001), 74.

reinterpretation demanded by our historical perspective today must somehow reflect aspects of the historicist philosophy of history as well.

This becomes clear as Race notes that the undermining of historical particularity alongside the endorsement of increased contact and awareness of other religions is not itself sufficient to effect the necessary change. For the variety of religious beliefs to be both myths *and* meaningful—not just disconnected, equally relative, and limited beliefs for Christian theology (i.e., for Christian theology itself to be meaningful)—Race's invoking of the principle of criticism points to the necessity of some additional interpretive framework. What he feels is needed, and what Race offers in pluralism, is "a theory which holds together the different types of religious experience in a creative tension."[38] Which brings us to Troeltsch's second principle of historical method, the "principle of analogy."

"The Principle of Analogy"

Troeltsch states his principle of analogy as follows: "Analogous occurrences that we observe both without and within ourselves furnish us with the key to historical criticism."[39] Coakley, cautiously rephrasing it as "historical events are not radically dissimilar from one another," notes that it has generally been understood as asserting the immutability of natural laws over and against a "supernaturalist" view of the miraculous, though she questions this interpretation.[40] This interpretation of Troeltsch's principle of analogy appears to be the one Race upholds.[41] On this view, the principle of analogy operates in a way similar to the principle of replication in the scientific method. Just as in the natural sciences, where an experiment's results are only valid if they are repeatable, so too is the historical world understood to be governed by the constant laws of nature, where any single event takes place under universal conditions which render in specific ways the possibility or impossibility of its occurrence. In other words, the principle of analogy rests upon a metaphysic reminiscent of that of Lessing and Strauss, wherein the possibility of any event in history is determined by the basic conditions under which all other events in history are rendered possible. The entry of the absolute into the external, public realm of history, or the occurrence of a completely unique, sui generis event like Jesus' incarnation, is denied a priori.

---

[38]   Race, *Christians and Religious Pluralism*, 104.
[39]   Troeltsch, "Historical and Dogmatic Method," 13.
[40]   Coakley, *Christ without Absolutes*, 24, n. 34; 108, n. 14.
[41]   Cf. Race, *Christians and Religious Pluralism*, 100ff., 113, 127.

Race argues that this principle creates serious concerns about the incarnation in two ways. First, it raises concerns about the incarnation's compatibility with insights drawn from the scientific and historical method vis-à-vis natural laws and the possibilities of their being "violated" by God.[42] Second, Race believes the principle of analogy raises questions relating to the historical particularity of the incarnation and its resonance within other religions.[43]

In the first case, Race's dispute with the Chalcedonian definition stems in part from concerns about certain infringements upon natural causal processes: "A belief which proposes that one person was related to the God of the universe and history in a unique manner and form cannot escape an encounter with modern changes in historical understanding."[44] The incarnation, Race concludes, must be interpreted as a myth to satisfy the metaphysical strictures entailed in the principle of analogy. In tallying the advantages of adopting "mythological" language in considering the incarnation of Christ, Race begins by focusing on the restrictions placed on divine intervention from the perspective of the principle of analogy:

> The attractions of treating the language of Incarnation as mythological are manifold. In the first place, it resolves the difficulties inherent in the notion of divine intervention. The metaphors of "sending" and "becoming" imply that God acts from outside to intervene in a world which, viewed scientifically and historically, is seen normally as a closed web of cause and effect. To speak of the Incarnation as myth is one way of separating the christological problem from the interventionist framework of divine action, which is now regarded by the majority of theologians as redundant.[45]

Yet Race, like Troeltsch, finds the idea of a radical separation between Creator and Creation unacceptable.[46] This is not just because of Race's understanding of God, but also because of his understanding of the human person, a concern which becomes particularly pointed again in the Chalcedonian idea of Christ's two natures.

For Jesus to be fully human, and therefore subject to the laws of nature underlying the historical method and the principle of anal-

---

42   Race, *Christians and Religious Pluralism*, 92.
43   Race, *Christians and Religious Pluralism*, 77–78.
44   Race, *Christians and Religious Pluralism*, 122.
45   Race, *Christians and Religious Pluralism*, 118.
46   Coakley, *Christ without Absolutes*, 84.

ogy, he cannot be said to have existed prior to his birth—"it is this belief which contradicts the assertion of his full humanity."[47] This, in turn, leads Race to conclude that "the problematic notion of the pre-existence of Christ is, in one form or another, the basic issue in the debate over the Incarnation."[48] In addition, it cannot be said of Jesus that he occupies any eschatological position at the end of history, as the "category of 'finality,' which was later transformed into the doctrine of the incarnation, itself has become deeply problematic in a historically critical age."[49]

According to Race, the principle of analogy, the historical method, and the historicist worldview in general subvert even the very idea of eschatology. Confusingly, this does not stop him from appealing to the possibility of "eschatological verification," echoing John Hick, in confirming "the genuineness" of religious experiences modeled after a metaphorical or mythological interpretation of Jesus' divine "sonship."[50] Citing Troeltsch, Race writes:

> Critical historical thinking, however, is likely to view *history as an interwoven process of cause and effect*, stretching into the unknown future, and with little need for a "final figure" to usher in a "final age." As a result of this assessment of history as a "continuous connection of becoming," to use Ernst Troeltsch's evocative phrase, there has been an immense theological shift towards viewing the whole of creation and history as the *locus* of the immanent presence of God. In turn, this has led to attempts to reinterpret the notion of the finality of Jesus and its successor, the doctrine of creation.[51]

Putting aside the apparent tensions between Race's rejection of eschatology, his own teleological view of history, and his invoking of Hick's "eschatological verification" to maintain the supposed epistemological rigor of theological pluralism, it should now be clear that Troeltsch's principle of analogy is partially utilized by Race in a metaphysically—not just epistemologically—restrictive sense. Its force is felt most strongly in Christology, where Race suggests it requires eschewing those Christian beliefs which might transgress the analogous uniformity of history,

47 Race, *Christians and Religious Pluralism*, 119.
48 Race, *Christians and Religious Pluralism*, 117.
49 Race, *Interfaith Encounter*, 67.
50 Race, *Interfaith Encounter*, 146.
51 Race, *Interfaith Encounter*, 68.

and demanding the mythological interpretation of the scriptures upon which they are based.

In the second sense of his appeal to the principle of analogy, Race applies the principle of analogy constructively, using it in an appeal for the universality of the world religions' salvific orientation and effectiveness. One of Race's most emphatic points is that any theology of religion must begin with an "empirical" analysis of the content and impact of the world religions.[52] Such analysis, Race argues, yields two very different—but complementary—insights. On the one hand, an empirical study of the world religions highlights just how culturally conditioned and particular each religion is—an insight resulting also from Race's implicit appeal to Troeltsch's third principle of correlation.[53] On the other hand, such particularity is mitigated by what Race suggests is a universal and analogous experience of the reality of the divine:

> Its corollary in religious truth is the hypothesis that the diverse forms and patterns of experience and belief, manifest in the religions, represent different "cultured responses" to the same ultimate divine reality. Christianity in this theory represents only one cultured response to the divine initiative; it cannot claim a monopoly of religious truth.[54]

Neither does Christianity *need* to claim a monopoly on such truth. For as Race sees it, all the world religions are also oriented toward "salvation"—a Christian term Race equates with more general notions of transcendence and transformation:

> The religions are distinct in the content of their culturally conditioned histories, belief systems and recommended spiritual and ethical practices. But they resemble one another in that they provide a comprehensive view of reality and a context for what can be termed "transcendent vision and human transformation." It is this distinctiveness combined with family resemblance that creates both a "strangeness" and a "resonance" in the relationships between the religions.[55]

[52]   Cf. Race, *Christians and Religious Pluralism*, 25. Race's view of the "impact" of religion is unclear but made primarily with soteriological language which stresses each religion's capacity to offer a "transcendent vision of human transformation." Race, *Christians and Religious Pluralism*, viii.

[53]   Race, *Christians and Religious Pluralism*, 76.

[54]   Race, *Christians and Religious Pluralism*, 76; cf. 101.

[55]   Race, *Interfaith Encounter*, 3.

Jesus, on this understanding, maintains theological significance because he provides a model of relationship between the divine and humanity which can be analogously observed across the world's religions.

In one sense, Jesus is culturally and contextually conditioned, and therefore a stranger to the world religions. Yet Jesus' focus on the possibility of having relationship with God (which Race isolates as his primary message) resembles salvific/transcendent/transformative aspects of other religions. Quoting the Catholic theologian Edward Schillebeeckx, Race asserts that Jesus' experience of union with God is one which was and is accessible to all humans:

> If salvation is understood . . . in terms of a personal relationship with the "'transcendent God,' with whom Jesus has made us familiar," then it is not essential to establish that a union existed between the divine and human in Jesus of a kind uniquely different from that in other human beings. What this implies is that the union represents the "focus" or "paradigm" of the union between man and God which we anticipate as the intended goal of salvation.[56]

This view of the incarnation as a demythologized paradigm of divine-human relationship represents Race's second, constructive use of Troeltsch's principle of analogy, whereby the particular tenets of individual religious traditions are rendered meaningful insofar as they are viewed as manifestations of a universal search for "salvation."

While Race employs the principle of analogy to negate the possibility of the incarnation as a historical event, he also uses it to affirm the significance of the incarnation as a universal religious ideal, suggesting it can be used to support the parity of the world's religions when "incarnation" is no longer applied to any one individual. Affirming the specific or historical incarnation of Jesus is held to be historically untenable, but the *idea* of the incarnation is at the same time held as having universal and ahistorical significance.

Race argues that only when the incarnation is viewed in this demythologized yet paradigmatic way will Christians be able to "be open to the possibility that the knowledge of God outside the Christian tradition is not so qualitatively different from that of the Christian tradition itself."[57] The incarnation as a metaphysical anomaly is rejected, while the idea behind the incarnation—union with the divine, as Race sees it—is posited as a

---

56 Race, *Christians and Religious Pluralism*, 132.
57 Race, *Christians and Religious Pluralism*, 28.

metaphysical universal, an objective both already present in each of the world religions and also increasingly brought to light through interfaith dialogue and religious interpenetration. In this way, Race takes Troeltsch's principle in two very different directions—undermining the metaphysical particularity of events such as the incarnation while also arguing for the metaphysical universality of incarnation as religious objective. This provides him with a purportedly empirical basis for a common search for salvation across humanity, even in the face of what appear to be disparate religious traditions.

"The Principle of Correlation"

This brings us to Troeltsch's third principle of the historical method, the principle of correlation, which confirms that all individual historical occurrences "are most closely correlated with a much larger historical context; they arise out of this context, they share its substance, and they must be understood in relation to it."[58] Coakley describes this as an affirmation that "historical events take place in contexts, which condition them, and which they themselves in turn affect."[59] The impact of this principle on Race's typology has been alluded to in the preceding discussion of the use of the principle of analogy as invoking the metaphysical limitations which impinge upon all historical phenomena yet which also ground the unity of seemingly disparate religious phenomena. "Taken together," Coakley, quoting Troeltsch, notes of the principles of analogy and correlation, "they assert both 'a basic consistency of the human spirit' and also the 'interaction of all phenomena in the history of civilization' . . . these principles issue from 'the *metaphysical* assumption that all things, including the activities of the human mind, are totally interconnected.'"[60]

Negatively, Race sees this metaphysical connectivity as a limitation:

> In one sense "all is relative"; that is, everything which exists does so in relation to everything else . . . all human apprehensions of truth are necessarily limited, partial, and conditioned by the environment of the subject. There is always a distinction between the knower and the known such that unconditioned knowledge can never be available, by definition, to persons limited by particular environments.[61]

---

58   Troeltsch, "Historical and Dogmatic Method," 17.
59   Coakley, *Christ without Absolutes*, 26.
60   Coakley, *Christ without Absolutes*, 26.
61   Race, *Christians and Religious Pluralism*, 77.

Positively, it points to the paradoxical unity-in-diversity of humanity:

> The more we realize our growing unity as a human race, the more we bump up against our indubitable multiplicity, our riotous diversity. In the midst of a growing sense of interconnectedness we recognize our ineradicable human plurality.[62]

Indeed, the principles of analogy and correlation can be seen as balancing out the two sides of a scale, uniting and dividing the totality of human experience. As such, amidst a compelling argument for limiting the scope of Troeltsch's relativism as it is commonly assessed, Coakley interprets the principle of correlation as conveying a conception of historical phenomena in which they are *united* by the shared *limitations* of their contextual conditioning, a "web of mutually interacting activities of the human spirit, which are never independent . . . but always interrelated."[63]

Similarly, Race employs the principle not just in an effort to explain the historically conditioned and contextual nature of religious truth, traditions, and experiences, but also as a means of inferring the significance of the many differences between religions. It therefore takes an epistemological turn in his typology, offering an account of how humans learn about a universal God (or transcendent reality) in the midst of historically particular and diverse settings—a partial knowledge, admittedly, but knowledge that will be verified and fulfilled eschatologically.[64] In this context, Race renders the principle of correlation in eschatological tones, accounting for the present limits of human knowledge while also hinting at how such epistemological limitation itself relates to that which is, finally, to be known.

To that end, Race takes the notion of historical correlation to highlight the overriding significance of dialogical engagement between individuals of different religions and of the empirical assessment of the texts, histories, and practices of such traditions.[65] Such empirical evaluation, as Race sees it, can only reasonably yield one conclusion, "the belief that there is not one, but a number of spheres of saving contact between God and man.

---

[62]   Race, *Interfaith Encounter*, ix. Race has a confused relationship with "paradox," using it constructively to respond to attacks against pluralism, as in the passage cited, yet using it critically to undermine Chalcedonian Christology and the doctrine of the incarnation. Cf. Race, *Christians and Religious Pluralism*, 15, 88, 114f.

[63]   Troeltsch, "Historical and Dogmatic Method," 15; cf. Coakley, *Christ without Absolutes*, 27.

[64]   Cf. Race, *Christians and Religious Pluralism*, 146.

[65]   Race, *Christians and Religious Pluralism*, 5; cf. J. A. Veitch, "The Case for a Theology of Religions," *Scottish Journal of Theology* 24, no. 4 (1971): 408.

God's revealing and redeeming activity has elicited response in a number of culturally conditioned ways throughout history.[66] So even while emphasizing the diversity that comprises the world religions, Race is wary of ascribing too much significance to this diversity, balancing it with an appeal to an eschatological verification that will confirm the true aspects of each religious tradition.[67]

Importantly, Race draws this notion of the final assimilation of different religions from *outside* the confines of any one religious tradition. The basic premise of his appeal to the unity of the world's religions cannot truly emerge from any one religion's internal doctrinal tenets, what Race (somewhat strangely) terms "a priori criteria":

> Truth, especially in religious matters, belongs within a whole context of life and culture. To say that the divine is manifest in different ways in different cultures is not to side-step the issue of truth in a religiously diverse world, but is to pave the way for a dialogue in which the cognitive discrepancies can be better evaluated in a wider setting . . . To believe otherwise, it seems to me, in an age of historical "enlightenment" would be an indefensible pre-judgment of truth . . . the pluralist theory willingly suspends the a priori application of criteria from the specifically Christian heritage in the search to distinguish the more from the less profound, the more from the less "true" religious belief, and looks to dialogue as the first step on the road to religious truth viewed from a world perspective.[68]

It is hard to determine exactly what Race means by "truth." He offers a contextual and relativized account of truth in which Christian criteria (which, it must be noted, are not derived a priori but are instead rooted in a posteriori reasoning pursued in light of claims concerning Jesus' life, ministry, death, and resurrection) are suspended, while maintaining that this suspension is done in the name of what are *in actuality* a priori criteria—Troeltsch's three principles, the Kantian separation of noumena and phenomenon and the epistemology this gives rise to, the unity of the transcendent, etc. What is clear is that Race sees the principle of correlation ("Truth . . . belongs within a whole context of life and culture") as the basis for a view of religious truth as depen-

---

[66]   Race, *Christians and Religious Pluralism*, 77, emphasis added.
[67]   Race, *Christians and Religious Pluralism*, 146; cf. John Hick, *Death and Eternal Life* (Louisville, Ky.: Westminster John Knox, 1994), 408, 416.
[68]   Race, *Christians and Religious Pluralism*, 143–44.

dent upon interfaith dialogue—called for and guided by external philosophical critiques and propositions.

Summary of Race's Use of Troeltsch's Three Principles

As it applies to Christianity and other religions, the principle of criticism is taken by Race to demand the centrality of historical criticism in theology, where new insights derived from biblical, sociological, philosophical, and even scientific research call into question the validity of Christian doctrines and the literal reading of scripture. The principle of criticism also grounds a historical relativism which undermines the durability of all religious beliefs oriented around particular historical events, persons, etc., demanding their continuous reappraisal and reformulation in line, first and foremost, with new historical conditions. While Race suggests that the principle of criticism means that any viable theology must take shape in light of new access to data from world religions, such data is itself only available and meaningful once it too has been chastened by historicism.

It has been suggested that the principle of analogy operates within Race's typology in two ways. Negatively, Race employs the principle to limit the possibility of metaphysical uniqueness, insisting that all events in history occur under universal conditions which render in specific ways the possibility or impossibility of their occurrence, subverting the notion of divine intervention operating within a Chalcedonian Christology. In this sense, the principle of analogy serves a restrictive purpose in Race's typology, limiting what is historically possible in relation to God's dealings with the world. Positively, and ironically, the principle of analogy also leads Race to "empirically" identify analogical correspondences between the world religions and their orientation toward an experience of the transcendent and ethical transformation. Specifically, it allows him to *negate* the historical possibility of the *particular event* of Jesus' incarnation while yet *affirming* and even *universalizing the idea* of "incarnation" for religious faith of all kinds.

As with the first sense of the principle of analogy discussed above, the principle of correlation in Race's typology yields an emphasis on the contextual nature of all religious experiences and truth statements. Yet, like the second sense of the principle of analogy, the principle of correlation for Race brings disparate religious doctrines into relation with one another—partly in this world but fully in the eschaton—because of their very disparateness. Where "incarnation" might be seen as a focal point in the epistemic context of the principle of analogy, for the principle of correlation, the metaphysical focus of Race's view of the principle of correlation might be "salvation." The very diversity and even discrepancy of religious conceptions of the nature and means of "salvation" paradoxically allows for its validity as a heuristic device for discerning the underlying unity of the world's religions, in both present experience and future orientation. No single religion can claim to be true, just as no religion can be deemed false. They are simply contextually colored manifestations of an underlying and intrinsic aspect of humanity's search for, and experience of, the transcendent. Neither can any religion's beliefs be separated from its historical environment, shaped by this as all historical phenomena are, nor can any one religion be interpreted in isolation, as they are viewed as interrelated responses to some general, human religious impulse. On this view, the foundation of a religion's true spiritual significance rests as much, if not more, on the acknowledgment of its limitations as it does on any particular scripture, tenet, or tradition. For Race, this signals an awareness of both the profundity of God's being and the related and apparently inevitable conclusion that seemingly opposing religious truths must be compatible.

The influence of Ernst Troeltsch and the significance of his three principles of historical method in orienting Race's typology cannot be overstated. His historicist principles serve to demarcate a legitimate view of history and the theological possibilities therein, dictating the typology's internal logic and the divisions between the types. The definition of exclusivism, in other words, is not premised on its embrace of the uniqueness of Jesus Christ, but its rejection of Troeltsch's historical principles. In constructing his typology upon a foundation of Troeltsch's historicism, Race makes the polemical thrust of his typology clear: The credibility of Christian belief begins with the affirmation of Troeltsch's historicism. Before the question of religious pluralism even comes up, exclusivism and inclusivism are relegated to the dustbin. It begins to appear as if pluralism being the only viable type in Race's typology has less to do with its particular position on the empirical fact of religious diversity and more to do with the antecedent philosophical and methodological commitments.

But this is not to say that it is Race's philosophical commitments that lead him to advocate for pluralism. There is certainly a structural bias within the typology regarding an approach to the historical method which renders it more of a polemic than a description. But this polemic is itself not geared toward a particular approach to religious pluralism itself, but toward an apologetic case for the rationality of religious faith. Race's argument in its entirety amounts to a restatement of historicism's argument against central aspects of Christian faith (e.g., Jesus' incarnation, miracles, and resurrection), followed by suggestions—epistemological and hermeneutical—as to how Christianity can render these problematic aspects plausible to those convinced by historicism's critique. In framing his description of possible positions within a Christian theology of religions as such, Race has set the critical philosophy of history as the narrow gate through which all Christians must pass toward theological legitimacy: "For religious faith, if it is to be credible in the modern world, must seek to answer the secular critique of religion while simultaneously demonstrating how it may provide secular culture with a religious foundation."[69] As such, it is not even clear whether religious pluralism is Race's primary concern or if it is simply fodder for his defense of faith in general.

Not only does the typology thus formed imply that those who do not accept historicism are themselves in theological error, but it also implies that the historicism of Troeltsch and others is indubitable. This being Race's view, his typology is best viewed as a philosophical apology for the historically viewed rationality of religious faith in general as a universal aspect of human experience. In that effort, having endorsed Troeltsch's historicist critique, Race turns to John Hick's epistemology of religious experience to bolster the apologetic force of his argument.

John Hick's Epistemology of Religious Experience

Race acknowledges that a theological accommodation of historicism alone leaves the validity of religious experience insecure, subject to the vicissitudes of a "debilitating relativism." Race concludes that Troeltsch's work cannot itself provide a theological justification for a theological pluralism that accounts for the underlying unity behind the world's religions:

> A weakness of Troeltsch at this point is that he gives no theological justification for the belief that all faiths derive from the same source and tend towards the same goal. The religions do characterize their inner meaning and essence differently. *If they tend towards the same goal, then the differing elements of religious experience within them will require careful alignment and comparison.*[70]

On the one hand, historicism's rejection of divine intervention or encounter within history's web of cause and effect suggests that the epistemic

---

[69]   Race, *Christians and Religious Pluralism*, 92.
[70]   Race, *Christians and Religious Pluralism*, 78, 81, emphasis added.

validity of religious knowledge itself must be defended. On the other hand, the commitment to the unity of transcendent source and goal in Race's religious pluralism means that this account of epistemic validity must also allow for the diversity of religious beliefs held between the world religions.

To this end, Race turns to Hick to argue that the global phenomenon of religion, though subject to all the stark limitations imposed by Troeltsch's historicism, can nonetheless be epistemologically sound and philosophically credible, provided the world religions come to be understood as diverse expressions of a single, universally accessible aspect of human experience.[71] Such experience, and our response to it, is diverse. But, first, because Hick insists religious faith, in any form, requires grounding in a single and impartial epistemology, and second, because of the shape such an epistemological argument takes, Hick concludes that religious diversity can be viewed as issuing from a common source. To better understand the centrality of experience in the epistemology upon which Race's typology is constructed, we will turn briefly to its development by Hick in his book *Arguments for the Existence of God*, where he provides a more concise presentation of the epistemology originally presented in *Faith and Knowledge*, before returning to consider how it shapes Race's typology.

Arguments for the Existence of God

Hick's forays into pluralistic theology, like Race's, appear to have been largely a byproduct of a different and more basic objective—making the case for the philosophical legitimacy of religious faith. Unlike Race, Hick embarked upon this journey as a self-described "very conservative Christian," seeking in *Faith and Knowledge* to defend Christian belief against charges of epistemological irrationality and invalidity. Only later did he take up his epistemic argument in the name of theological pluralism.[72] In *Arguments for the Existence of God*, Hick describes and critiques the most influential "proofs" for a Christian God, such as the design, teleological, probabilistic, cosmological, moral, and ontological arguments. At the end of this survey, Hick draws two general conclusions on their insufficiency. First, Hick argues that none are philosophically sound:

> We have seen that it is impossible to demonstrate the reality of God by *a priori* reasoning, since such reasoning is confined to the realm of concepts; impossible to demonstrate it by *a posteriori* reasoning,

71   Race, *Christians and Religious Pluralism*, 83.
72   John Hick, *An Autobiography* (Oxford: Oneworld, 2005), 70–73.

since this would have to include a premise begging the very question at issue; and impossible to establish it as in a greater or lesser degree probable, since the notion of probability lacks any clear meaning in this context.[73]

Second, Hick argues that theologically, such arguments are entirely foreign to the perspective of the biblical authors and wholly absent from the Bible itself:

> Indeed, to the biblical writers it would have seemed absurd to try to establish by logical argumentation that God exists. For they were convinced that they were already having to do with him and he with them in all the affairs of their lives. They did not think of God as an inferred entity *but as an experienced reality.* Many of the biblical writers were (sometimes, though doubtless not at all times) *as vividly conscious of being in God's presence as they were of living in a material world.* It is impossible to read their pages without realizing that to them God was not a proposition completing a syllogism, or an idea adopted by the mind, *but the supreme experiential reality.*[74]

This leads Hick to question whether, in the face of the philosophical failures and the biblical emphasis on experience, proof of God's existence is theologically warranted, much less possible.

Hick finds a path forward by shifting the objective of such proofs from substantiating God's *existence* itself to merely confirming the validity of knowledge drawn from *experiences* of God's presence. Here Hick makes a crucial, and questionable, move for his argument, collapsing the distinction between religious belief and experience:

> The claims of religion are claims made by individuals and communities on the basis of their experience—and experience which is none the less their own for occurring [sic] within an inherited framework of ideas. We are not dealing with a merely conceivable metaphysical hypothesis which someone has speculatively invented but which hardly anyone seriously believes. *We are concerned, rather, with convictions born out of experience and reflection and living within actual communities of faith and practice.*[75]

---

[73]   John Hick, *Arguments for the Existence of God* (London: Macmillan, 1970), 101.
[74]   Hick, *Arguments for the Existence of God*, 102, emphasis added.
[75]   Hick, *Arguments for the Existence of God*, 108, emphasis added.

While he rejects on philosophical and theological grounds efforts toward proving God's existence, Hick maintains that the need for proof is not something we can simply ignore, and that such proof might be based not in arguments of logic but in an epistemology of religious experience.[76] He writes:

> The question is not whether it is possible to prove, starting from zero, that God exists; the question is whether the religious man, given the distinctively religious form of human existence in which he participates, is properly entitled as a rational person to believe what he does believe?[77]

Such an argument, Hick acknowledges, will not provide irrefutable proof of God's existence to those who have not had religious experiences of their own, but can at least answer the question of whether a believer "is acting rationally in trusting his own experience and in proceeding to live on the basis of it."[78] In other words, Hick's epistemology of religious experience is not an attempt to describe the nature of religious faith and the kind of knowing that leads to and from it, but instead is an argument for a particular kind of knowing that Hick identifies as the only appropriate (philosophically speaking) basis of religious faith. In Hick's epistemology, we encounter an apologetic argument for what religious faith must be if it is to survive in the modern world, one motivated by slightly different concerns than Race's but which becomes the first step in Race's reconstrual of religious faith in the wake of historicism's disruption.

Hick argues that there is an epistemologically analogous relationship "between the religious person's claim to be conscious of God and any man's claim to be conscious of the physical world as an environment, existing independently of himself."[79] So Hick first turns his attention to truth statements drawn from perceptual experience, arguing that just as nonreligious sensory experience provides a rational basis for the formation of beliefs about external reality, so too does religious experience. The religious believer "cannot help believing either in the reality of the mate-

---

[76]   Hick, *Arguments for the Existence of God*, 103.
[77]   Hick, *Arguments for the Existence of God*, 108. For other versions of this argument, see Richard Swinburne, *Faith and Reason* (New York: Oxford University Press, 1984); William Alston, *Perceiving God* (Ithaca, N.Y.: Cornell University Press, 1991); Alvin Plantinga, *Warranted Christian Belief* (New York: Oxford University Press, 2000).
[78]   Hick, *Arguments for the Existence of God*, 109.
[79]   Hick, *Arguments for the Existence of God*, 110.

rial world which he is conscious of inhabiting, or of the personal divine presence which is overwhelmingly evident to him . . . it is *as* reasonable for him to hold and to act upon the one belief as the other."[80]

While Hick's defense of the epistemic validity of religious belief is initially focused on the Christian tradition and theistic religious experience more broadly, he acknowledges that the scope of the argument is far wider:

> The principle which I have used to justify as rational the faith of a Christian who on the basis of his own religious experience cannot help believing in the reality of "the God and Father of our Lord Jesus Christ," also operates to justify as rational the faith of a Muslim who on the basis of *his* religious experience cannot help believing in the reality of Allah and his providence; and the faith of the Buddhist who on the basis of *his* religious experience cannot help accepting the Buddhist picture of the universe; and so on.[81]

Hick here provides an initial response to the epistemological challenges to religious faith raised by historicism. By orienting his defense of religious belief around individual experience and perspectives, not historical occurrence, Hick has tried to outflank historicism's criticism. But as noted above, this line of thought raises at least one other, equally thorny, problem: how this general epistemic validity of religious belief can be maintained in light of the existence of apparently conflicting religious beliefs. Hick describes this as the question "of the ultimate public verifiability and falsifiability of religious faiths."[82] Significantly, he addresses it as an eschatological issue.

In brief, Hick sees two possible answers. He acknowledges that the "non-eschatological religions" and "most atheistic and naturalistic theories" believe that there will be no future eschatological verification.[83] The second answer, Hick suggests, is offered in eschatological religions such as Christianity and Islam and in "one type of Judaism and perhaps in one type of Buddhism," which maintain that the universe has a definite structure and character which it will become impossible to avoid acknowledging at some point in the future.[84]

[80]   Hick, *Arguments for the Existence of God*, 116.
[81]   Hick, *Arguments for the Existence of God*, 117–18; cf. idem, *The New Frontier of Religion and Science* (Basingstoke, UK: Palgrave Macmillan, 2010), 142–45.
[82]   Hick, *Arguments for the Existence of God*, 118.
[83]   Hick, *Arguments for the Existence of God*, 118, emphasis added.
[84]   Hick, *Arguments for the Existence of God*, 118; cf. idem, *An Interpretation of Religion: Human Responses to the Transcendent*, 2nd ed. (New Haven, Conn.: Yale University Press, 2004), 180–89.

As Hick has been "investigating the rationality of the *Christian* belief in God," it is this second path to which he turns, considering two subsequent possibilities in determining the relationship between divergent religious beliefs.[85] Will seemingly conflicting, or at least dissimilar, religious beliefs be eschatologically revealed as compatible or incompatible? Hick acknowledges the possibility of incompatibility from a Christian perspective but quickly abandons it by making a theological argument that Race will echo, invoking "a specifically Christian reason . . . that belief in the redeeming love of God for all his human creatures [which] makes it incredible that the divine activity in relation to mankind should have been confined to those within the reach of the influence of the Christian revelation."[86]

While Hick's epistemology of religion is supplemented by an appeal to theology, it is largely window dressing. He makes no mention of alternative strands in scripture or doctrine that challenge this theological universalism. Tradition here is an afterthought, invoked only insofar as it can provide confirmation of philosophical conclusions ex post facto. Indeed, Race will appeal to Wilfred Cantwell Smith's phenomenology of faith—conceived as an internal experience strictly differentiated from both external, historical tradition and beliefs that are attached to tradition—to provide an empirical basis for his argument for the compatibility of what appear to be contradictory religious beliefs, rather than appealing to aspects of different traditions themselves that might point in this direction.

In the end, Hick concludes that if Christian religious beliefs are to be considered epistemologically valid and rational, Christians must also "postulate a divine reality of which the different religions of the world represent different partial experiences and partial knowledge."[87] Hick has made the philosophical and ipso facto (from his perspective) theological case for how the general epistemic validity of religious faith is consistent with the existence of different religions with *apparently* conflicting beliefs. But while the transcendental idealism, or "anti-realism," implicit in Hick's argument might allow for some basic and noncontroversial claims of epistemic validity of apparently conflicting beliefs, it neither *guarantees* their transcendent harmony nor does it provide a positive criterion for *identifying* the underlying commonality across

85   Hick, *Arguments for the Existence of God*, 118.
86   Hick, *Arguments for the Existence of God*, 119.
87   Hick, *Arguments for the Existence of God*, 120.

disparate traditions.[88] But what it does provide Race with is of no less importance—an epistemological account in which transcendent experiences and certain conclusions drawn from them are legitimized without contradicting Troeltsch's historicism, such that religious faith *in general* is protected while beliefs attached to particular and historical traditions are disavowed. So, we turn now to consider the formative influence Hick's epistemology exerts on Race's model.

Hick's Epistemology in Race's Typology

Race's adoption of Troeltsch's historicism raises difficult questions about religious faith. Troeltsch himself wrote: "Give the historical method an inch and it will take a mile."[89] The challenge for Race is to find a way to honor Troeltsch's historicism and its undermining of claims concerning God's particular acts in history, like the incarnation, while avoiding its degeneration into a "wretched historicism"—"a collapse of human values and the abandonment of any criteria, any controlling standard for the interpretation of religious-cultural history."[90] This leads Race to confront two basic questions: (1) Is there a way of protecting the rational validity of religious faith—across history—without appealing to specific, historical religious traditions, scriptures, and practices? (2) If such a universal key to understanding the nature and rationality of religious faith is determined, how can we interpret the manifest diversity of religious views as flowing from a common source?

It is in Hick's epistemology of religious experience that Race finds the answer to the first of these questions, and in W. C. Smith's phenomenology, the answer to the second. Hick's epistemological justification of religious experience preserves the critical force of Troeltsch's historical theory without abandoning a commitment to the possibility of authentic religious experiences, and to a limited degree, the awareness of religious truth which emerges from such experiences, occurring in history. The apologetic objective of this focus on experience is clear. For as historicism and

---

[88]   Christopher J. Insole, *The Realist Hope* (New York: Routledge, 2016), 117–33. Hick claims the inherent indeterminacy of the noumenal, transcendent source of religious experience. But Insole notes that he repeatedly violates his own claims of such indefinable ineffability by making substantial claims about its nature—claims that, while unjustified according to his own metaphysical framework, are vague enough to support his pluralistic hypothesis without saying much beyond affirming that the noumenal is transcendent, ontologically and conceptually, and accessible to being authentically experienced in many faiths.

[89]   Troeltsch, "Historical and Dogmatic Method," 16.

[90]   Race, *Christians and Religious Pluralism*, 81.

historical criticism has undermined religious traditions, Race insists that "[in] such circumstances, for religious traditions to survive they must seek to understand and appropriate the underlying experiences at the roots of their respective traditions."[91]

Race summarizes the significance of Hick's argument as follows: "at the level of experience the religions portray a genuine, though different, encounter with the divine."[92] In answer to historicism's undermining of religious *traditions*, Race finds in Hick's epistemology a means of relocating the basis for the rationality of religious faith in *experience*. With Hick's epistemology of religious experience, Race seeks to maintain the full force of historicism's critique of religious traditions while still protecting the possibility of religious experience and, therefore, the validity of religious truth claims of some sort. Race's typology insists that upholding the plausibility of religious faith as a justified response to some actual state of affairs demands the acceptance of pluralism. But as the religious experiences and traditions of people around the world appear to have stark differences, how can they be viewed as responses to a single transcendent source? As Hick puts it, "since one could restate the argument . . . from the point of view of many different religions, with their different forms of religious experience and belief, the question arises whether the argument does not prove too much."[93]

This is a concern that Race shares, one that echoes his worries about Troeltsch's relativism. While Hick's epistemology and its differentiation between tradition and experience rebuffs historicism's apparent undermining of the validity of religious faith itself, the risk of affirming a "wretched" religious relativism is far greater for Hick than for Troeltsch. Yet, although Race defines Troeltsch's "wretched historicism" in terms that imply relativism—"a collapse of human values and the abandonment of any criteria, any controlling standard for the interpretation of religious-cultural history"—it should be pointed out that historicism only threatens human values, criteria, or controlling standards for interpretation of history's meaning founded on an appeal to "ahistorical" events in history, e.g., the incarnation of Jesus.[94] This may be unsavory for those who are committed to the existence of harmony between philosophy and faith, but it is not in itself the start of the inex-

91   Race, *Christians and Religious Pluralism*, 141.
92   Race, *Christians and Religious Pluralism*, 83.
93   Hick, *Arguments for the Existence of God*, 117.
94   Race, *Christians and Religious Pluralism*, 81.

orable drift toward a full-throated metaphysical or even moral relativism which Race implies.

Hick's epistemology, on the other hand, which might be described as a kind of neo-Kantian perspectivism, risks precisely the kind of moral relativism Race hopes to avoid, and may even be construed as depending upon an affirmation of metaphysical relativity.[95] Left to its own devices, it concludes that all values, criteria, and standards for interpretation drawn from experience (absent mitigating factors like mental illness), no matter how contrary to one another they might be, are epistemologically valid and legitimately upheld. *This* is where the threat of relativism—epistemological and moral at least, and potentially metaphysical—is most pointed, and it is the cost of adopting Hick's epistemology.[96] To mitigate it, Race turns to Smith's phenomenology of faith. Though he acknowledges at the outset that, phenomenologically speaking, "any simple assertion of complementarity" is disallowed, citing Hick's reliance upon the Kantian distinction between the noumenal and phenomenal, Race argues that "a distinction between 'God as infinite being' and 'God as finitely experienced'" can, phenomenologically, be shown as present in all the major religious traditions.[97] Not only that, but phenomenological analysis can also elucidate the difference between *faith* as the internal response to the transcendent, and *tradition* or *belief*, which is faith's historically conditioned expression.

Summary of Race's Reliance upon Hick's Religious Epistemology

Exploring the animating force of Troeltsch's historicism within Race's thought led to Hick's epistemology of religious experience, which Race positions as a theological safety net beneath historicism's unrelenting inclination

---

[95]   Harold Netland, *Encountering Religious Pluralism: The Challenge to Christian Faith and Mission* (Downers Grove, Ill.: IVP, 2001), 140–42; cf. Hans Frei, "Niebuhr's Theological Background," in *Faith and Ethics: The Theology of H. Richard Niebuhr*, ed. Paul Ramsey (New York: Harper & Row, 1957), 38; idem, "Remarks in Connection with a Theological Proposal," in *Theology and Narrative*, 31–32, 37–40; idem, "Theological Reflections on the Accounts of Jesus' Death and Resurrection," in *Theology and Narrative*, 87–91; idem, "On Interpreting the Christian Story," in *Reading Faithfully*, 1:72.

[96]   Of course, Hick himself makes several substantial, metaphysical claims—the inherent indeterminacy of the noumenal, transcendent source of religious experience—thereby contradicting his own rejection of substantialist claims about God. The rather strange upshot of this, as Christopher Insole points out, is that the only thing preventing Hick's epistemology from descending into a thoroughgoing metaphysical relativism or "anti-realism . . . is his preparedness to break his own rules and covertly make substantial claims about God." Insole, *Realist Hope*, 133.

[97]   Insole, *Realist Hope*, 85.

to push religion over the cliff and into the briar-patch of "wretched historicism." On this view, religions—if they are to be accorded any explanatory power—should not be seen as traditions which emerge in response to public events or occurrences, as such a historical underpinning would defy the three principles of historical criticism advocated by Troeltsch and render them void. Rather, if they do speak to a transcendent reality, religions must be conceived as external expressions of the *internal*, and in that sense, ahistorical religious experiences of their founders and adherents.

Although Hick describes them as perceptual and therefore in some way interfacing with the historical world surrounding the experiencing individual, such experiences can only truly evade the clutches of historicism if they are fundamentally interior experiences. Indeed, the basic content of these experiences, encounters with the universal *Real*, is understood as ahistorical—even though they are necessarily tinted by the historical context of the experiencing person. To Race, this historical haziness or phenomenal tinting is the explanation of religious pluralism that we must acknowledge and then peer through if we are to enter into interfaith relationships built on a foundation of mutual respect, vulnerability and interest.[98] With this in mind, we turn now to the work of W. C. Smith, whose phenomenological hermeneutic attempted to address "empirically" the problem of relativism that arises from Hick's epistemological perspectivism, making a theological distinction between external and historically contingent religious traditions, and the personal faith of individuals.

W. C. Smith's Phenomenology of Faith

Wilfred Cantwell Smith's phenomenological interpretation of religion is employed by Race as a means of integrating the historicist and epistemological commitments just outlined. Of course, Smith's work has been greatly influential in theology of religions and in pluralist theology. But of particular interest to the interrogation of Race's typology of the theology of religion itself is that Smith's early methodological critique of the *academic* study of religion serves as the foundation of the *theological* methodology of phenomenology he developed later in his career. Where his academic method advocated for "personalism"—taking seriously the lived experiences and expressions of an individual's faith—Smith's theological method expands upon this, assuming what might be called an ide-

---

[98]   Cf. Philip L. Quinn, "Towards Thinner Theologies: Hick and Alston on Religious Diversity," *International Journal for Philosophy of Religion* 38, no. 1 (1995): 145–64.

alist anthropology, where *faith* in the transcendent is posited to be what might be described as an anthropological constant, existing prior to and independent of any external stimuli, but which can nonetheless be phenomenologically tracked and traced through the external expressions resulting from it. Where Smith's academic method insisted that academic accounts of a religion must be intelligible to those within that tradition, his theological method—particularly his principle of "corporate critical self-consciousness"—further demands mutual intelligibility between faith traditions themselves and between *all* faith traditions and philosophy.

Whatever significance Smith's academic personalism exercises in his theology, it is ultimately subverted by his anthropological and phenomenological rendering of faith. Smith's theology only accepts those claims that can be endorsed by both those of another faith tradition *and* a philosophically trained academic. Smith's theological methodology preserves from his academic methodology the primacy of etic philosophical criticism over and against the emic resources (scriptural, doctrinal, and others) of a faith tradition. So, Race's adoption of Smith's theological methodology for pluralism is itself the selection of an academic methodology for theology, subordinating the particulars of any religious tradition to the generalities of his anthropological account of faith as a universal human attribute that can be phenomenologically analyzed.

Smith, a historian whose early work focused on Islamic history, follows Troeltsch in upholding critical historical inquiry as foundational to the study of religion.[99] Unlike Troeltsch, who was a philosopher and theologian and ended up focusing much of his work on history, Smith was a historian who ended up focusing much of his work on theology and philosophy. Troeltsch's most enduring impact on the study of religion might be his arguments *for* the imposition of historical limits on theological statements. Smith's abiding contribution takes an inverse approach, in his arguing *from* the limitations inherent in historical phenomena toward an expansive vision of theological possibility.

He does this most famously in his 1963 book *The Meaning and End of Religion*, where etymological and conceptual analysis of the term "religion" is put in service of a methodological argument that suggests theologians and scholars have come to focus their attention on the external aspects of *tradition* when they should instead be focusing on the internal

---

[99]   W. C. Smith, *The Meaning and End of Religion* (Minneapolis: Fortress, 1991), 133–41; cf. idem, *Belief and History* (Charlottesville: University of Virginia Press, 1977).

dynamics of *faith*. This subsequently became the central focus of his work, culminating in his 1989 *Towards a World Theology*, where he presents his historical and methodological work in explicitly theological terms.[100]

In *Meaning and End*, Smith insists that the study of religion must accept "that the 'nature' either of religious traditions or of faith is not an intellectual desideratum nor a metaphysical reality; we are dealing here rather with historical actualities, which must be explored as such."[101] So it is ironic that in attempting to deal with religious traditions as historical realities, he ends up casting history aside by positing a metaphysical distinction between tradition and faith, where tradition is the historically tainted expression of the internal and universal phenomenon of human faith:

> There are plenty of merely mundane and many repugnantly perverse elements clearly visible in the religious history of humankind (one's own and others'); these elements may without too much trouble be sorted out. They cloud, but need not eclipse, the divine. To discriminate them (whether in one's own or in all traditions) is (in one's own has long been) the responsibility of faith.[102]

On display here is the strange logic of pluralist theology: invoking the importance of history only to circumvent it when positing the true nature of humanity's encounter with the transcendent; appealing to academic or philosophical disciplines and methods as the only legitimate means of waging a theological argument; enshrining the responsibility to discard beliefs not simply in one's own tradition but "in all traditions" in an argument for a theology that is supposedly marked by its affirming of the importance of the beliefs of said religious traditions. This strangeness is a function of its apologetic objective. For, the thought apparently goes, if the independent and unbiased tools of academic inquiry can demonstrate the legitimacy of religious faith, a skeptical world can reconsider its doubt without giving up its claim to critical objectivity—no matter how this might distort the views on and expressions of faith held by those who are already believers.[103] With its central role in Race's account of pluralism,

---

[100]   W. C. Smith, *Towards a World Theology* (Basingstoke, UK: Macmillan, 1981); idem, *What Is Scripture?* (Minneapolis: Fortress, 1994).
[101]   Smith, *Meaning and End*, 195; cf. idem, *Faith and Belief* (Princeton, N.J.: Princeton University Press, 1979).
[102]   Smith, *World Theology*, 185; cf. James C. Livingston, "Religious Pluralism and the Question of Religious Truth in Wilfred C. Smith," *Journal of Religious and Cultural Theory* 4, no. 3 (2003): 64f.
[103]   Smith, *World Theology*, 50–55, 145–51.

we can see in Smith's theological method and the pluralist theology to which it points, the prioritization of philosophy and etic discourses over and against emic and self-descriptive discourses.

Race sees Troeltsch's historicism as having exposed a fatal flaw in traditional Christian theology in general (and Christology in particular), and Hick's argument for the epistemic validity of religious experience as having rescued the rationality of faith. But in the wake of their acceptance, Race argues that what "is needed is a philosophical means by which the specificities of 'transcendence,' found in the different traditions are honored while their 'facets' as part of a greater whole are brought into relationship more clearly."[104] It is in Smith's phenomenology that Race finds an account of the possibility of discerning the unity of faith that underlies the diversity of the world's religious traditions.

Equally important, Race finds in Smith's work not just a phenomenological understanding of faith that seems perfectly fitted to filling the gaps left by Troeltsch and Hick, but also a theological methodology that issues from this framing of faith and which purportedly provides support for it. Following Smith, Race identifies this methodology as interfaith dialogue, though this moniker ignores the overriding influence of philosophy and other academic disciplines in delineating the legitimate content of such dialogue: "In dialogue, participants will be aware that Ultimate Reality will be possessed of a richness which can sustain different manifestations of the fullness of its hidden truth."[105] Race finds that Smith's phenomenology of faith supports Hick's "optimistic confidence in the processes of discursive dialogue [which] render what appear contradictory differences as complementary truths."[106] Indeed, Hick deems Smith "the father of contemporary religious pluralism."[107] At the same time, Smith's phenomenology is supported by the insights of historicism and Hick's religious epistemology.[108] So the three strands exist, within Race's typology, in a reciprocal relationship from which emerges a whole that is, from Race's perspective, greater than the sum of its parts—pluralist theology.

Looking ahead to the next chapter, it is perhaps worth noting here that Frei conceives of the quest for Christ's presence in the world in a way that in some

---

[104]   Race, *Interfaith Encounter*, 110.
[105]   Race, *Interfaith Encounter*, 110.
[106]   Race, *Christians and Religious Pluralism*, 90.
[107]   Hick, *Autobiography*, 261.
[108]   Race, *Interfaith Encounter*, 110.

important respects resembles Smith's phenomenology.[109] Most significantly, Frei, like Smith, argues that God's presence is not limited to the church or the Bible, and that the place to look is not in systems of thought but in the patterns of our enacted, communal lives. Unlike Smith, Frei's quest for God's presence in the world, beyond scripture and sacrament, is not oriented around inner experience, much less an interior experience of faith framed in opposition to an exterior body of beliefs. Frei describes the discernment of God's presence in history in largely moral terms, where it is discerned in examples of the "ordinary kindness and natural gentleness" of communal life—figures of the identity of Jesus Christ enacted and discerned in the unsystematic and unpredictable unfolding of history.[110] So Frei adopts something akin to a phenomenological approach to discerning the patterns of God's presence in the world, but on very different terms than Smith's. For Frei, the search for God's presence in the world is both an inherently Christocentric endeavor and one that cannot simply bypass or explain away external and historical events, the uniqueness and particularity of which are constitutive of their theological significance. It is therefore best described not as phenomenological, but *figural*, as will be explained in the next chapter.

Relatedly, Frei, unlike Smith, does not begin his theology with an anthropology, and to the extent that it implies one, it describes a very different understanding of the human person. Smith's existentialism yields an anthropology that prioritizes the interior and transcendental over the public and communal,[111] an approach that, in spite of his claims otherwise, explains away external differences in its appeal to their common transcendent source.[112]

From Comparative Religious History to Theology:
The Shifting Context of Smith's Methodology

With a background in religious studies and the history of religion, including a particular focus on Islam, Smith's early work focused largely on a

[109] See further ch. 3.
[110] Hans Frei, "The Encounter of Jesus with the German Academy," in *Theology and Narrative*, 136.
[111] Frei, *Types of Christian Theology*, 136.
[112] Cf. Hans Frei, "Interpreting the Christian Story," 70f.; idem, "History, Salvation-History, and Typology," in *Reading Faithfully*, 1:152f. As we will see, Frei's refusal to "go behind history" in an effort to identify some universal ontological locus of transcendent encounter ends up, on the other hand, suggesting that our historical encounters with events and individuals in whom we discern the pattern of Christ's presence might force us to alter our understandings of Jesus in profound ways.

constructive methodological critique of the philosophical, historical, and sociological approaches to the study of religion.[113] His argument, particularly in *The Meaning and End of Religion*, was compelling enough to receive a favorable review by Lesslie Newbigin—although the potential for their future theological discord is discernible even there.[114]

In criticizing the methodology of religious studies and the history of religion, Smith sought to discredit the prevailing approach as "objectivist," concerned only with the external manifestations of humanity's religious life. He believed that this reflected a misapprehension of human nature, erroneously placing emphasis on the external aspects of our lives, to the detriment of the inner aspects of our being:

> The traditional form of Western scholarship in the study of other men's religion was that of an impersonal presentation of an "it" . . . A fundamental error of the social sciences, and a fundamental lapse even of some humanists, has been to take the observable manifestations of some human concern as if they were the concern itself.[115]

So, Smith suggests replacing this objectivist methodology with personalism, prioritizing the expressions and experiences of persons of faith over and above the orthodox accounts contained in scriptural canons and doctrinal corpuses. Though he initially expressed this distinction simply in terms of "external" and "internal" religion, he would come to cast the divide as one between *belief*—the historically contingent, doctrinal or ritual forms which result from futile attempts to interpret and define ultimate reality—and *faith*—an existential response to transcendent experience and a universally shared human capacity.[116]

---

[113] Cf. W. C. Smith, *Islam in Modern History: The Tension between Faith and History in the Islamic World* (Princeton, N.J.: Princeton University Press, 1957); idem, "Comparative Religion: Whither—and Why?" in *The History of Religions: Essays in Methodology*, ed. Mircea Eliade and Joseph M. Kitagawa (Chicago: University of Chicago Press, 1959), 31–58.

[114] Lesslie Newbigin, review of *The Meaning and End of Religion* by W. C. Smith, *Theology* 82, no. 688 (1979): 294–96. For an account of their contentious encounters at Tambaram 1988, see Lesslie Newbigin, *Unfinished Agenda* (Edinburgh: St. Andrew Press, 1993), 243; Geoffrey Wainwright, *Lesslie Newbigin: A Theological Life* (Oxford: Oxford University Press, 2000), 197, 200, 229.

[115] Smith, "Comparative Religion," 34–35; cf. Smith, *World Theology*, 56–80.

[116] For the earlier external/internal distinction, see Smith, "Comparative Religion," 34–39; for the subsequent faith/belief formulation, see Smith, *Meaning and End*, 170–92; idem, *Faith and Belief*, 160–66, 196.

Smith initially portrays this distinction as a methodological one, aimed at criticizing the colonial and patronizing tenor of the comparative or academic study of religion. But the theological significance of the divide between faith and belief soon becomes his primary concern, culminating in a book published late in his life, *Towards a World Theology*.[117] This shift in subject matter should not be mistaken for a shift in method, for this academic methodology remained a central aspect of Smith's later, more theological work. Indeed, what began as an academic methodology is rather easily transformed into an explicitly theological methodology. Race hints at this when he suggests that "the notion of a 'Christian Theology of Comparative Religion' gives way for Cantwell Smith to 'A Theology of Comparative Religion for those among us who are Christians.'"[118]

In a 1959 essay titled "Comparative Religion—Whither—and Why?" Smith suggests that we can see the academic study of religion as unfolding in stages—from the objective to the personal. The objective stage is characterized by "the accumulation, organization and analysis of facts."[119] This empirical period gave way to the analytical period of the nineteenth century, when universities "gradually enshrined Oriental studies and anthropological studies and here and there established chairs of *Religionswissenschaft*, the study of religion."[120] Though objective research continues, rightly in Smith's view, he believes that the interpretive framework appropriate to its analysis has undergone a fundamental shift in which "the exciting new frontiers of inquiry and of challenge lie at a new and higher level."[121] That is, the personal, because "the study of a religion is the study of persons . . . Faith is a quality of men's lives."[122]

Again, it would not be until *The Meaning and End of Religion* that Smith formally differentiated between "faith" and "belief" as the interior and exterior aspects of "religion."[123] In the early 1959 essay, the distinction is offered in a rather limited methodological suggestion: that analysis of the observable facts be corroborated and conditioned in reference to the roles they play in people's lived experience.[124] Though they are not identical, in

---

[117]   Cf. Smith, "Comparative Religion."
[118]   Race, *Christians and Religious Pluralism*, 102; cf. James L. Cox, *A Guide to the Phenomenology of Religion* (London: T&T Clark, 2006), 195.
[119]   Smith, "Comparative Religion," 31–32.
[120]   Smith, "Comparative Religion," 32.
[121]   Smith, "Comparative Religion," 32.
[122]   Smith, "Comparative Religion," 35.
[123]   Smith, *Meaning and End*, 111.
[124]   Smith, "Comparative Religion," 39.

this personalist methodology are discernible traces of Smith's later isolation and elevation of faith as the interior site of transcendent encounter.

Smith's advocacy of a personalist approach is accompanied by another methodological principle which also will carry greater theological significance in Smith's later work. What he will come to describe in theological terms as the principle of "corporate critical self-consciousness" is present in 1959, though there without a name and applied as a methodological principle for the academic study of religion: "*it is the business of comparative religion to construct statements about religion that are intelligible within at least two traditions simultaneously.*"[125] At this point in Smith's career, the second tradition is "academia," though there are already here suggestions of a more explicitly interfaith agenda.[126] And insofar as Smith's essay is intended for scholars of religion, the insistence of mutual intelligibility is an important scholarly acknowledgment of the significance of a person's self-understanding of their actions in the face of another person's divergent analysis. But its real force lies in its insistence upon the objective intelligibility of theological statements.

Smith here, as later, maintains the prioritization of academic criticism, insisting that "it is possible both in theory and in practice for an outside scholar to break new ground in stating the meaning of a faith in, say, modern terms more successfully than a believer."[127] Smith would have it as incumbent upon an academic to inquire directly into an individual's perspective on the meaning of their scripture, ritual, or the like. But such self-description, for Smith, is better serviced by someone with a Western, academic pedigree: ". . . it is imperative that our new enterprise [transcendentology] not leave the Western philosophic tradition on the outside."[128]

So even while he presents his methodology as more focused on religion's "personal lived qualities," academic and/or philosophical analysis retains pride of place in Smith's methodology. Again, this is perhaps unsurprising insofar as Smith's project is advancing an academic methodology. But in Smith's later, more theological work, the retention of this academic priority ends up dictating the terms of *theological* reciprocity between adherents of different religions. In other words, though rooted in Smith's early rejection of academic objectivism, understood as a focus on external dogmas and practices, the principle of corporate critical self-consciousness and its

---

125   Smith, "Comparative Religion," 52; cf. idem, *World Theology*, 56–80.
126   Smith, "Comparative Religion," 52.
127   Smith, "Comparative Religion," 43.
128   Cf. Smith, *World Theology*, 182–83.

prioritization of philosophy asserts the objectivity of religious truth such that all religious truth must be philosophically or academically acceptable and, as such, actual disagreement between religions is rendered an impossibility, the perception of which is simply an unfortunate byproduct of taking too seriously the historical traditions and particular beliefs of the world's religions.

If anything, his later theological work presents an even more stringent account of the philosophical requirements that accompany mutual intelligibility in theology: ". . . any statement about personal faith should in principle be *intellectually persuasive* both to him or her or those whose faith it is and to the perceptive outside observer."[129] This insistence of intellectual intelligibility and persuasiveness of faith statements both dissolves any divide between academic analysis and theological description *and* proposes philosophical coherence, however vaguely defined, as a basic criterion for theological legitimacy. Smith's theological methodology seemingly relies on philosophy and perpetuates objectivism in the study of religion more forcefully than does his academic method.

The Anthropology of Faith, the Mythological Interpretation of Scripture, and the Phenomenology of Faith

Smith's methodological program for the academic study of religion sets the stage for his subsequent theological agenda, and it is his anthropological account of faith and the related phenomenological interpretation of religion that are of central importance in this transition.[130] For his redirection of religious study's object toward the inner life of humanity depends upon an idealist anthropology that prioritizes this interior life as the site of transcendent encounter, a view with theological implications similar in some ways to those of Hick's epistemology. To understand the true nature of the human person is to strip away the ephemera of historical existence and access the inner life of the mind. While this has resonance with Hick's epistemology, Smith's priority is less to demonstrate that faith is epistemically valid but more to show that it is ubiquitous, an inherent feature of the human person.[131] In other words, there is already implicit in Smith's phenomenological

---

[129]   Smith, *World Theology*, 101, emphasis added; cf. idem, *Belief and History*, viii. For a slightly different take on the progression of corporate critical self-consciousness, see Cox, *Phenomenology of Religion*, 201–3.

[130]   Smith never appears to have used the term "phenomenology" to describe his own work, preferring instead "comparative religion," but it is both a term Race uses in his typology and one that has been applied to Smith by other scholars. Race, *Christians and Religious Pluralism*, 84f., 96f., 150; Cox, *Phenomenology of Religion*, 171.

[131]   Cf. Cox, *Phenomenology of Religion*, 67.

method an anthropological assumption of the underlying unity of the world's religions. His interpretation of religion provides the means of not simply describing different religions, but of explaining how their external diversity emerges from a universal anthropological attribute. As Smith sees it, "one's faith is given by God, one's beliefs by one's century."[132]

Smith's phenomenological method is therefore focused on discerning traces of the internal experience of faith in external phenomena like scripture and tradition, so that phenomenological analysis purportedly reveals a pervasive unity only masked by the limitations and impositions of historical context that inevitably creep into descriptions of this ineffable and internal encounter. Smith's phenomenological method is designed to uncover the unity of this universal aspect of human life. That said, Smith does pursue an understanding of "scripture" as a phenomenon itself, akin to other features of cumulative traditions, such that scripture appears to be a universal response to transcendent experience.[133]

But scripture as a phenomenon is for Smith always subsidiary to faith. Even before its contents are considered, any one scripture is viewed by Smith as a limited and historically restricted specimen, though evoked within a universal process propelled by the basic human capacity for the experience of the transcendent, or "faith" in Smith's terms. In this sense, even as Smith insists that too strong a focus on scripture limits our ability to discern the universal truths that are shared across religious traditions, the existence of scripture in different religions is also treated as evidence of this anthropological constant.

Smith is candid about the apologetic orientation of his phenomenological method, which he describes as in the service of a "new task" for theology. By yielding an interpretation of empirical evidence that casts faith as a universal experience inherent to human existence, Smith's phenomenology claims to free faith from the difficult limitations imposed upon it by history-bound traditions—limitations which have themselves rendered faith intellectually untenable in modernity. The "new task" for theologians, scholars and religious adherents is "to interpret intellectually the cosmic significance of human life generically, not just for one's own group specifically."[134] In so doing, the apologetic endeavor of justifying the philosophical legitimacy of religious faith becomes imminently

---

[132]   Smith, *Belief and History*, 96; cf. Philip C. Almond, "W.C. Smith as Theologian of Religions," *Harvard Theological Review* 76, no. 3 (1983): 337f.
[133]   Smith, *What Is Scripture?* 212.
[134]   Smith, *World Theology*, 187.

achievable, for "the problem of religious truth is in principle not different, but in practice much improved, if one take the whole of religion rather than a sector of it as the question's field."[135] Interpreted phenomenologically, "scripture" is rendered not only as a manifestation of an interior faith available by virtue of human nature itself, but as a testament to the existence of a transcendent force for those who do not believe.

Of course, if the *meaning* of scripture is limited to the *concept* of scripture alone, it becomes impossible to place emphasis on the actual contents of any particular text:

> We shall be arguing presently that the true issue is not scripture itself. Rather, what is requisite is an *understanding* of scripture, and of the place in human life that it has filled when and where it was important . . . a *general theory* . . . a new conception of scripture . . . it will be critical of all, and must move well beyond them, to supersede.[136]

This hermeneutical supersession of scripture brought about by adopting the phenomenological interpretation of scripture allows Smith to eschew the problems posed by different scriptural accounts of the divine, replacing them with a general affirmation of faith as an anthropological constant: "Scripture . . . can be understood only in relation to a community of persons . . . this human component, when taken seriously, raises in new form the question of transcendence (and the immanence that is involved with it)."[137]

So with regard to the specific contents of scripture, Smith suggests his phenomenological interpretation means abandoning those hermeneutical stances in which scripture is "specifying something originally celestial" in favor of an interpretation which views scripture as "characterizing various matters on this earth" and its influence on the expression of the "transcendent significance" that led to their creation in the first place.[138] But it is important to note that this account risks obscuring the anthropological and hermeneutical idealism of Smith's phenomenological interpretation. The theological significance of scripture's account of "various matters on this earth" is not tied to the specific matters themselves, but rather to the theological ideals that such matters represent *apart from* their historical

---

[135]   Smith, *World Theology*, 187.
[136]   Smith, *What Is Scripture?* 213–14, 216, emphasis added.
[137]   Smith, *What Is Scripture?* 221.
[138]   Smith, *What Is Scripture?* 221.

particularity. The contents of scripture are meaningful on an experiential level, where "experience" is something sufficiently generic such that it is intelligible across religious traditions. Smith writes that, "rather than saying that Jesus Christ is the full revelation of God, I would say rather that He is a revelation of God to me, and has been to many other people, though I know others to whom He has not been."[139]

Elsewhere, Smith displays some confusion about the Christological implications of his phenomenological hermeneutic. In a chapter he authored for the 1987 book *The Myth of Christian Uniqueness*, he first rejects the notion that his theology demands the undermining of central theological commitments such as the divinity of Christ, writing: "It has been widely felt that the divinity of Christ is centrally at stake in the pluralism debate; even that this is a crucial matter. The divinity of Christ is not, however, at issue in these discussions. In fact, in some ways it could become a serious distraction to the question before us."[140] Yet Smith concludes this very same chapter by asserting that the incarnation is best appreciated as a myth.[141] Smith's reticence in tracing out the Christological implications of his phenomenological hermeneutic is something even supporters like Hick noted with apparent frustration.[142] In the end, as Hick's criticism highlights, Smith's attempt at circumventing historicist skepticism with a phenomenological argument for the universality of faith seems unavoidably dependent upon a mythological account of the diverse normative claims and particular narratives of individual scriptures. Scripture, for Smith, is not "a central issue" but "it can serve as one clue to what is, indeed, a central issue."[143]

The central issue is the existence of faith as an internal, anthropological constant. Smith's claims of making an academically defensible case for faith as a universal human feature rely on his analysis of the external and subsidiary phenomena of scripture and tradition.[144] This analysis

[139] W. C. Smith, *Questions of Religious Truth* (New York: Charles Scribner's Sons, 1967), 91.

[140] W. C. Smith, "Idolatry: In Comparative Perspective," in Hick and Knitter, *Myth of Christian Uniqueness*, 61.

[141] Smith, "Idolatry," 66.

[142] John Hick, "On Wilfred Cantwell Smith—His Place in the Study of Religion," *Method and Theory in the Study of Religion* 4, nos. 1–2 (1992): 15–16.

[143] Smith, *What Is Scripture?* 238.

[144] Francis Schüssler Fiorenza, "Religion—A Contested Site in Theology and the Study of Religion," *Harvard Theological Review* 93, no. 1 (2000): 17.

rests upon his idealist anthropology and the notion of faith as a universal human quality. In Smith's words:

> Such, then, is my thesis on faith . . . that which saves, universally. But I do not quite arrive at that [by] tautology. My concept of faith as a generic human quality is partly inductive, empirically derived from a study of man's religious history throughout the world, and partly is derived from and continuous with the concept in the history of Christian doctrine . . . The concept does not pretend to be exactly the same as any other one Christian thinker's . . . just different enough to cope with modern knowledge.[145]

Again, the apologetic orientation of Smith's theology toward satisfying intellectual or philosophical standards is explicit. Like Race, Smith's primary point in differentiating his theology from other Christian theologies is that his is able to cope with modern knowledge.[146] For Smith believes that the phenomenological analysis of internal faith in external tradition is the basis upon which the correspondence between philosophical and theological truth is discerned. Scripture, rituals, and other externals are emptied of any actual or specific theological significance.

When held up against Smith's assertion that "personalism" in the study of religion will yield greater respect for the lived experiences and expressions of a person's faith, it appears as if Smith's program is less about respecting religious differences and more about predetermining what aspects of a person's religious experiences and expressions deserve respect. The true meaning and value of any religious tradition and its sacred texts can only properly be discerned through phenomenological analysis, which is to say that the meaning of religion, writ large, is only fully available to an academic like Smith. The theological value of any one religion's practices and traditions is dependent upon the overarching connection phenomenological analysis makes between diverse external phenomena and the unity of their underlying transcendent significance. Any statement of faith is unwarranted until it can be connected with other religious phenomena *and* pass philosophical muster. Only in meeting these standards is the spiritual significance simultaneously affirmed and discerned.

With the anthropological account of faith, Smith believes he is in possession of a theological key to uncovering the common essence of the superficial diversity across the cumulative traditions; with phenomeno-

---

[145]   Smith, *World Theology*, 172.
[146]   Cf. Cox, *Phenomenology of Religion*, 199.

logical analysis of faith in cumulative traditions, Smith believes he is in possession of an empirical and philosophically sound argument for the existence of this underlying transcendent source. "Faith is not belief," Smith writes, "none the less (or: therein) one is committed to intellectual integrity. This includes the integrating of what one says theologically and what one knows and thinks and understands generally, as well as the integrating of what one knows and what one is."[147]

Corporate Critical Self-Consciousness

It was suggested at the start of this section that Smith is an integrating force within Race's account of pluralism. Race responds to the challenge laid out by historicism with an implicit appeal to an epistemology like Hick's, which provides epistemological plausibility to religious faith but does so by risking the religious relativism Race seeks to avoid. In response, Smith's phenomenological analysis is presented as both mitigating the relativizing concerns entailed in an epistemological appeal alone *and* providing empirical proof that justifies religious faith. In this sense, though Smith's theology does not depend upon Troeltsch's historicism or Hick's epistemology, it has a kind of symbiotic relationship with both. Smith himself writes that the "task of attaining an epistemological sophistication that will be historically self-critical as well as universalist, is interlinked with, not prior to, our task of attaining corporate critical self-consciousness in the religious realm."[148]

This approach is formalized in his principle of "corporate critical self-consciousness," inchoate in his 1959 personalist academic methodology and, later, placed at the center of his theological methodology as a "scientific" and "decisive principle of verification":

> The intellectual pursuit in humane studies of corporate self-consciousness, critical, rational, empirical, is scientific in various senses; *including that of its being subject, and it alone being subject, in the deepest sense, to a valid verification procedure.* In objective knowledge, that a first observer's understanding has done justice to what is observed is testable by the experience of a second and a third observer. In corporate critical self-consciousness, that justice has been done to the matter being studied is testable by the experience of other observers but also by that of the subject or subjects . . . *No*

---

[147]   Smith, *World Theology*, 82.
[148]   Smith, *World Theology*, 189.

statement involving persons is valid, I propose, unless theoretically its
validity can be verified both by the persons involved and by critical
observers not involved.[149]

Again, it should be abundantly clear that for all of Smith's emphasis on
"personalism" and the value of subjective transcendent experience, corporate critical self-consciousness is hardly an abandonment of the objectivism he decries.

On the one hand, corporate critical self-consciousness demands that
any particular description of a religion must be acceptable in the eyes of
most adherents of that religion: "No statement about Islamic faith is true
that Muslims cannot accept. No personalist statement about Hindu religious life is legitimate in which Hindus cannot recognize themselves."[150]
But on the other hand, philosophical coherence is identified as the final
arbiter of theological legitimacy:

> It is also the case, however, that these statements are made by out-
> siders, presumably honest; so that first of all they must satisfy the
> non-participant, and *satisfy all the most exacting requirements of*
> *rational inquiry and academic rigor.* They must be more than objec-
> tively true; not less. *Thus, no statement about Islamic faith is true that*
> *non-Muslims cannot accept. No statement about Hindu religious life*
> *is legitimate in which the Hindus' non-Hindu neighbors cannot recog-*
> *nize them[selves].*[151]

For all the emphasis theological pluralism places on the supposed prioritization of interfaith intelligibility, the above passage clearly reveals it to be
secondary to, and even contingent on, satisfying the requirement of philosophical validity. The principle of corporate critical self-consciousness
gives different religions the power of veto over each other, but philosophy
and "critical modern thought" retain ultimate authority, determining the
very premises of what is and is not defensible theological thought. Not
insignificantly, this suggests that if "rational inquiry and academic rigor"
deem a statement or claim of faith inadmissible—e.g., the occurrence of
miracles—it remains unacceptable no matter how many religious traditions affirm it.

---

[149]   Smith, *World Theology*, 59–60, emphasis added; cf. Cox, *Phenomenology of*
Religion, 201–2.
[150]   Smith, *World Theology*, 97; cf. Smith, *Meaning and End*, 196–202, 323, 329.
[151]   Smith, *World Theology*, 97, emphasis added.

This is a direct result of Smith's apologetic approach to theology. For him, the principle of corporate critical self-consciousness ensures theology need no longer be viewed as antiquated, anti-intellectual, or irrational. Having philosophical cogency determine theological legitimacy represents for Smith a refusal "to let faith wallow innovatingly [sic] in sentimental a-rationality." Instead, it affirms that it "belongs to faith . . . to move upwards, not downwards, intellectually from the past."[152] So anchored to philosophical validation, Smith's view of theology is one that demands *progress*. The only viable theology today is one that *continuously* strives to conform to the developing requirements of philosophical intelligibility. Smith acknowledges that faith unresponsive to philosophical critique might "presumably continue," but such faith, rooted in and responsive to a particular tradition, is inferior to the universalism of the philosophically yoked faith of theological pluralism:

> Perhaps because I believe seriously in the unity of knowledge, and believe seriously in the unity of mankind, I rather imagine that the only answer to our question that will satisfy the non-Muslim and the only answer that will satisfy the Muslim will in coming years be identical . . . I am deeply persuaded that in the twentieth and twenty-first centuries the religious history of mankind will be taking a major new turn . . . I cannot see how in principle any answer to our question can be truly adequate for a Christian unless it were also and simultaneously truly adequate for a Muslim . . . Reactions to the universe, the existential religious response, may presumably continue to be a personal or group adventure . . . on the other hand, it is the business of those of us who are intellectuals to universalize.[153]

The Primacy of Philosophy and the Apologetic Promise of W. C. Smith's Theology of Comparative Religion in Race's Typology

Toward the end of his exposition of the pluralist type, Race writes:

> Some form of pluralism in the Christian theology of religions is inevitable, I have said, if historical studies are treated seriously. For many reasons, however, a clear formulation of the pluralist position

---

[152]   Smith, *Faith and Belief*, 167; cf. Livingston, "Religious Pluralism and the Question of Religious Truth," 64; Schüssler Fiorenza, "Religion—A Contested Site," 16–17; Cox, *Phenomenology of Religion*, 203.
[153]   Smith, *Religious Truth*, 61.

is not easily forthcoming. The main problem concerns the "debili-tating relativism" which it seems, at least potentially, to espouse.[154]

In light of the significance of Troeltsch and Hick for his pluralist theology of religions, Race acknowledges that accepting their respective historicism and epistemology leads to a conflicted position, affirming the inevitability of religious pluralism while also risking a descent into a pervasive religious relativism. Left to its own devices, a wholesale affirmation of the theories of Troeltsch and Hick renders humanity's relationship with the transcendent as one that is individualistic and discordant. If God cannot act in "external" history, and relatedly, if the only rational basis of religious faith for a person is some sort of *interior* (but, perhaps confusingly, also sensory) experience, then everyone's religious experiences must be considered authentic and the theological claims they draw therefrom remain rational—no matter how much they might conflict. The situation Race apparently wants to avoid is a relativistic pluralism that depicts humanity's encounters with the transcendent as valid but divided, impenetrable to anyone other than the experiencing individual, where what is theologically "true" capriciously depends upon each person's experiences (or lack thereof).

Smith's work does not merely suggest the universalism of religious experience, but crucially provides a way of framing this universalism without "proving too much," in the words of Hick. This is then perhaps the most significant aspect of Smith's influence on the typology and in overcoming the threat of relativism—the rearrangement of theological structures of hermeneutical authority as a function of his phenomenological approach. In Smith's theological methodology, Race finds both a critique of authority as it has historically been understood in religious traditions and a new vision of authority, both philosophical and theological, which he believes inoculates pluralism from the relativistic threat. By reframing theological interpretation phenomenologically—directing the interpreters gaze away from the text or traditions themselves and toward the generalized treatment of the phenomena of scripture and tradition—Smith provides Race with an apologetic argument for theology's ability to accommodate philosophical critiques by reworking the configuration of theological authority to include non-Christians and *wissenschaftlich* academia.

On this view, Race's theological pluralism appears less concerned with accounting theologically for the *fact* of religious pluralism than with answering philosophical criticisms. Without descending into the impen-

---

[154]   Race, *Christians and Religious Pluralism*, 97.

etrable and unproductive terrain of authorial motivation and intention, from what has been covered above it should be clear that waging an apologetic argument for the legitimacy of religious faith by affirming the compatibility of theology and philosophy is one of Race's foremost concerns. Race's typology appears to take its shape from a driving interest in subjecting theological claims to philosophical scrutiny—with the force of other faith traditions' theologies only coming into play as a result of this philosophical chastening. In this light, it seems impossible to avoid the conclusion that the superiority of pluralism over exclusivism and inclusivism is closely tied to, if not entirely determined by, its acceptance of the primacy of philosophy. Race's account of pluralism is revealed to be more an argument for the apologetic imperative of granting philosophy's authority over Christian theology than it is an argument for pluralism's own theological or even ethical superiority.

Both Race and Smith assert that the traditional sources of authority within individual traditions—scriptures, rituals, priesthoods—should be emptied of their power to adjudicate the legitimacy of theological formulations and conclusions. Religious traditions may shape and color such experiences or truth claims, but they are themselves wholly unsuited to weighing in on historical and epistemic questions—which are, for Race and Smith, questions of theological legitimacy—and as such cannot be trusted to provide an acceptable hermeneutic within and without particular religious groups. Following Smith, Race will claim that the legitimacy of theological interpretation—of scripture, ritual, etc.—depends upon its being untethered from the particularities of any religious community. For Race at least, this applies even when tradition is used to support claims that might resonate with pluralism. Using the example of a Christian reliance upon the Bible in accounting for the diversity of religious experiences outside of Christianity, Race argues that "other forms of religious experience . . . make their own claims upon us. To render other forms of experience as also examples of 'salvation history' could be a sleight of hand when based on biblical considerations alone."[155] For Christians to acknowledge other faiths as "salvific" from a Christian framework is insufficient for Race. For, having accepted the historicist and epistemic premises drawn from Troeltsch and Hick, any tradition-bound theologizing is rendered untenable, regardless of where it ends up—even as he himself employs the Christian notion of salvation as the telos of all

---

[155]   Alan Race, *Making Sense of Religious Pluralism: Shaping Theology of Religions for Our Times* (London: SPCK, 2013), 6–7.

forms of religious faith. Smith's phenomenology is revealed as a universal religious hermeneutic, displacing those interpretive habits and traditions derived within the community and vested with theological authority, with a one-size-fits-all anthropological phenomenology of faith.

In other words, the question of theological authority, not the reality of religious diversity, is the central concern of Race's typology. Pluralism as a type is recommended because it adopts apologetically potent and philosophically grounded guiding principles and structures of authority. As Race writes, "the argument for pluralism . . . employs insights from a sociological perspective and reflects on the influence of the so-called modern secular consciousness, which is spreading to all parts of the world, on the *authority* of religious traditions."[156] Race's case for theological pluralism's superiority rests primarily on its turn to alternative authority sources beyond tradition that are purported to prove their own validity, whether rationally or empirically, as in Hick's epistemological argument for religious experience and Smith's phenomenological empiricism, respectively.

On this view, Race (like Troeltsch, Hick, and Smith) does not appear to be a relativist in any robust metaphysical or even theological sense, although he certainly displays some confusion on the matter.[157] Surprisingly, even such astute philosophical theologians as then-Cardinal Joseph Ratzinger have fallen into the trap of designating pluralists like Hick and Paul Knitter as relativists.[158] One could perhaps consider them soteriological relativists. But their teleological account of the progress of religious understanding and their appeals to the objectivity of critical reasoning make it difficult to ascribe any relativism beyond this. Indeed, as Ratzinger himself notes in the same article in which he labels them relativists, it is the very "exclusivism" of their construal of the relationship between philosophy and theology that represents the most problematic aspect of pluralism and the threefold typology Race designed in its support.

Of course, this is made plain in Race's repeated expressions of concern in avoiding a "debilitating relativism" or a "wretched historicism." Writing specifically about Troeltsch, Race asserts that such relativism defies that which we know is true *philosophically*, which we must therefore conclude is *theologically* true:

---

[156]   Race, *Christians and Religious Pluralism*, 140; Cf. Race, *Making Sense*, 6.
[157]   Race, *Christians and Religious Pluralism*, 76.
[158]   Joseph Ratzinger, "Relativism: The Central Problem for Faith Today," *Origins* 26 (1996): 309–17.

There is some unease about Troeltsch's discussion at this point. It derives from the intellectual and psychological instinct that something cannot be true *for us* without also being true for all mankind . . . [Troeltsch] Having abandoned himself to the historical method *in toto*, the "wretched historicism" could only be overcome after a survey of the cultural history of the whole world.[159]

Overcoming relativism by way of a cultural survey is precisely what Smith's phenomenological hermeneutic claims to provide. Race's typology in general, and his account of theological pluralism in particular, can therefore be seen first and foremost as an argument *against* theological relativism. Appealing to the supposed objectivity of philosophical thought as *the* source of theological authority allows Race to reassert the rationality of religious faith. Although it is religious diversity, among other things, that has called into question the rationality of faith, pluralism's affirmation of a single transcendent source which unites all religious experiences despite their superficial diversity is essentially a byproduct of Race's philosophical argument for the rationality of religious faith. Such authority is anchored in a conglomeration of epistemology, anthropology, and phenomenology, surpassing the authoritative role of religious traditions and practices and making the intellectual viability of faith difficult, if not impossible, to impugn.

It is worth summarizing Race's account of theological authority. Smith's theory of faith as an anthropological constant, empirically demonstrated through a phenomenological hermeneutic, is presented as a theological method that honors Troeltsch's historicism and Hick's epistemology while rebuffing the threat of relativism they would evince on their own.[160] So it is in light of pluralism's apologetic appeal to philosophical authority that religious tenets derive their legitimacy:

> Not all beliefs and practices of the religions are acceptable. Deciding between good and bad, true and false religions is now a matter of cross-cultural and cross-religious dialogue, as well as engaging with critical thinking in the light of what we know of the world through knowledge which is gained from many disciplines.[161]

---

[159]   Race, *Christians and Religious Pluralism*, 80, emphasis added.

[160]   Race, *Christians and Religious Pluralism*, 81. For an account of Troeltsch's work that suggests he did in fact anticipate the threat of relativism and provide a path forward similar to the one Race provides, see Mark D. Chapman, *Ernst Troeltsch and Liberal Theology* (Oxford: Oxford University Press, 2001), 104.

[161]   Race, *Making Sense*, 41; cf. Race, *Interfaith Encounter*, viii.

Having spurned tradition as a source of theological authority, Race follows Smith in replacing it with a vision of "critical thinking" in service of a phenomenologically attested vision of faith as an anthropological constant.

Smith's principle of corporate critical self-consciousness encapsulates the logic of authority within Race's typology.[162] Though Race never specifically invokes the principle as such, its presence is hard to miss in passages such as the concluding paragraph in the preface to the second edition of *Christians and Religious Pluralism*:

> Christian self-consciousness has undergone profound changes as a result of the encounter with critical thought, especially with the challenges posed by historical, scientific and philosophical studies. We can expect no less, once religious studies becomes the new dialogue partner . . . Who we are is a function of our interdependence.[163]

Indeed, in his introduction to Smith's contribution to pluralism later in the book, Race begins by quoting a passage from Smiths *Towards a World Theology* which also implicitly invokes the principle as the defining feature of "comparative religion":

> The study of comparative religion is the process, now begun, where we human beings learn, through critical analysis, empirical enquiry, and collaborative discourse, to conceptualize a world in which some of us are Christians . . . Muslims . . . Hindus . . . Jews . . . sceptics; and where all of us are, and recognize each other as being, rational men and women.[164]

It is Smith's principle of critical corporate self-consciousness, built upon a notion of faith as an anthropological quality and the phenomenological hermeneutic which provides that notion with empirical support, that supports Race's demotion of traditional bodies of hermeneutical authority and the replacement of them with philosophy, as he construes it.

A lengthy passage from Race sums up the path traced so far, underlining the question of authority as the basic criterion for distinguishing between the theology of religion types as Race depicts them:

> Sociologists, historians, phenomenologists may be able to map the basic religious alternatives at the level of religious experience, but

---

162   Race, *Christians and Religious Pluralism*, 92–93; idem, *Making Sense*, 7–8.
163   Race, *Christians and Religious Pluralism*, viii.
164   Smith, *World Theology*, 101, quoted in Race, *Christians and Religious Pluralism*, 99.

thereafter the question of a normative standard which transcends the comparison between the different forms of religious expression belongs within the domain of the theologian. . . . The pluralist theory willingly suspends the *a priori* application of criteria from the specifically Christian heritage in the search to distinguish the more from the less profound, the more from the less "true" religious belief, and looks to dialogue as the first step on the road to religious truth viewed from a world perspective.[165]

Race's view of theological and/or hermeneutical authority involves a rejection of the a priori application of Christian criteria, turning the theologian invoked in the passage into what sounds more like a philosopher, capable of determining the "normative standard." Yet this dismissal of inferred standards is limited. Race appears to be unaware that he, following Troeltsch, Hick, Smith, and others, assumes certain beliefs as criteria in his own philosophical and theological endeavors. This lack of awareness is evident in Race's exclusively derogatory use of "a priori." But of course, Troeltsch himself famously described the "religious a priori" while also acknowledging a priori commitments operative within his epistemology and philosophy of history.[166] Similarly, Hick and Smith assume Kant's epistemological distinction between the phenomena and noumena as a basic premise of their theological argument.[167]

Race, Hick, and Smith, and perhaps Troeltsch, might respond that such assumptions are better understood as hypotheses, which are subsequently and continuously confirmed through phenomenological analysis. But what threat could such inquiry impose when theological possibility is *a function* of philosophy? Short of a definitive philosophical proof of the nonexistence of the divine, Race's pluralism posits that all theology need do is respond and reform to philosophical insights or criticisms as they arise, to zig when philosophy zigs and zag when it zags. Theology, now philosophy's handmaiden, can no longer be philosophically undermined.

---

[165] Race, *Christians and Religious Pluralism*, 144, quoting Smith, *World Theology*, 172.

[166] Ernst Troeltsch, "*Logos* and *Mythos* in Theology and Philosophy of Religion," in *Religion in History*, 57f.; idem, "On the Question of the Religious A Priori," in *Religion in History*, 33–45; idem, "Modern Philosophy of History," in *Religion in History*, 302, 307; cf. Chapman, *Ernst Troeltsch*, 111–37.

[167] Cf. John Hick, "The Outcome: Dialogue into Truth," in *Truth and Dialogue: The Relationship between Christianity and World Religions* (London: Sheldon, 1974), 149; idem, *God Has Many Names* (Philadelphia: Westminster, 1982), 42; Smith, *Faith and Belief*, 129.

It is merely amended accordingly. If theological authority *is* philosophical authority, then philosophy *cannot* undermine religious faith, for to do so would be to undermine itself. Race's typology, and his pluralist type, are best viewed as apologetic efforts to safeguard theology from philosophical critique. With this in mind, we turn to Race's three types and the authority-related differences through which they are identified.

Exclusivism, Inclusivism, and Pluralism

With Troeltsch's historicism, Hick's epistemology, and Smith's phenomenology set forth as the basic premises of theological authority within Race's typology, the real basis of Race's typological distinctions should be plain, even if Race himself is less clear on it. In spite of this ambiguity, or perhaps because of it, Race's types have profoundly influenced the theology of religions discourse. It is worth considering why some have defended the typology, particularly those who are not pluralists themselves. To this end, we will look briefly at the work of Paul R. Eddy, a critic of pluralism in general and Hick in particular, who also supports the typology and argues forcefully for its theological value.

In arguing for the value of the threefold typology, Eddy provides a helpful analysis of the different senses in which its organizing principle might be interpreted.[168] Eddy argues that there is a basic divide between those who see the typology as soteriological and those who see it as alethic. Within this general divide, Eddy identifies three views on the typology: (1) alethic-philosophical, (2) alethic-religious, and (3) soteric.[169] Eddy himself argues that the typology is best viewed as soteric. Yet, puzzlingly, he does not distinguish between the three senses in his own criticism of "the pluralist paradigm":

> Possibly the most challenging issue that faces adherents of the pluralist paradigm involves . . . the "conflicting conceptions of the divine" problem . . . If all the great world religions are roughly co-equal in terms of their soteriological efficacy and religious truth, how does one explain the fact that their conceptions of ultimate Reality . . . are so different—at times, even mutually contradictory—in nature? It seems safe to say that no other philosophical (as opposed to purely theological) issue has presented as persistent and challenging a

---

[168]   Paul R. Eddy, *John Hick's Pluralist Philosophy of World Religions* (Eugene, Ore.: Wipf & Stock, 2002), 1–17.
[169]   Eddy, *John Hick's Pluralist Philosophy*, 11.

conundrum to pluralists as has the conflicting conceptions of the divine problem.[170]

Arguing that Race's typology and the pluralist type should be viewed as soteric, Eddy suggests in almost the same breath that pluralism's biggest challenge is alethic. This assertion that the biggest problem facing pluralism is not soteric but alethic, offered in defense of a soteric interpretation of the typology, suggests that Eddy's own engagement with the typology is confused and undermines his argument that it is in fact best interpreted as soteric. Beyond the passage quoted above, this criticism is further justified in two respects. The preceding exposition of the historical, epistemological, and phenomenological foundations of Race's typology makes it evident that Race views historicism and epistemology—not soteriology—as the sources of the most pressing challenges confronting Christian theology in general and that these challenges are evinced most clearly in the encounter between Christianity and other religions. In Race's account, the biggest questions, and problems, facing Christian theology are not soteriological, and not even alethic-religious but, fundamentally, alethic-philosophical. Race's entire interrogation of the doctrine of the incarnation is organized under three headings—"philosophical, theological, historical"—where even the theological problems are philosophical in nature, "centered on the credibility of the belief that one person could embody two natures . . . [and] whether the Incarnation is best comprehended as a religious myth."[171]

Eddy's argument for the soteric interpretation takes shape around his rebuttal of Gavin D'Costa's criticism of theological pluralism, accusing D'Costa of not adequately acknowledging the distinction between the typology's alethic and soteric interpretations and their distinct implications. Arguing that D'Costa's designation of pluralists as advocating a position no different from exclusivists, he interprets D'Costa as

> narrowing his use of the threefold typology to address the alethic-philosophical issues alone . . . merely to say that pluralists, as much as anyone else, hold to the "exclusive" view that they believe their own position to be true and those which claim otherwise to be false . . . [suggesting] that an inherent and necessary link exists between the

[170] Eddy, *John Hick's Pluralist Philosophy*, 15–16.
[171] Eddy, *John Hick's Pluralist Philosophy*, 117.

alethic-religious and soteric uses of the typology [which] is simply descriptively false.[172]

Eddy correctly notes that D'Costa's criticism attends to the typology's alethic-philosophical commitments and implications. But the suggestion that the problem is the imposition of a false link between the alethic-religious and soteric uses is precisely to miss the point.

Indeed, D'Costa's criticism is better interpreted as expressing Eddy's "alethic-religious" interpretation of Race's typology, precisely because it reveals that pluralism's account of the *relationship* between truth claims from specific traditions is at the same time an account of their *meaning* (as symbols or myths, in the case of truth claims like the incarnation which threaten the historical boundaries Race imposes upon them). Significantly, this also helps to explain why it seems that pluralism's account of divine transcendence is depicted as being *at odds with* exclusivist faith, rather than contextualizing and including it. Because the exclusivist's interpretation fails to affirm such a relationship between the truth claims of different traditions, the exclusivist fails to grasp the meaning of the truth claims of their own tradition—which at the very least indicates that the exclusivist's experience of or relationship to the transcendent source expressed within those claims is *intrinsically* flawed.[173] In arguing that the typology is primarily soteric, Eddy does not see that it is Race's alethic-philosophical commitments (to Troeltsch's historicism, Hick's neo-Kantian epistemology) which entail an inherent and necessary link between the alethic-philosophical and the alethic-religious interpretations of the typology, thereby rendering both the legitimacy and the meaning of the particular truth claims from different religious traditions in terms of their philosophical legitimacy. D'Costa's claim that pluralism is a form of exclusivism points out that it is the typology's philosophical commitments upon which Race's analysis of alethic-religious claims legitimacy and meaning is grounded and therein, crucially, their soteric implications.

Simply put, Race is adamant that if Jesus' meaning is to have universal salvific implications, (alethic-religious) beliefs about him must conform to the dictates of Race's philosophical accounts of history, knowledge, and transcendence. For example, let us say that Jesus is who Race's pluralist account claims he is—a universal paradigm of relationship to the transcendent who

---

[172]   Eddy, *John Hick's Pluralist Philosophy*, 12.
[173]   Gavin D'Costa, *The Meeting of Religions and the Trinity* (Edinburgh: T&T Clark, 2000), 22ff.

can only be recognized as such alongside the rejection of an account of his identity as the particular incarnation of God. An exclusivist's interpretation of him, as Race himself frames exclusivism, is not only an explicit affirmation of Jesus as the incarnate Son of God but also an explicit rejection of Jesus' identity as the universal paradigm of transcendent relationship. If an exclusivist's interpretation of Jesus rests upon precisely the identity Race claims *he must have* to secure *legitimate* religious significance, the inevitable conclusion would seem to be that pluralism maintains not only that exclusivist truth claims about Jesus are false, but most problematically for pluralism's own internal coherence, that the exclusivist *experience* of him (whether in scripture, prayer, the eucharist) is not really an experience of *him* (a non-incarnate exemplar of transcendent relationship) or of *the Transcendent*, at all.

In this sense, contrary to Eddy's rejection of an inherent link between the spheres of interpretation he identifies, the alethic-philosophical commitments embedded in and organizing Race's typology *do* necessarily shape the meaning of alethic-religious claims—which, at least in the case of Jesus, is inseparable from his soteric interpretation. Eddy, in arguing that soteric and alethic-religious interpretations of the typology are truly distinct, points out that while John Hick believes "that the truth-claims of all religions are literally false vis-a-vis the ultimate reality, he is nonetheless a soteriological universalist."[174] But this phrasing is very misleading. Hick's soteriological universalism is not at odds with but *is premised upon* the falsity of all alethic-religious truth claims precisely because it is, at root, a function of his alethic-philosophical beliefs. Thus, pluralism would seem to imply the same logic Race attributes to exclusivism. This is all to say that Race's typology is primarily alethic-philosophical but, therein, imposes (what it necessarily frames as) subsidiary truth claims of the alethic-religious and soteric sorts upon the types in accordance with its philosophically prioritized account of truth and its ensuing account of the transcendent nature of reality.

Second, and more simply, interpreting the typology as essentially soteric would render it as a binary typology rather than tripartite—either salvation is universally accessible or it is not. Inclusivism would seem inevitably to be a form of pluralism on a soteric interpretation. Not only does Eddy's soteric interpretation of the typology encourage a similar collapse of the three types, but it also runs counter to Race's own view

[174]   D'Costa, *Meeting of Religions*, 12.

that any conflation between the types would be between exclusivism and inclusivism—"exclusivist and inclusivist understandings look like two sides of the same coin, in so far as neither are fully able to absorb the real implications of historical consciousness"—a distinction which rests entirely upon their alethic-philosophical differences.[175]

Eddy's defense of the typology, and the notion that salvation is its primary concern, appears difficult to maintain. But his distinction between the possibilities in interpreting its organizing principle remains useful. For we might now say that Race's typology is best interpreted as prioritizing alethic-philosophical questions, the responses to which it presents as determining the alethic-religious and soteric positions within each type. This of course leads us to the same conclusion reached above: What differentiates each type is their understanding of theological authority—the degree to which they are capable of *theologically* accommodating *philosophical* critiques, and particularly those concerning historical possibility and epistemic warrant.[176] Significantly, this interpretation of Race's typology is neither imposed upon it nor deftly extracted from its insinuating logic. Rather, it is the way Race himself explicitly describes the typology in general and the differences, problems and merits of its three types.

Indeed, Race is far more explicit in addressing the philosophical problems of traditional Christian faith than he is on the issue of salvation. Although Race does not provide a formal account of his philosophical commitments in the typology or elsewhere—he variously describes it as "critical thinking," "critical reasoning," and "the normal means of human enquiry and reasoning"[177]—perhaps the most basic statement of his perspective is the following claim he makes in his chapter on "Incarnation and the Christian Theology of Religions":

> The logical problem is perhaps the most intractable of all the problems
> associated with the Incarnation . . . neither is it sufficient to point out
> this difficulty in conceptual definition and then go on to claim that
> God did become man as though there was no need for clarification

[175]   Race, *Christians and Religious Pluralism*, 156; cf. Frederick Quinn, "Toward 'Generous Love': Recent Anglican Approaches to World Religions," *Journal of Anglican Studies* 10, no. 2 (2012): 167.

[176]   Race, *Christians and Religious Pluralism*, 28.

[177]   Race, *Interfaith Encounter*, 11–14; cf. idem, *Christians and Religious Pluralism*, viii, 28, 32–33, 78, 99, 154; idem, "Theology of Religions in Change," in *Christian Approaches to Other Faiths*, ed. Alan Race and Paul M. Hedges (London: SCM Press, 2008), 7–9.

of the logical issue. The difficulty is to know where to place the burden of proof. It is reasonable to claim that this must be shouldered by those who wish to uphold some traditional form of the Incarnation, and that a *prima facie* case exists for those who argue that a logical fallacy lies at the heart of it.[178]

However it is labeled, some version of what could loosely be called "Enlightenment reason" appears to be Race's basic philosophical stance, blended with some existentialism.[179] Perhaps this is also the most straightforward way of describing Race's basic philosophical perspective, which is evident in his many affirmations that "there can be no access to Christian truth apart from the role played by the processes of interpretation and critical reason that have become so much part of theological accountability today."[180]

In sum, for Race, theological authority is almost entirely subservient to philosophical authority—a principle which grounds both his endorsement of pluralism and the typological distinctions he makes in service of that endorsement. It is also the basis of his affirmation of interfaith dialogue as the only viable method for future theological insight, as the very content of such dialogue is necessarily limited to what really amounts to philosophical and ethical critique and agreement:

> In the final analysis, all traditions are rafts (to use a Buddhist image), means to an end, and they conceptualize these means and ends according to the best conceptual matrices that are available. But all matrices are necessarily limited . . . and this is because religious language depicts but does not reproduce the ultimate truth of our condition and the meaning of life. The infinity of ultimate reality is the deeper ineffable ground of the many phenomenal manifestations of religious insight and truth. An empirical justification for hypothesizing this is that the traditions show themselves to be comparable at the empirical level—producers of both good and bad in spiritual insight and practice.[181]

---

[178]   Race, *Christians and Religious Pluralism*, 113–14, emphasis added.

[179]   Paul Badham, analyzing Hick's epistemology, argues that his implicit assumption is "that authentic knowledge must be restricted to what all would recognize as indisputably true." Paul Badham, "John Hick's *An Interpretation of Religion*," in *Problems in the Philosophy of Religion*, ed. Harold Hewitt Jr. (London: Macmillan, 1991), 92, quoted in David S. Nah, *Christian Theology and Religious Pluralism: A Critical Evaluation of John Hick* (Cambridge: James Clarke, 2013), 53.

[180]   Race, *Christians and Religious Pluralism*, 154.

[181]   Race, *Making Sense*, 69.

Race's pluralist theology of religions conceives of philosophy as a theological winnowing fork, separating the traditionalist chaff from the transcendent grain and revealing the conditions necessary for the formulation and identification of more accurate theological truths. The question of philosophical cogency is *the* organizing logic of the typology, the basis upon which Race differentiates between the types and determines the degree to which they can be supported.

Conclusion

For Race, Christian theology is primarily accountable to the academy and not the church. This is the vision of Christian faith and theology that lies at the base of Race's own acceptance of pluralism and the typological construction he proposes. Race's types do not depict the range of theological possibilities, but three responses to his assertion of academic and philosophical primacy in theological discourse. They are not designed to describe but to persuade—and not merely to persuade us that God might be present outside the confines of Christian faith. Rather, the typology itself is designed to frame the reality of religious pluralism as the final straw in a fight over the nature of Christian theology waged since the Enlightenment. Exclusivism as a type is not defined by its perspective on pluralism but by its outright rejection of the philosophical axioms Race views as nonnegotiable. But of course, by defining exclusivism in light of its rejection of Race's philosophical commitments, these philosophical commitments themselves are affirmed as definitive for Christian faith. Their assumed authority is such that Christian faith ends up being defined in terms of its embrace or rejection of them. Exclusivism is not a type of theology of religions so much as a type of theological reaction against a particular set of philosophical claims—a reaction which, as we will see in the next chapter, ends up misconstruing the particularity of Jesus by virtue of its rejection of a philosophical account of universality.

In viewing differences within the "theology of religions" as essentially differences in understanding to whom (or what) Christian theology is responsible and how it should therefore be conducted, we are able to differentiate between the many different manifestations of the Christian theology of religions based on their very understanding of what Christian theology is itself, *not* by subsequent alethic or soteriological conclusions concerning other religions. Indeed, the preceding analysis of this typology shows that this is in fact what Race is already doing by insisting that to be intellectually and socially responsible, theology must take philosophy (or more accurately, the neo-Kantian philosophical tradition to which Race ascribes) as its guide, and then identifying three supposed theological types in relation to their accommodation of this claim.

The critique of Race's typology and the analysis of the premises upon which it is constructed should not be taken as a criticism of pluralism's concerns regarding the possibility of God's universal presence. Rather, acknowledging that Race's theological pluralism is largely conditioned by philosophy and exploring the problems with that conditioning frees us to approach those same concerns from different angles. To that end, we turn now to Hans Frei's typology and his direct grappling with historicism, epistemology, and phenomenological hermeneutics to show that concerns about God's universal presence can be honored and shared outside of pluralism, and that Race's typology only inhibits our ability to grasp this.

3

Hans Frei, Christian Theology, and the Question of Authority

Introduction: Race and Frei—Similar Concerns, Dissimilar Priorities

Hans Frei is a theologian rarely mentioned in the theology of religions discourse, but his work intersects with Race's in significant ways. Though surprisingly similar in certain respects, their theological visions are ultimately very different. The most obvious of these differences might *appear* to be the role that the world religions play in orienting their work. Race's entire theological focus is supposedly on the theological implications and practical concerns raised by the world religions for Christians—i.e., the "theology of religions." Frei mentions the world religions in general or specific individual traditions only infrequently, and makes no specific reference to the theology of religions whatsoever. Yet this is a superficial difference and one that emerges out of a more basic disparity in their theological sensibilities, a disparity which might be best exposed by focusing on what the two *share*.

Indeed, Race and Frei have in common some basic concerns and interests. Most notably, both share a faith in God's presence to those outside the Christian faith and church and even agree that it is important that Christians seek to discern God's presence in the world. While seeking the presence of God outside of Christian scripture and community is obviously central to Race's work, it is something of a lodestar in Frei's theology as well, even if he insisted it was a question that could only be addressed after others, namely that of the identity of the God who is present. Other areas of overlap between Race and Frei are found in their shared interests in the relation of historicism and historical criticism to biblical interpretation and Christian dogmas like the Chalcedonian definition, as well as in the epistemology of faith and the impact of the phenomenology of religion on biblical hermeneutics. So, although neither mentions the other in their work, they have ruminated on many of the same issues.[1]

The differences between them in their work on these areas are rooted in their contrasting views on the responsibilities of Christian theology and on the relationship between faith and philosophy—a matter that Frei's work covers extensively. Indeed, the relation between theology and "external discourses" is one that Frei sees as a basic, profound, and unsettled issue in Christian theology. It is, in his view, a question that has persistently pestered academic Christian theology, emerging out of the debate in nineteenth-century German universities, especially Berlin, about the status of theology faculties.[2]

Frei described the debate as a question of Christian theology's relation to *Glaube* and *Wissenschaft*, or faith and philosophy. Frei defines *Glaube* as "either a religiously committed disposition of trust or personal devoutness . . . a set of Christian beliefs or propositional claims, or . . . various combinations of the two," and more simply, as "faith" or "Christian self-description."[3] *Wissenschaft* might variously be understood as "untrammeled critical inquiry . . . the exercise of Reason as a universal speculative capacity, applicable to Christianity as to all other areas of reflection because it is of the essence of human nature and of reality," what Frei will broadly describe as "philosophy."[4]

---

[1]   Cf. Paul Knitter, *Introducing Theologies of Religions* (Maryknoll, N.Y.: Orbis, 2002), 181; idem, *One Earth, Many Religions* (Maryknoll, N.Y.: Orbis, 1995), 51–53; Stanley J. Samartha, *One Christ—Many Religions* (Maryknoll, N.Y.: Orbis, 1991), 156, n. 10; Veli-Matti Kärkkäinen, *A Constructive Christian Theology for the Pluralistic World*, vol. 1, *Christ and Reconciliation* (Grand Rapids: Eerdmans, 2013), 7, 12, 18, 132; idem, *A Constructive Christian Theology for the Pluralistic World*, vol. 2, *Trinity and Revelation* (Grand Rapids: Eerdmans, 2013), 84, 90; idem, *The Trinity: Global Perspectives* (Louisville, Ky.: Westminster John Knox, 2007), 257, n. 2; Tim S. Perry, *Radical Difference* (Waterloo, Ont.: Wilfrid Laurier University Press, 2001), 92–94; Lesslie Newbigin, *Proper Confidence* (Grand Rapids: Eerdmans, 1995), 72; idem, *The Gospel in a Pluralist Society* (Grand Rapids: Eerdmans, 1989), 99.

[2]   Hans Frei, *Types of Christian Theology*, ed. George Hunsinger and William C. Placher (New Haven, Conn.: Yale University Press, 1992), 95–132; idem, "David Friedrich Strauss," in vol. 1 of *Nineteenth Century Religious Thought in the West*, ed. Ninian Smart et al. (Cambridge: Cambridge University Press, 1985), 216.

[3]   Frei, "Strauss," 216; idem, *Types of Christian Theology*, 3ff.

[4]   Frei, "Strauss," 216; cf. idem, *Types of Christian Theology*, 2–3.

Frei, though sensitive to the concerns raised by philosophy, construes its force and, correspondingly, theology's response in an entirely different manner than does Race. For Frei, theology is not "part of that general mapping out of the intellectual universe, the natural academic offshoot of which is the liberal arts curriculum replete with graduate studies."[5] Rather, theology is one "aspect of the self-description of Christianity as a religion . . . an inquiry into the coherence and appropriateness of any given instance of the use of Christian language in the light of its normative articulation, whether that be Scripture, tradition, the Christian conscience, a mixture of these and other candidates."[6] Frei considered the relationship between philosophy and theology in general, and historicism, epistemology, and hermeneutics in particular, with an interest and concern hardly befitting Race's exclusivist type and its supposed rejection of the theological significance of all criteria outside of Bible and doctrine. The same can be said regarding the inadequacy of labeling Frei as a "particularist" where, because "every 'universal' truth is universal only for its particular filter . . . our religious language and stories" are seen as "*creating* the world we live in," rendering moot questions of universal truth.[7] Rather, Frei's argument is for the subordination of philosophy to theology, not their exclusivity. More importantly, regarding the unfitness of Race's typology, Frei's emphasis on the unsubstitutability of Jesus' identity, which philosophy can help us describe but not explain, is what undergirds the hope for universal salvation—a position at odds with all three of Race's types.[8]

Race insists that modern faith needs a validating authority beyond anything the Bible, doctrines, or the like can provide. If the modern world's discovery of critical reasoning has undermined the authority of scripture and of the doctrines and dogmas that extrapolate from it—particularly that of the incarnation—Race argues that it is these traditional sources or shapers of faith which need modifying. Philosophy sets the terms upon which faith

---

[5]   Frei, "Interpretation of Narrative," in *Theology and Narrative: Selected Essays*, ed. George Hunsinger and William C. Placher (Oxford: Oxford University Press, 1993), 96.

[6]   Frei, "Interpretation of Narrative," 96.

[7]   Knitter, *Theologies of Religions*, 176, 181. Here Knitter uses the terminology of the "Acceptance Model" as including Frei's theology, but he later replaces this with the term "particularism." Idem, "Comparative Theology Is Not 'Business-as-Usual Theology': Personal Witness from a Buddhist Christian," *Buddhist-Christian Studies* 35 (2015): 183.

[8]   Hans Frei, *The Identity of Jesus Christ* (Eugene, Ore.: Wipf & Stock, 1997), 193f.; idem, "Of the Holy Ghost," in *Reading Faithfully: Writings from the Archives*, ed. Mike Higton and Mark Alan Bowald, 2 vols. (Eugene, Ore.: Cascade Books, 2015), 1:194f.

is first undermined and then made viable. It is therefore theology's task to work in concert with philosophy and other disciplines to achieve a modification satisfying to all.[9] Yet Frei argues that this very arrangement is mutually injurious, gutting both theology and philosophy of the strengths of their convictions. Echoing David Friedrich Strauss' rejection of Schleiermacher's insistence on the "compatibility between faith and a scientific-historical perspective on the facts," Frei argues that such an arrangement results in "the worst of both worlds."[10] Even while acknowledging the force questions asked within these philosophical areas might have for Christian theology, Frei views the relationship between philosophy and theology in a very different way than Race does. Frei insists on the distinctiveness of *Glaube* and *Wissenschaft*, not to isolate theology from the philosophical, but to better honor their autonomy. This in turn provides them with the possibility of both *mutual* criticism and *unexpected*, ad hoc, consonance.

Hans Frei's Ad Hoc Historicism

Frei, like Race, saw the questions concerning history and faith raised by the likes of G. E. Lessing, Kant, Herder, and, particularly, D. F. Strauss and Troeltsch as important considerations for Christian theology.[11] On the one hand, Frei notes that for all of the anxiety that came with modern understandings of history, philosophy, and science, the questions they raise concern the same Christological dilemma that plagued the fourth- and fifth-century endeavors "to describe both the indivisible unity of the person of Christ and the presence of two unabridged natures, divine and human in him."[12] On the other hand, Frei acknowledges that the issue gained force during and after the Enlightenment. For the "modern shift in categories from those of substantialist personhood to self-conscious, inward and at the same time historical personality gave the problem a new urgency and changed its expression . . . it became most urgent when Christocentric faith was to be reconciled with the assumptions and judgments of modern historical inquiry."[13]

Yet, after driving theology to distraction for well over a century, the problem, as Frei saw it, suddenly fell out of focus. In a 1976 letter to

---

[9]   Cf. Alan Race, *Christians and Religious Pluralism: Patterns in the Christian Theology of Religions* (London: SCM Press, 1993), 107.
[10]   Frei, "Strauss," 253, 251.
[11]   Frei, "Letter to Van Harvey," in *Reading Faithfully*, 1:26; cf. Mike Higton, *Christ, Providence and History: Hans Frei's Public Theology* (London: T&T Clark International, 2004), 19, 35.
[12]   Frei, "Strauss," 254.
[13]   Frei, "Strauss," 254.

Van Harvey, Frei praised a recently completed essay of Harvey's for drawing attention to the neglected issue:

> The essay was reassuring because the question of the continuity between Jesus and faith (or whatever one calls the issue Strauss put before us) suddenly and distressingly ceased to be discussed nearly a decade ago. Nothing much had been solved (I personally believe none of us had as yet stated rightly the whole issue) when all of a sudden it appeared almost as if there were a conspiracy to *forget it* and escape into a bunch of trivial issues and trivial affirmations. *It was a disservice to the morality of belief* . . . There may be a community of us recalling theologians to some of their central topics. I'd like to be able to help at least that much.[14]

As to why the issue was neglected, Frei suggests that questions surrounding the relationship between "Jesus and faith" had divided Christianity into its "conservative" and "liberal" wings.[15] Eventually, it appeared as if these two wings were operating from entirely different and irreconcilable premises—like the portrayal in Race's typology of the divide between exclusivists and pluralists. The question lost its bite, for without any common ground, each Christian contingent could retreat into the safety of their respective corners.

Frei sees this problematic situation as a symptom of a more deep-seated confusion afflicting Christian theology. For in addressing the question, Frei suggests that both liberals and conservatives had unwittingly and unquestioningly allowed philosophy to set the theological agenda. In his view, this has been a constant struggle within Christianity from its early days, though again, it became particularly problematic in the wake of the Enlightenment. Frei narrates this tale in detail in *The Eclipse of Biblical Narrative*. There, he argues that the rise of empirical philosophy, Deism, and historical criticism created confusion concerning the relationship between the Bible's syntactical or grammatical sense, and its ostensive reference, i.e., its "signified subject" or its *meaning*.

Previously, Frei observes, the "Western Christian tradition" had demonstrated an agreement on the unity of these two senses as aspects of the *sensus literalis*, the plain or literal sense of the narrative. As Frei understands it, the "literal sense" of the Gospels is not an affirmation of inerrancy but of "the identification of Jesus Christ as the *ascriptive* subject of

---

[14]   Frei, "Letter to Van Harvey," 26, emphasis added.
[15]   Hans Frei, "Historical Reference and the Gospels," in *Reading Faithfully*, 1:95.

the descriptions or stories told about and in relation to him."[16] Frei's usage of "literal" therefore is better understood as "plain" or "surface," meaning simply that the subject matter of the Gospel stories "is not something or someone else, and that the rest of the canon must in some way or ways, looser or tighter, be related to this subject matter or at least not in contradiction with it."[17] Significantly, for Frei to prioritize the *sensus literalis* is not only to engage in a mode of scriptural interpretation that takes the Gospels to be about Jesus, but also to participate in a mode of communal self-description for the church. It is both the "unity of grammatical/ syntactical sense and signified subject" and "use-in-context."[18] In some important respects the prioritization of the plain sense limits the scope of the Gospel text's subject matter to Jesus. But at the same time, Frei points out that it is the very prioritization of the literal sense which demands interpretive leeway and room for contestation.[19]

The Enlightenment's undermining of the integrity of the biblical text itself and the historical plausibility of the miraculous events depicted therein led many to lose trust in the accuracy of the biblical narrative. But that this loss of trust occurred *alongside* a persistent commitment toward the meaningfulness of Christian scripture, is what Frei believes truly compromised the literal sense and, ipso facto, this interpretive flexibility, drawing theologians toward one of two poles.[20] Rejecting the force of philosophy and *wissenschaftlich* discourses for Christian faith, conservatives turned toward a firm insistence on the historical reliability of the biblical accounts, collapsing the Bible's syntactical sense into its historical reference. For them, the Bible's meaning is equated with the historical occurrence of the events depicted in it. Like exclusivism, this position only emerges as a possibility *in response* to the preceding philosophical critiques. Conversely, liberals, embracing the *wissenschaftlich* criticisms, separated the meaning of the biblical narratives from the question of its historical occurrence, appealing instead to the mythological or allegorical meaning of the Bible. "In either case," Frei

[16]   Frei, *Types of Christian Theology*, 5.

[17]   Frei, *Types of Christian Theology*, 5.

[18]   Frei, "Theology and the Interpretation of Narrative," in *Theology and Narrative*, 110.

[19]   Jason Springs, *Toward a Generous Orthodoxy: Prospects for Hans Frei's Postliberal Theology* (Oxford: Oxford University Press, 2010), 149; cf. Karl Barth, *Church Dogmatics*, IV.1, trans. G. W. Bromiley et al. (Edinburgh: T&T Clark, 1956), 763.

[20]   Hans Frei, *The Eclipse of Biblical Narrative: A Study in Eighteenth and Nineteenth Century Hermeneutics* (New Haven, Conn.: Yale University Press, 1974), 5.

writes, "the *meaning* of the stories was finally something different from the stories or depictions themselves," giving license to interpretations that, for different reasons, similarly stretched the literal sense of the biblical stories to the breaking point.[21]

The scriptural text cannot fully capture the historical world, much less the extraordinary events surrounding the life, death, and resurrection of Jesus. But incomplete is not the same as inadequate. As Frei sees it, the Christian faith is centered not just on a belief in the historical occurrence of the resurrection, but also on a trust in God's graceful and miraculous allowance of the *adequacy* of the Gospels' historical reference. To affirm the historical possibility of Jesus' resurrection is of course contrary to the historicism of Troeltsch and Strauss. But in rejecting an appeal to idealism in its construal of the Gospels' meaning, Frei's theology ends up affirming the historical particularity of the world, appearing in some important respects to have more in common with historicism than with so-called mediating theologies.

Strauss and Troeltsch against Schleiermacher and Mediating Theology

Race sets the acceptance of the modern historical method (and the historicist metaphysics from which the method issues) as the decisive criterion for differentiating between types of Christian theology.[22] In this regard, non-Christian religions occupy a less significant role in his typology and pluralist theology than he suggests, serving primarily as a foil against which Christianity is forced to take philosophical stock. His critical account of exclusivism is formed negatively, not in terms of its theological affirmation of Jesus' identity as both historically particular and universally significant, but in terms of its rejection of the previously described philosophical dictums of historicism:

> Exclusivism has no answer to the questions raised by epistemological considerations or the new historical perspective . . . evident in the fact that the positions we have outlined either refuse to engage in the debate with philosophy or history, or they severely limit the application from these disciplines for theological method. The shortcomings

---

[21]   Frei, *Eclipse of Biblical Narrative*, 11–12; cf. idem, "The 'Literal Reading' of Biblical Narrative," in *Theology and Narrative*, 118–49.

[22]   Cf. Ernst Troeltsch, "Historical and Dogmatic Method in Theology," in *Religion in History*, ed. and trans. James Luther Adams and Walter F. Bense (Edinburgh: T&T Clark, 1991), 22.

of the exclusivist approach are probably best considered in respect of the debate with history.[23]

Race sees the historicism advanced by Troeltsch and, to a lesser degree, Strauss, as emerging out of and reinforcing a basic divide between two types of biblical interpretation: one that takes an "a priori" affirmation of scripture's literal sense (i.e., one that affirms the incarnation and resurrection of Jesus Christ) and one that finds theological truth in what can be "affirmed only on the basis of the historical method."[24] In Race's telling, Strauss and Troeltsch fought against a pervasive and rigid theological dogmatism, a position which historicism showed to be indefensible. In response arose liberal Christian theology, from which the theology of pluralism emerged.[25]

Frei presents a different picture of historicism as it is worked out by both Troeltsch and Strauss. Like them, he agrees that a view of Christianity which prioritizes dogma in its interpretation of the Bible is wrong-headed.[26] Although he certainly agrees that appeals to supernatural explanations for religious beliefs are untenable for Troeltsch and Strauss, Frei depicts the historicist work of both as rooted in disputes, not with conservatives, but with mediating theologians like Schleiermacher, Albrecht Ritschl, and Wilhelm Herrmann.[27] This is counter to Race's depiction of the historicism of Troeltsch and Strauss, and to his suggestion that Schleiermacher, whom Race describes as a foe of exclusivism and as the founder of the liberal Protestant tradition, charted a course for theology that leads inevitably to pluralism, the type that takes historicist concerns most seriously.[28]

Frei shows that, although Schleiermacher was no dogmatist, he still earned the scorn of historicists, especially Strauss.[29] Schleiermacher attempted to chart a course in which the uniqueness of Jesus Christ could

[23]   Race, *Christians and Religious Pluralism*, 36.
[24]   Race, *Christians and Religious Pluralism*, 78–79.
[25]   Race, *Christians and Religious Pluralism*, 127–37.
[26]   Frei, *Types of Christian Theology*, 124; cf. idem, *Eclipse of Biblical Narrative*, 3f. For a compelling argument differentiating between Frei and Lindbeck on this point, see Paul DeHart, *The Trial of the Witnesses* (Oxford: Wiley-Blackwell, 2006), 149–239.
[27]   Frei, *Eclipse of Biblical Narrative*, 128, 284–85; idem, "Niebuhr's Theological Background," in *Faith and Ethics: The Theology of H. Richard Niebuhr*, ed. Paul Ramsey (New York: Harper & Row, 1957), 54–64. Cf. Brent W. Sockness, *Against False Apologetics: Wilhelm Herrmann and Ernst Troeltsch in Conflict* (Tübingen: Mohr Siebeck, 1998).
[28]   Race, *Christians and Religious Pluralism*, 142.
[29]   Race, *Christians and Religious Pluralism*, 18, 142.

be upheld without appeal to dogmas like the virgin birth and the resurrection. He did this, in part, by differentiating between "absolute" and "relative" miracles. Absolute miracles involve an interruption of the natural order which cannot be supported. But relative miracles are simply occurrences that produce faith in an individual; events which no matter how they are perceived *are not* supernatural or violations of natural law.[30] Not only did Schleiermacher reject supernatural explanations vis-à-vis the miraculous, but when pushed beyond the explanatory capacities of the relative/absolute distinction, as in the question of the resurrection, he opted for a purely natural explanation: "a deep coma followed by withdrawal and natural death."[31] Schleiermacher is not a dogmatist, supernaturalist, or an exclusivist. Race suggests that he was the fountainhead of Christian pluralism, arguing that that the "liberal Protestant tradition, which looks to Schleiermacher as its founder . . . leads to the pluralist conclusion."[32]

Yet Frei shows that Schleiermacher and the mediating theologians who followed in his wake were theological adversaries of both Strauss and Troeltsch, though Troeltsch also found much to be admired in Schleiermacher as well.[33] But with his emphasis on Troeltsch's role in advancing the historicist underpinnings of pluralism, and the association of Schleiermacher with pluralism, it appears as if Race has construed the foundations of pluralism as resting upon oppositional figures. Strauss and Troeltsch contended that Schleiermacher, unlike the supernatural dogmatists, tried to honor both *Wissenschaft* and *Glaube* and, thus, did a disservice to both. Troeltsch goes so far as to describe Schleiermacher's attempt at proffering a philosophically and historically sound exposition of Christian dogma as "a travesty in the shape of an ecclesiastical Biblicist dogmatics."[34]

[30]   Friedrich Schleiermacher, *The Christian Faith*, trans. H. R. Mackintosh and J. S. Stewart (London: T&T Clark, 1999), 71–73, 180–83; cf. Frei, "Strauss," 247–51. This account has some affinity with that of Hick's "experiencing-*as*," especially in its earliest form as an epistemological justification for the specific rationality of Christian faith as presented in *Faith and Knowledge* (London: Macmillan, 1967). But we will see that Frei differentiates Schleiermacher from the likes of Race and Hick *hermeneutically*, contrasting Schleiermacher's preservation of the plain sense of scripture with those whose philosophical priorities lead to a mythical or metaphorical interpretation.

[31]   Frei, "Strauss," 253; cf. Schleiermacher, *Christian Faith*, 417–21.

[32]   Race, *Christians and Religious Pluralism*, 142.

[33]   Cf. Robert Morgan, introduction to Ernst Troeltsch, *Writings on Theology and Religion*, ed. and trans. Robert Morgan and Michael Pye (London: Duckworth, 1977), 4–5.

[34]   Ernst Troeltsch, "The Dogmatics of the History-of-Religions School," in *Religion in History*, 92; cf. idem, "*Logos* and *Mythos* in Theology and Philosophy of Religion," in *Religion in History*, 47–49; Frei, "Niebuhr's Theological Background," 54.

Similarly, for Strauss, as Frei explains, this is "the worst of both worlds—the conjunction of reduced Christology with hobbled scientific exegesis."[35] According to Frei, both Strauss and Troeltsch, who like Schleiermacher sought to avoid historicism's descent into an unchecked materialism, nonetheless saw Schleiermacher's mediation between *Wissenschaft* and *Glaube* as more harmful than helpful. For his very construal of theology as separate from philosophy yet congruent with its insights "sundered it from all theoretical and universally valid understanding, especially from philosophy and historical method."[36]

Indeed, Troeltsch argues that Schleiermacher's advancing Christian theology along these lines, depicted in terms that evoke Race's pluralism, ensures the collapse of the credibility of theological statements:

> A different escape from the chaos of world religions was to be found in another direction. Here . . . the individual, personal, and irrational factors involved in personal affirmation were stressed . . . if Christianity asserts that its convictions rest upon an experience wholly incapable of objective measurement, there remains no basis for opposition.[37]

From this perspective, it is in the very insistence upon the compatibility of faith and science that Schleiermacher has sown the seeds of his theology's own demise. As Frei explains,

> the demand for *compatibility* between faith and science governs (and has to govern) Schleiermacher's reading of the personal description of Jesus and the events of his life fully as much as the *independence* of science from faith. But if it governs as much, it in fact governs completely. And then all the features of the dogmatic conception of Christ, based on the supposed need of Christian experience, come floating in as hermeneutical tools for interpreting the data of the Gospel portrait.[38]

It is not a defense of miracles, but Schleiermacher's appeal to a *natural* explanation for the resurrection, while still maintaining its religious significance as a relative miracle that yields faith, that is for Strauss the most flagrant and troublesome example of the problems that arise from

[35]   Frei, "Strauss," 251.
[36]   Frei, "Niebuhr's Theological Background," 54.
[37]   Troeltsch, "*Logos* and *Mythos*," 48–49.
[38]   Frei, "Strauss," 251; cf. Troeltsch, "*Logos* and *Mythos*," 48–49.

attempts at mediation between faith and science like those that Schleier-macher advocates.

In the attempt to appease both *Glaube* and *Wissenschaft*, Strauss and Troeltsch see Schleiermacher mounting an argument that seeks to derive theological conclusions from a scientific procedure, an effort which assumes their mutual and consistent agreement but therefore strips the latter of its critical force.[39] Strauss views Schleiermacher's Christology as a brazen endeavor to co-opt elements of the scientific method to defend his vision of faith in the face of philosophical criticisms. His Christ has been stripped of "the powerfully miraculous redemptive character" presented in the Gospels while still failing to "meet modernity's demand for a natural man."[40]

Troeltsch highlights similar attempts made in the early twentieth cen-tury as indicators of this continued malaise besetting Christian theology. In a previously cited polemical essay against Friedrich Niebergall, a con-temporary of Troeltsch and a leader of the "practical theology" movement within German liberal theology, Troeltsch lambasts him for charting a theological course that pays lip service to empirical and historical-critical procedure to shore up the credibility of Christian dogma.[41] The result is a theology that "has been deeply affected by the spirit of historical criti-cism, analogy and relativity. Indeed, it has been almost destroyed. All that remain are some pathetic and quite general claims. *In this respect, the older dogmatic doctrine was better and more understandable.*"[42] Troeltsch finds the unabashed "supernaturalism" of what he calls "the dogmatic method" preferable to the mediating theology of Schleiermacher and his heirs, which seeks to tame the "historical method" by employing it in the service of dogmatic apologetics.

What Strauss and Troeltsch most object to, then, as Frei's account shows, is the attempted *immunization* of Christian faith from scientific contagion. A simple dogmatic appeal to the truth of Christian theology would no doubt be discounted by both outright. But both Strauss and

---

[39]   David Friedrich Strauss, *The Christ of Faith and the Jesus of History*, trans. Leander E. Keck (Philadelphia: Fortress, 1977), 159–69.

[40]   Frei, "Strauss," 253.

[41]   Ernst Troeltsch, "Historical and Dogmatic Method in Theology," in *Religion in History*, 11–32; cf. Angela Dienhart Hancock, *Karl Barth's Emergency Homiletic, 1932–1933* (Grand Rapids: Eerdmans, 2013) 142, 155–56, 166. Cf. Sarah Coakley, *Christ without Absolutes: A Study of the Christology of Ernst Troeltsch* (Oxford: Claren-don, 1988), 83–84.

[42]   Troeltsch, "Historical and Dogmatic Method," 31, emphasis added; cf. idem, "Dogmatics of the History-of-Religions School," 92.

Troeltsch affirm in no uncertain terms that, for all the failings of the dogmatic approach, it has the benefit of not pretending to evade, or even worse, satisfy, the demands of philosophy and historical criticism. Supernatural justifications of the incarnation and resurrection dogmas may be absurd in their eyes, but it is this very absurdity in modern eyes which limits the scope of their damage. Attempts at mediating the encounter between faith and science toward apologetic and dogmatic ends, however, discredit both faith and philosophy.

Concerning Race's typology, Strauss and Troeltsch would perhaps take greatest issue with inclusivism's attempt to affirm the ultimate significance of Jesus Christ and the historical events of his life, death, and resurrection, alongside the possibility of his saving presence, unmediated by history, within other historical religions.[43] But pluralism is also implicated. Indeed, when confronted with Niebergall's suggestion that "in the ground of the soul there remains *a gap in the causal nexus* . . . that provides full scope for the operation of a higher power," Troeltsch responded: "Should one admire a theology that has come to the point of finding its foundation ultimately in a gap?"[44]

Interestingly, Frei notes that such attempts to systematically reconcile science, philosophy, and faith are rejected with equal force by a theologian of a very different sort—Karl Barth. While Race frames Barth in opposition to historicists like Strauss and Troeltsch, Frei (without minimizing the distance between them) helps us to see their similarities. Like Strauss and Troeltsch, Barth "desired to break through the 'relational' or 'practical-mediating, agnostic' understanding of revelation in theology, the total separation between faith and normative understanding (or reason)."[45] This suggests that Race's typology is more rigid than it should be, obfuscating what is at stake in the confrontation between historicism and Christian faith, creating false equivalencies between historicism and mediating theology, and inhibiting an appreciation of the "non-apologetic" approach characteristic of a historicism like that of Strauss or Troeltsch—an approach that connects those whom Race sees as inherently opposed. And on that note, we will now turn to look more closely at Frei's critical

43   Cf. Coakley, *Christ without Absolutes*, 103–35, 190–97.
44   Troeltsch, "Historical and Dogmatic Method," 31, emphasis added; cf. Coakley, *Christ without Absolutes*, 157ff.
45   Frei, "Niebuhr's Theological Background," 59f.; idem, *Types of Christian Theology*, 78ff.

engagement with Troeltsch's historicism and his appreciative reading of its "non-apologetic" tenor.

Ernst Troeltsch's Non-apologetic Historicism

Race engages with Troeltsch insofar as he provides him with useful historical claims and criticisms that undermine the Gospels' literal sense, Chalcedonian Christology and the scope of all religions' universal truth claims tied to historical events, individuals, or communities. Yet he faults Troeltsch for not going farther and providing a *constructive* argument for the possibility of unity across disparate religious traditions. In fact, he contends that the very "unlimited relativism" Troeltsch sought to avoid is precisely where he ends up.[46] It is Troeltsch's most full-throated affirmation of Christianity's historical and theological parity with other religions in an essay he wrote at the end of his life which was delivered at Oxford in absentia, "Christianity among World-Religions," which Race upholds as the triumph of Troeltsch's historicism over his prior attempts toward affirming Christianity's superiority. Yet it is at this point that Race views Troeltsch's position as most vulnerable to the threat of relativism.[47]

Race believes John Hick's epistemological case for religious belief lays the groundwork for the philosophical validity undergirding Smith's phenomenological argument for the empirical evidence of faith as a universal constant, confirming the reality of a transcendent connection behind the world's diverse religious traditions while avoiding relativism. Even here, however, Race makes a distinction between "levels" of mystery which are tolerable. Race argues that while it is impermissible for Christians not to conceive of other religions as setting out different "paths of salvation," "we do not need to know the answers to questions about the origins of life, eschatology, and so on."[48] Race is happy for the salvific mechanisms to be relativized, but apparently does not extend this to the goal of salvation itself. It is Troeltsch's strong emphasis in this final essay on the historical

---

[46]   Cf. Troeltsch, "The Essence of the Modern Spirit," in *Religion in History*, 255; idem, "Historical and Dogmatic Method," 27.

[47]   Ernst Troeltsch, "The Place of Christianity among World-Religions," in *Attitudes toward Other Religions: Some Christian Interpretations*, ed. Owen C. Thomas (London: SCM Press, 1969), 73–91.

[48]   Race, *Christians and Religious Pluralism*, 164; cf. John Hick, *An Interpretation of Religion: Human Responses to the Transcendent*, 2nd ed. (New Haven, Conn.: Yale University Press, 2004), chs. 19 and 20; idem, "The Buddha's Doctrine of the 'Undetermined Questions,'" in *Disputed Questions in Theology and the Philosophy of Religion* (Basingstoke, UK: Macmillan, 1997), 105–18.

specificity of the world's religions to which Race objects, faulting Troeltsch for not concluding that all religions strive toward the same salvific end. Race laments Troeltsch not having provided a historical apologetic for the unity of the world religions' origins and goals. Without such an apologetic, historicism is, for Race, wretched.

Frei has a different take on Troeltsch, applauding him for his refusal to bend his commitment to historicism for the sake of a comfortable religious apologetic. The power of Troeltsch's thought is, for Frei, a function of its dedication to its critical *philosophical* principles, a commitment which serves as the basis of his *theological* humility.[49] This is neither to say that Troeltsch did not harbor more grand ambitions, nor to say that, as Frei reads him, Troeltsch denied an underlying unity across religious traditions. Indeed, Troeltsch himself was adamant about the importance of apologetics, arguing that the very attempt to reject apologetics is itself apologetic—a critique Frei echoes in his typology.[50] Rather Troeltsch, like Frei, affirmed the significance of apologetics not as a systematic and achievable endeavor, but as something which must be ceaselessly attended to despite its inevitable failures—an ad hoc apologetics.[51]

In the absence of a systematic defense, Frei takes Troeltsch's affirmation of the unity across religions as *a statement of faith*—not of philosophy. Similarly, Frei views his refusal to provide a comprehensive explanation of and argument for this unity as a result of the humility which Troeltsch saw as a constraint natural to the inherent limitations of both historicism and theology. As Frei sees it, "Troeltsch saw the purpose of history hidden in divine spirituality which must never be confused with the finite spirits of men and cultures that are informed by it."[52] For Troeltsch, the historical variety of religious forms and claims is an inevitable product of *how* we know and *what it is possible* for us to know given the nature of history and historical existence. This variety is so vast and complex, caught up in a myriad of contingent and unique historical happenings, that to subject it to any *comprehensive* interpretive system would be to overstep the bounds of historicism. It would also overemphasize the disparity between modern historicism and the old-world dogmatism. For Troeltsch, the divide is not

---

[49]   Frei, "Niebuhr's Theological Background," 60.

[50]   Morgan, introduction to Troeltsch, *Writings on Theology and Religion*, 6; cf. Frei, *Types of Christian Theology*, 46–55.

[51]   Morgan, introduction to Troeltsch, *Writings on Theology and Religion*, 6; cf. Troeltsch, "Historical and Dogmatic Method," 23ff.; Frei, *Types of Christian Theology*, 161.

[52]   Frei, "Niebuhr's Theological Background," 61.

actually that sharp. In his view, the modern world "is not a contrast to or an aberration from ecclesiastical culture, but its successor and heir; the heir has assimilated much of the inheritance, and also acquired much that is new."[53]

It is this element in Troeltsch's thought and his understanding of culture that Frei describes as "nonapologetic":

> Cultures were to [Troeltsch] phenomena admirable in themselves and with their own direct relation to God. They must not be vulgarized by an apologetic, at best provincial and aggressively defensive, that would assimilate the mysterious diversity of culture to a preconceived theological framework . . . if, as a result, Troeltsch fragmentized his conceptual scheme unnecessarily, he did not, at any rate, domesticate the vision of God after the fashion of that relational or "practical-mediating" tradition in theology which he viewed with a disapproval surprisingly generous as a well as incisive.[54]

Frei goes on to contrast Troeltsch's historicism with that of later German theologians like Friedrich Gogarten and Rudolf Bultmann, implicitly perhaps invoking the earlier divide between Troeltsch and Wilhelm Herrmann, who had accused Troeltsch of attempting to replace a Hegelian historical apologetic with an ontological apologetic in *The Absoluteness of Christianity*.[55] Frei describes Troeltsch's "ontology of history," again, as more of a statement of faith than philosophy, and so he is far less critical of it than Herrmann. Indeed, for Frei, hermeneutical, anthropological, and ontological claims are inevitable for Christian theology, no matter how it is conceived.[56] As such, Frei is both not especially troubled by Troeltsch's ontological claim of humanity's direct relation to God and able to applaud Troeltsch's reluctance to pursue a systematic explanation of the nature of this relation across history. From this perspective, it appears as if the so-called relativism that Race *laments* in Troeltsch is *praised* by Frei as a commendable example of nonapologetic philosophical rigor and theological humility.

---

[53]   Troeltsch, "Essence of the Modern Spirit," 269.
[54]   Frei, "Niebuhr's Theological Background," 61.
[55]   Sockness, *Against False Apologetics*, 36.
[56]   The key for Frei, as Mike Higton puts it, is to keep them "low key and secondary . . . they should retain the status of clarifications along the path of careful reading [of the Gospels], rather than be allowed to become rigidly defined theoretical positions which may henceforth govern that reading." Higton, *Christ, Providence and History*, 10; cf. Frei, *Types of Christian Theology*, 125, 143; idem, "The Specificity of Reference," in *Reading Faithfully*, 1:104ff.

Finding History in Faith: The Resurrection, the "Miracle"
of Reference, and the Adequacy of the Literal Sense

We turn now to look at Frei's view on the relationship between scripture's syntactical sense and its ostensive reference. It is worth noting at the start of this section that Frei's position, though typically framed in opposition to liberal theology, has come under equal fire from evangelical theologians—an important counterpoint to those descriptions of Frei's work simply as "postliberal," a term that is not so much incorrect as it is incomplete.[57] If Frei is postliberal, he is "postconservative," too. Frei charts a course that almost inevitably frustrates those on both sides of the aisle, challenging the presuppositions upon which the very divide between "conservative" and "liberal" Christianity is based. Indeed, although Frei's tendency, especially early in his career, is to focus his critiques on liberal, or mediating, theology, he argues in *The Eclipse of Biblical Narrative* that both conservative and liberal Christians are, at root, making the same error, even if the results of this error vary widely between them. Both, in Frei's view, mistake the Bible in general and the Gospels in particular for texts whose meaning is a function of its external reference over, and often against, its syntactical sense.[58] Both decide *first* to what scripture refers, in other words, and then interpret it accordingly.

Fundamentalists, evangelicals, or conservatives primarily locate this reference in the past, in a chain of factual events starting in the Garden of Eden, running through the Gospels and the apostolic period. Liberals, equally emphatic on the basic significance of scripture's "ostensive reference," locate this reference in the present. Eschewing the historical reference of scripture, they instead locate its meaning in terms of its contemporary relevance and resonance with general, existential situations, both individual and communal. To this end, philosophy and anthropology are viewed as essential hermeneutical guides.[59] The more radical of such liberal interpretations are found in the "mythical school" founded by Strauss, for whom the "'historical Jesus' has neither historically nor theologically (or philosophically) any connection with the 'Christ of faith.'"[60] On the

---

[57]   See Knitter, *Theologies of Religions*, 181; idem, *One Earth, Many Religions*, 51–53; For responses to such a one-sided interpretation of Frei, see Springs, *Generous Orthodoxy*, 132–35; DeHart, *Trial of the Witnesses*, 241–82; C. C. Pecknold, *Transforming Postliberal Theology: George Lindbeck, Pragmatism and Scripture* (London: T&T Clark, 2005), 1–12.

[58]   Frei, *Eclipse of Biblical Narrative*, 87.

[59]   Frei, *Eclipse of Biblical Narrative*, 18, 43–50.

[60]   Frei, *Eclipse of Biblical Narrative*, 234.

conservative extreme is biblical literalism and its insistence upon the inerrancy and historical factuality of the Bible, which has come increasingly
to draw upon archeology and other scientific discourses to support its
interpretive approach.

In response to the rising influence of historicism, empirical philosophy, and Deism, Frei shows how conservatives and liberals alike sought
meaning in something behind or beyond the text, such as historical facts
or ethical ideals, in hopes of shoring up its contemporary significance.
In Frei's estimation, this caused the "realistic or history-like element" of
scripture to be obscured, turning the focus of its interpretation from the
narrative—the words of scripture—to the predetermined subject matter
or referent. He writes:

> The apologetic urge from left to right, for which explication and
> application had to walk in harmony, was only one reason for the
> strange eclipse of the realistic narrative option in a situation in which
> many observers actually paid heed to that feature. Hermeneutics
> stood between religious apologetics and historical criticism, and
> these two worked against the narrative option.[61]

An additional casualty of the loss of the narrative option, an approach
oriented around the plain or literal sense of scripture, was *figural reading*,
a way of interpreting the Bible's different history-like narratives in relation
to one another under an appeal to God's providential plan while affirming
the historical particularity of the different events or persons. Frei views the
unity of literal and figural reading as the traditional practice of Western
Christianity and the most fitting interpretive approach to the history-like
narratives within the Bible. Regrettably, this unity was sundered through
the apologetic moves of both conservatives and liberals:

> When the identity of literal sense and historical reference is severed,
> literal and figural reading likewise no longer belong together. Sim-
> ilarly, when the pattern of meaning is no longer firmly ingredient
> in the story and the occurrence character of the text but becomes a
> function of a quasi-independent interpretive stance, literal and fig-
> ural reading draw apart, the latter gradually looking like a forced,
> arbitrary imposition of unity on a group of very diverse texts. No
> longer an extension of literal reading, figural interpretation instead

---

[61]   Frei, *Eclipse of Biblical Narrative*, 134.

becomes a bad historical argument or an arbitrary allegorizing of texts in the service of preconceived dogma.[62]

The loss of figural interpretation profoundly hobbled Christian theology's capacity to imagine a connection between the historical uniqueness *and* providential significance of historical events and persons.

This summary of *Eclipse* points us in the direction of Frei's positive account of scripture's reference, which in turn directs attention to the other book Frei published during his lifetime, *The Identity of Jesus Christ*. This book is both a prequel of sorts and "an exegetical test" of the kind of interpretation Frei argues for in *Eclipse*.[63] But Frei most explicitly considered the question of historical reference and scripture, particularly the resurrection, in several journal articles, essays, and lectures, which will be considered alongside *Identity*.

Together in these works, we see that for Frei, the meaning of scripture, and the identity of Jesus Christ, is best approached by prioritizing a literal reading of the Gospel narratives, especially the crucifixion and resurrection accounts, such that they are also rendered interpretable figurally. For nonbelievers, this means the miraculous claims made within the Bible can be taken as constitutive of the meaning of its narratives, even if their actual occurrence is denied. For believing Christians, this literal sense does indeed imply an equivalent historical reference, but this does not exhaust or confine the import of the narratives themselves and their description of Jesus' identity to a simple constellation of historical events alone. The Gospels are not "histories" but they are *history-like*, "having a textual shape like a historical account, that is, the linguistic form of verisimilitude."[64] The Gospels employ "realistic narrative . . . history-like—in its language as well as its depiction of a common public world (no matter whether it is the one we all think we inhabit), in the close interaction of character and incident, and in the non-symbolic quality of the relation between the story and what the story is about."[65] It is this "history-likeness" that also points to the importance of figural interpretation in discerning, however dimly, the providential relation between contemporary historical life and the Gospel narrative.

---

[62]   Frei, *Eclipse of Biblical Narrative*, 37.
[63]   Frei, *Eclipse of Biblical Narrative*, vii.
[64]   Hans Frei, "Conflicts in Interpretation," in *Theology and Narrative*, 162; cf. idem, "'Literal Reading,'" 128f., 139f.
[65]   Frei, *Identity of Jesus Christ*, 59.

Again, Frei rejects the prioritization of ostensive reference over syntactical sense in the interpretation of scripture, the foregrounding of an account of theological meaning prior to an engagement with theological texts. But it is important to note that the doctrine of providence sets out what might be described as a horizon of significance for the *sensus literalis*, affirming whatever particular meaning we might discern while prioritizing the plain sense of scripture and the historically particular events and contexts which it depicts, while affirming the significance of these accounts for those who read them today. The providential affirmation of this significance, crucially, does not impose a particular frame of interpretation upon scripture—rendering its meaningfulness as a function of its historical accuracy, psychology, morality, or the like—but merely affirms that they remain meaningful.

It is also important to emphasize that Frei's appeal to the primacy of the literal sense in the interpretation of the Gospels is hardly a claim of historical inerrancy. Rather, Frei advocates a literal reading of the Bible in which the interpreter can affirm that, "whether or not these stories report history (either reliably or unreliably), whether or not the Gospels are other things besides realistic stories, what they tell us is a fruit of the stories themselves."[66] So Frei insists that an affirmation of the historical reference of the Gospels and crucifixion/resurrection accounts, though an essential component of Christian faith, is nonetheless secondary or subsidiary to their interpretation as realistic narratives.

For Frei, the *Christian* affirmation of the historical reference of the Gospel accounts of the resurrection is grounded not in a general metaphysical, epistemological, existential, or ethical account which would indicate either its possibility or, worse, its inevitability. Rather, affirming the historical reference of the Bible is for Frei an outworking of faith, akin in many ways to Troeltsch's affirmation of the unity of world religions. As such, the affirmation of this historical reference is tied to an acceptance of the limitations of any narrative account, written or otherwise, of a miraculous event, which by its very nature defies the possibility of a complete reckoning. So for those Christians who, upon reading the Gospels, are inclined to believe the resurrection transpired in history, the Gospels can only be said to refer *miraculously* to such historical events, even while they are acknowledged as necessarily limited accounts.[67] Moreover, the

---

[66]   Frei, *Identity of Jesus Christ*, 59.
[67]   Frei, "Response to 'Narrative Theology: An Evangelical Appraisal,'" in *Theology and Narrative*, 211f.

providential connection between the literal and figural means not only that such historical reference is inextricably tied to the present, but even that contemporary historical occurrences *might* be interpreted—with great restraint and deference to the mystery of God's providence—as shedding some light on the meaning of events narrated in the Bible and even on the identity of Jesus Christ. Reflecting on the apostle Paul's account in Romans 11:29-32 of the "mysterious fitness between God's choice of the Gentiles in and by his rejection of his own chosen people, Israel, and the salvation of this same people," Frei writes:

> The interaction pattern here worked out may serve as a possible parable for the providential presence of God in Jesus Christ to the history that takes place in the interaction of the church with humanity at large. In a sense, that means that the really significant events may well transpire among the "Gentiles" from whom the church ("Israel") receives the enrichment of her own humanity. Humanity at large is the neighbor given to the church, through whom Christ is present to the church. It follows that, even though events in history, such as the imperative move toward church reunion, are important, there are other events in the history of mankind at large that may parabolically bespeak the presence of Christ in a far more significant and evident way.[68]

Such interpretation is too cautious to be deemed "optimistic" but at the same time cannot be less than "hopeful."[69]

Frei on Reference and the Resurrection

Clarification is here in order as Frei's account of reference has subsequently come under considerable attack. Unease with Frei's position typically takes two forms.[70] Some, especially conservative Christians like Carl Henry, read Frei as rejecting the question of historical reference altogether.[71] Others, particularly certain Barth scholars, argue that Frei's account of scripture's meaning as "identical with the text" posits a "linguistically

---

[68]   Frei, *Identity of Jesus Christ*, 192.
[69]   Higton, *Christ, Providence and History*, 86.
[70]   Here following the observation of Springs, *Generous Orthodoxy*, 85–103.
[71]   Carl Henry, "Narrative Theology: An Evangelical Appraisal," *Trinity Journal* 8, no. 1 (1987): 3–19; cf. Henri Blocher, "Biblical Narrative and Historical Reference," in *Issues in Faith and History: Papers Presented at the Second Edinburgh Conference on Dogmatics*, ed. Nigel M. de S. Cameron (Edinburgh: Rutherford House, 1989), 102–22.

idealist" portrayal of revelation which, contrary to Barth's realism, turns the Bible itself into the "linguistic presence" of God.[72]

We can add a third source of such discomfort which mirrors the first—the interpretation of Frei as rejecting *philosophical* reference and descending into "pure narrativism."[73] Similar to the first in its insinuation that Frei isolates the Bible from all external reference, it is different in that the concern here is not simply for historical reference but for the supposed rejection of scripture's external reference altogether, including the possibility of meaningful exchange with contemporary philosophical and scientific views and social conditions. It was suggested in the preceding chapter that the question of reference in this regard is of paramount importance to Alan Race.[74] On this view, Frei's rejection of overarching philosophical and hermeneutical theories leaves the Bible hopelessly isolated from and irrelevant to contemporary life. We will focus on the first and last of these criticisms, i.e., the evangelical and liberal critiques.

Given his view of the centrality of the resurrection in the Gospels' description of the identity of Jesus Christ and, therefore, its centrality in orienting Christian interpretation of scripture, Frei tends to focus the question of reference specifically in terms of the Gospels' resurrection claims. In Frei's telling, liberals might claim the historical reference of the resurrection statements is not any actual events that befell Jesus, but a mythological expression of the disciples' experience of faith in Jesus, rendering the notion of the resurrection's meaning in idealist and existentialist terms alone. This makes the very question of the resurrection's historical occurrence superfluous to the cogency of Christian faith.[75] On the other side, conservatives tend to insist that the resurrection claims must be interpreted as direct historical reporting, describing the physical "manner of his resurrected state, e.g. . . . whether his resurrected body was or else was not subject to the laws of gravity."[76]

Frei's response to these opposing accounts of the resurrection's reference displays a characteristic humility, undoubtedly tied to his awareness of both the power and the inadequacy of the prevailing options:

[72] Frei, "Interpretation of Narrative," 108; cf. Springs, *Generous Orthodoxy*, 86. Cf. Bruce McCormack, *Orthodox and Modern Studies in the Theology of Karl Barth* (Grand Rapids: Baker Academic, 2008), 123.

[73] Gary Comstock, "Truth or Meaning: Ricoeur versus Frei on Biblical Narrative," *HTS Teologiese Studies / Theological Studies* 45, no. 4 (1989): 743.

[74] Race, *Christians and Religious Pluralism*, 131–32.

[75] Frei, "Historical Reference," 95.

[76] Frei, "Historical Reference," 95.

My dilemma is the obvious one: the first set of remarks seems to me a pure evasion of the texts and implies a willingness to surrender what seems to me an indispensable aspect of what makes the gospel good news. The second I find impossible to believe.

A properly modest and realistic self-appraisal is imperative at this point: can one find another way that is honest to the texts?[77]

Frei's unease with the options modern theology has laid before him is an important element in framing his own notion of reference. In response to Henry, Frei describes his vision of theology as "a kind of generous orthodoxy which would have in it an element of liberalism . . . and an element of evangelicalism."[78]

Frei sees the question of historical reference and the resurrection as unavoidable in the interpretation of scripture yet also secondary in some sense to the Bible's syntactical sense. One possible way of understanding this is to say that no amount of archeological evidence or historical proof of Jesus' resurrection, however doubtful the acquisition of such evidence might be, could ever supplant the primary importance of its narrative account in scripture. Indeed, he distinguishes between "historical reference" and "textual reference," where, for believing Christians, the latter means that "the text is witness to the Word of God, whether it is historical or not."[79] This is not to say that the historical reference of the Gospels is irrelevant for Christians. But it is for Frei neither the primary question in determining the meaning of the text nor the basic condition upon which the text can retain its claim to being the Word of God.

This being the case, one might wonder what role, if any, Frei allows for historical criticism in biblical interpretation. While Race argues that, if the meaning of the incarnation (and, by extension, the resurrection) is specific to them (and not a function of a universal transcendent meaning of which they are mythological expressions), this *depends* on historical study confirming them "as the only reasonable and complete interpretation of the life and work of Jesus."[80] First we establish that the incarnation and resurrection are verifiable historical occurrences, then, and only then, can we affirm that their theological significance is particular to them. This

---

[77]   Frei, "Historical Reference," 95; cf. idem, "Strauss," 251–53.
[78]   Frei, "Response to 'Narrative Theology,'" 208.
[79]   Frei, "Response to 'Narrative Theology,'" 209.
[80]   Race, *Christians and Religious Pluralism*, 35; Hans Frei, "Of the Resurrection of Christ," in *Reading Faithfully*, 1:187f.; idem, "Response to 'Narrative Theology,'" 209ff.

is the position implicitly occupied by exclusivism as Race formulates it, insofar as exclusivism's reduction of the meaning of scripture to a historical record assumes the verifiability of these events. It is also a position that Frei rejects. The nature of the resurrection claim itself—the supposed occurrence of a wholly unique and exceptional event within the normal, causally determined order of the historical world—means the resurrection is necessarily beyond the ken not only of historical verifiability but also of comprehensive literal description. The text should be "understood primarily as the adequate testimony to, rather than an accurate report of, the reality."[81]

> [Some] read the [resurrection] accounts as meaning what they say, so that their subject is indeed the bodily resurrected Christ Jesus. They also believe that a miracle—the miracle of the resurrection in particular—is a real event; however, it is one to which human depiction and conception are inadequate, even though the literal description is the best that can be offered, not to be supplanted or replaced by any other and therefore itself not simply metaphorical in character. In this view, text and reality are adequate, indeed, indispensable to each other but not identical.[82]

If the resurrection did occur, Frei argues that it would neither be a part of the causal nexus of history—participation in which is the basis for historical confirmation—nor would it be capable of complete encapsulation or depiction in a literal or history-like narrative.

Moreover, and unlike other historical events, because the resurrection is depicted in scripture and has been interpreted by Christian communities up to the present day as impinging directly upon our lives as our "salvation from sin and death," it is necessarily distinct from all other historical events, none of which are described as bearing a similar import. Elsewhere, Frei asks: "To what historical or natural occurrence would we be able to compare the resurrection . . . ?" His response: "None. There appears to be no argument from factual evidence or rational possibility to smooth the transition from literary to faith judgment."[83] In

---

[81]   Frei, "Resurrection of Christ," 187. Although Frei appears to have struggled with the question of the contemporary, empirical verifiability of the risen Christ, his position on historical verifiability does not entail a denial of its possibility. Cf. Frei, "Historical Reference," 97.

[82]   Frei, "Resurrection of Christ," 187.

[83]   Frei, *Identity of Jesus Christ*, 183.

other words, "if the resurrection is true, it is unique," and historical crit-icism or excavation could not hope to confirm it; "but if false, it is like any other purported fact that has been proved false: there is nothing unique about it in that case."[84]

It is therefore important to emphasize that historical investigation does, for Frei, have a role to play in understanding the resurrection of Jesus Christ and its import. Like Strauss and Troeltsch, Frei acknowledges the power of historical investigation to *disconfirm* the factuality of histor-ical events. Of equal importance, unlike Strauss, Troeltsch, and Race, Frei frames the possibility of such disconfirmation as empirical rather than philosophical. Although Frei is reluctant, for the reasons just outlined, to qualify the resurrection as *fact*, a designation which would in some way be disrespectful of both faith and history, he agrees that "fact" is the closest conceptual analog at our disposal. As such, "reliable historical evi-dence *against* the resurrection would be decisive."[85] Archeological efforts in Jerusalem might one day yield incontrovertible proof that Jesus did not undergo a bodily resurrection. But until such factual evidence emerges, the resurrection remains for Frei *the* necessary and defining affirmation of Christian faith. Whereas Race's pluralism renders the validity of human faith in the transcendent as impervious to *any* criticism, including the his-torical or philosophical, for Frei, Christian faith is plainly vulnerable to historical evidence.

At the same time, and especially regarding those depictions of Jesus beyond the resurrection, the question of the historical accuracy of the events narrated and its status as the Word of God is not a zero-sum game for Frei. Given the inherent inadequacy of finite and literal depic-tion of an encounter with the infinite—as Frei understands Christ's resurrection—the text cannot be considered a *complete* retelling, but as an *adequate* description. Moreover, while Christian faith does hinge on an affirmation of the historical reference of the resurrection accounts, this is not true for all passages of the Gospels or the Bible. For Frei, the status of scripture as the Word of God, and its adequacy for Christian faith, is entirely dependent upon God's grace, not the accuracy of histori-cal reporting of its human authors. But as *Christian* faith in God's grace is inextricably tied to a faith in the occurrence of the resurrection, it is there that the Christian must affirm, in faith, the overlap between syntactical sense and historical reference.

---

84   Frei, *Identity of Jesus Christ*, 183.
85   Frei, *Identity of Jesus Christ*, 183.

In other words, while we must acknowledge the limitations of scripture in conveying that which is impossible to convey through language (e.g., the causal unfolding of miracles), we must also grant that even passages about Jesus which *might not* have a historical basis must still be conceived as truthfully or accurately referring to a realistic state of affairs, namely, the identity of Jesus Christ as the resurrected Son of God.[86] For Frei, above all else, the Gospels depict the crucial particular of Jesus' identity to be his crucifixion and resurrection. As such, all the other aspects of their narratives find their meaning and truth in relation to it, whether or not they are historically accurate.

In this way, we see that Frei turns the question of historical reference, as conceived by Strauss, Troeltsch, Race, and others, on its head. It is the resurrection which limits the reach of historicism. But it is also the resurrection itself which inescapably and provocatively raises the question of the significance of historical reference for Christian faith. In other words, the question of historical reference is a question in the first place because of the Bible's accounts of miracle, especially the miracle of the resurrection, and the church's reading of them in this way. Any hermeneutical take on the Gospels that seeks to circumvent the resurrection in this regard is therefore inherently flawed. For it is not external, metaphysical postulates or historical criticism that force us to ask if the resurrection accounts refer to actual historical events—the question is raised by the resurrection accounts themselves and their creedal and ecclesial interpretation. It is the resurrection which raises the question of historical reference while also asserting its own centrality in the meaning and reference of all other aspects of the Gospel narratives.

---

[86]   Frei, "Response to 'Narrative Theology,'" 208; cf. Springs, *Generous Orthodoxy*, 90–91. William Placher helpfully explains this potentially confusing aspect of Frei's view of reference as follows:

> Reading these stories, one learns who Jesus is—that is, one learns both the characteristics of his human life and the fact that human life was somehow the self-revelation of God. Many of the individual episodes serve as biographical anecdotes, *"true" if they illustrate his character authentically even though the particular incident they narrate never happened, and the overall shape of the narrative portrays something of Jesus' identity.* While such an identity description need not be correct in all its particulars in order to get someone's identity right, its general themes do have to capture a person's essential features, and *some* of its particulars may be crucial . . .

William C. Placher, *Narratives of a Vulnerable God: Christ, Theology, and Scripture* (Louisville, Ky.: Westminster John Knox, 1994), 92, quoted in Springs, *Generous Orthodoxy*, 207, n. 18.

Contrary to those who argue that Frei ignores the question of histor-ical reference, or those who suggest that he advances a view of it which is entirely fideistic, Frei takes the referential concerns of both liberal and evangelical Christians seriously while also showing them to be herme-neutically misplaced. The resurrection accounts, for Frei, cannot avoid the question of historical reference. But for him, this must be viewed as a question of the referential sufficiency or adequacy of the finite narrative description in relation to its infinite referent—a sufficiency or adequacy that is grounded in the miracle of God's grace.

Epistemology and Apologetics

We saw in the last chapter that Race principally links historicist criticisms to questions concerning the epistemic rationality of faith. Historicism sug-gests that scriptural traditions, replete with stories of miraculous events, are unreliable and not a suitable basis for an intellectually plausible faith. Therefore, Race concludes, the epistemic legitimacy of religious faith must be derived independently of scripture.

Frei discerns a similar trajectory in post-Enlightenment theology more broadly. He notes, with evident frustration, that concerns over the Bible's historical reference led theologians to focus on providing apologetic argu-ments for the epistemic viability of Christianity.[87] Following Barth, and in line even with Hick's own presentation in *Faith and Knowledge*, Frei views most epistemological accounts of faith as apologetic endeavors focused on appeasing philosophical critiques, not as descriptions of the epistemology implicitly recommended in Christianity itself. As Frei wrote at the start of a 1967 lecture delivered at the Harvard Divinity School,

> Kant's *Religion Within the Limits* contains *in nuce* almost all the problems systematic theologians have worried to and fro since his day . . . we have lived for almost three hundred years in an era in which an anthropologically oriented theological apologetic has tried to demonstrate the notion of a unique divine revelation in Jesus Christ is one whose meaning and possibility are reflected in general human experience . . . To say it another way: Theology has to validate the *possibility* and hence the meaning of Christian claims concerning the shape of human existence and divine relation to it . . .[88]

---

[87]   Frei, *Eclipse of Biblical Narrative*, 130–42.
[88]   Hans Frei, "Remarks in Connection with a Theological Proposal," in *Theol-ogy and Narrative*, 29.

The same idea is succinctly put forward by Nicholas Wolterstorff: "Ever since Kant, the anxious questions, 'Can we? How can we?' have haunted theologians, insisting on being addressed before any others."[89] Again, one of the primary areas in which theologians became convinced they needed to appease philosophy was that of history and historical criticism. In turning to Frei's reflections on epistemology, it is important to keep in mind that hermeneutics, which for Frei is essentially biblical exegesis under the auspices of the doctrine of providence, precedes epistemology in the ordered operations of Christian faith. Put simply, Frei refuses to force his reading of scripture through a Bible-shaped hole created by an epistemological theory arrived at independently of that reading.[90]

Epistemology and Apologetics: The Order of Belief and
the Order of Coming to Believe

While Race appeals to John Hick's argument for the epistemic validity of religious belief as theological pluralism's response to the challenges set by historicism, Frei instead situates the encounter between faith and epistemology on very different terms. Frei differentiates between "the order of belief" and "that of coming to believe," such that theology is primarily aligned with the former and conceived as a *descriptive* rather than *explanatory* endeavor—but one that still might point toward possible, if provisional, philosophical points of agreement.[91]

Frei's disinclination toward advancing a systematic apologetic in response to historicist critiques has been misinterpreted as a wholesale rejection of philosophy and *wissenschaftlich* inquiries as significant for theology. This, in turn, has led some to claim that Frei's epistemology is simply fideism. Related to but distinct from this suggestion is the charge that Frei rejects the significance of the resurrection's historical occurrence altogether. N. T. Wright, for example, accuses Frei of "arguing that we should not try to investigate the resurrection historically because the resurrection is itself the ground of Christian epistemology . . . [leaving] Frei's proposal, in the last analysis . . . always in danger of describing a closed epistemological circle, a fideism from within which everything can be seen clearly but which remains necessarily opaque to those outside."[92]

---

[89]   Nicholas Wolterstorff, "Is It Possible and Desirable for Theologians to Recover from Kant?" *Modern Theology* 14, no. 1 (1998): 15.
[90]   Cf. Frei, "Remarks," 27.
[91]   Frei, *Identity of Jesus Christ*, 58; idem, "Remarks," 30.
[92]   N. T. Wright, *The Resurrection of the Son of God* (London: SPCK, 2003), 21.

It is important to note at the outset of this section that Frei rejects claims that his project is fideistic, that he insists that philosophy *is* an essential interlocutor in Christian theology, and that he distinguishes between his own philosophical proclivities independent of theology and those he sees as proper for a Christian theologian.[93] In other words, Frei neither rejects the significance of philosophy or epistemology for theology nor are his own philosophical inclinations decided by determining which support his Christian faith best.[94] Refusing to let epistemic concerns dictate the terms of Christian theology, he nonetheless affirms the importance of exploring the epistemological questions which inevitably arise when Christian theology confronts *wissenschaftlich* discourses and critiques—provided this is not used as a means of differentiating between licit and illicit hermeneutical approaches.

Indeed, though Frei does take modern theology to task for its obsession with philosophical appeasement, he is equally critical of those, like D. Z. Philips, who advocate a rejection of any relationship whatsoever between theology and philosophy. This is partly because such a rejection, as Frei sees it, often relies upon a philosophical apologetic of its own, such that the two extremes of philosophical appeasement and rejection end up meeting "like a snake curled in on itself."[95] But it is also because Frei *does* retain a place within his theology for apologetics—though neither as a starting point nor as a systematic endeavor. Like Barth, Frei wants to affirm the possibility of a provisional overlap between theology and philosophy to which we should be sensitive and which might indicate ad hoc apologetic points of contact.[96]

In what follows, we will see how Frei differentiates between apologetic epistemologies like Hick's neo-Kantian perspectivism and descriptive theological epistemologies like Barth's analogical account. But how Frei orders the relationship between epistemology and hermeneutics is just as significant. For Frei's theology calls into question not just which epistemology is preferable for Christian faith but the *entire scheme* Race contrives in which a Christology, chastened by historicism and the overarching concern with making faith philosophically plausible, undergirds a demand for Christians to accept of a neo-Kantian epistemology. Against accusations of fideism, it will be argued that the key for Frei in navigating the ad hoc relationship between theology and philosophy is neither to make philosophy accommodate Christological dogma nor to make Chris-

---

93   Frei, "'Literal Reading,'" 142.
94   Frei, "Remarks," 30.
95   Frei, *Types of Christian Theology*, 51.
96   Frei, *Types of Christian Theology*, 51.

tology accommodate philosophy, but rather to see what philosophical claims might shed light on Christology.

In this vein, we will see that, rather than bowing to historicism, or being content to simply restate Barth's affirmation of the "ontic fact" of the incarnation, Frei's Christology summons a more pronounced emphasis on the particular, *historical* person of Jesus of Nazareth than does Race's supposedly historically attuned, pluralist theology. Following Barth's reading of Anselm in outlining what might be loosely described as an analogical epistemology, Frei provides an epistemological account not of how belief is *possible*, but of the order of Christian belief itself. Building off his criticism of Barth's potential "epistemological monophysitism," Frei orients this analogical epistemology to provide an even greater emphasis both on Jesus' life as narrated in scripture and on the possibility of encountering his presence *today*. In this way, we can see reflected in Frei's analogical epistemology Troeltsch's concern for history, the particularity of historical occurrences and the way in which we "know" things in the historical world, alongside Barth's prioritization of the "ontic fact" of the incarnation and its providential figuration in history.[97]

Frei draws the outlines of a Christian epistemology which reflects an appreciation of history's particularity governed by a faith in history's positive relation to God and in God's providential plan for creation. This plan is disclosed in the life, death, and resurrection of Jesus Christ as narrated in the Gospels. It is also discernible in the analogical or figural interpretation of the present in relation to the history-like narrative of the Gospels, a relation that persists throughout the course of history's providential unfolding.[98] This analogical account took shape in response to two epistemological approaches to the question of faith and its relation to history which Frei found unsatisfactory—relationalism or perspectivism and epistemological monophysitism.

Relationalism, Perspectivism, and the Freedom of God, Humanity, and History

Looking at Schleiermacher and Barth, Frei sees two opposite, yet oddly similar, epistemological responses to the confrontation between faith and history. On the one side are those like Schleiermacher whom Frei termed

---

[97]   Cf. Hans Frei, "Theological Reflections on the Accounts of Jesus' Death and Resurrection," in *Theology and Narrative*, 91; idem, "'Literal Reading,'" 122; Higton, *Christ, Providence and History*, 90, n. 2.

[98]   Cf. Higton, *Christ, Providence and History*, 59.

"relationalists" and the more extreme camp of "perspectivists."[99] For both, history, in all its real and manifold particularity, is viewed as a veil behind which lies a transcendent reality and through which this transcendent reality is *given universally* to humanity.[100] There is an organic relationship between God and humanity built into the very structure of reality, which renders the significance of our historical existence strictly in terms of its capacity to provide us with epistemic access to this ahistorical, ultimate truth. As we saw in the last chapter, this is Hick's approach.

In fact, Hick goes well beyond Schleiermacher and Troeltsch in his epistemological apologetic for the universal rationality of faith. Frei sees that Schleiermacher maintained a Christocentrism within his relationalism, such that revelation is "not only a matter of a given, present relation but also of a given historical relation (somehow united to the present relation) behind or beyond which one cannot go for concrete contact with God."[101] And Troeltsch kept his idealism as a formal feature of his theology, refusing to extrapolate from it a theory synthesizing the historical manifestations of faith in toto. Yet Hick puts his transcendental idealism, or, as he calls it, critical realism, to work in a far-reaching apologetic for the rationality of religious belief and for a theology of pluralism, which Race invokes as the only approach to Christianity which satisfies the epistemological problems raised by historicism.[102]

Frei sees in this apologetic impulse a prioritization of humanity's freedom of faith over and against God's freedom, and Hick confirms this: "Our essential personal freedom is preserved by the epistemic distance—a distance not in space but in knowledge—between ourselves and the divine reality."[103] Race's criticism of Barth echoes this concern by suggesting that "Barth's epistemological model . . . involves the most extraordinary by-passing of the normal means by which knowledge comes before the human subject."[104] In line with Frei's portrayal of relationalism and perspectivism, Race and Hick are committed to viewing human agency as the primary apparatus of faith, which remains a free act particularly inso-

---

[99]   Cf. Frei, "Niebuhr's Theological Background," 38; idem, "Historical Reference," 100; idem, "Remarks," 31–32, 37–40; idem, "Accounts of Jesus' Death," 87–91; idem, "On Interpreting the Christian Story," in *Reading Faithfully*, 72, 78f.; idem, "History, Salvation-History, and Typology," in *Reading Faithfully*, 1:152–56, 158f.

[100]   Frei, "Remarks," 37ff.; cf. Higton, *Christ, Providence and History*, 40–41.

[101]   Frei, "Niebuhr's Theological Background," 38.

[102]   Christopher J. Insole, *The Realist Hope* (New York: Routledge, 2016), 3ff.

[103]   John Hick, *The Fifth Dimension* (Oxford: Oneworld, 2004), 43.

[104]   Race, *Christians and Religious Pluralism*, 28.

far as it is an act of reason. *Crucially, this means that the constraints upon the operation of our reason in connection with the transcendent are not located in the transcendent—there is no incongruity between our reasoning and its transcendent object, or between our free will to know God and the free will of God to reveal Godself—but in history.* Indeed, the threats to this free act are not—cannot—be located in the nature of the transcendent or divine, as the employment of critical reasoning is essential for the proper interpretation of the transcendent nature itself. Rather, the epistemological limitations of Hick's perspectivism are essentially a function of the contextual and contingent nature of historical existence: "Surely the medium through which we receive God's light is so much part of our ordinary world that we cannot help but judge and evaluate it from our position within the world. It is not that we cannot step aside from the light of God as it shines, but that we are unable to step aside from the world as we receive the light."[105]

So relationalists, perspectivists, perhaps inclusivists, and certainly pluralists take the view that God's presence is a universal constant of human experience. Whereas for some Christian relationalists (like inclusivists), this *given* is still viewed through a Christological lens and therefore as a relation founded upon God's act in Christ, for perspectivists and pluralists even this Christological condition is removed. On this view, transcendent presence being a basic attribute of human experience means that our various approximations of the transcendent must in some sense hold true even if they appear contradictory.

But as Frei notes in a lecture later in his career titled "Is Religious Sensibility Accessible to Study?" seeking to prioritize human freedom and accounts of history's metaphysical limitations, perspectivism and relationalism appear to *undermine* the freedom of humanity and history:

> It's the old ploy about your not being able to understand music if you're tone-deaf, but—it goes on—fear not, for in fact you're *not* tone-deaf. (As a matter of fact you couldn't be if you tried.) But your musicality or your affinity for religion is not a specific, given content of your consciousness; it's a pre-given, transcendental condition for understanding any specific instance of it that comes to be given to consciousness. That's what makes it universal and, in its own indirect way, accessible.[106]

---

[105]   Race, *Christians and Religious Pluralism*, 28.
[106]   Hans Frei, "Is Religious Sensibility Accessible to Study?" in *Reading Faithfully*, 1:145.

Frei's criticism of relationalism as transgressing not only God's freedom but the freedom of humans and history as well, plainly holds true for theological pluralism. For in its insistence on universal access to transcendent experience and its characterization of such experience as ahistorical and of faith as perspectival, pluralism undermines not only the freedom of God and the contingency of history, but even the human freedom to believe or not to believe—"fear not, for in fact you're *not* tone-deaf . . . you couldn't be if you tried."

In short, Frei found relationalism's attempt at bridging the divide between God and humanity, as well as history and the present, untenable. And while he never addressed Race's "pluralism" directly in his work, it seems clear that he would have felt similarly toward it. For pluralism goes even farther than relationalism in constraining not only God's freedom but also our own. For pluralists, what qualifies as revelation itself has been passed through the winnowing fork of Hick's neo-Kantian epistemology and its perspectivism. Neither is God free to reveal Godself to humanity in a way that would conflict with the metaphysical idealism of perspectivism nor are humans free to affirm the particular significance of any aspect of their faith or religious tradition outside of this idealism. Moreover, and despite Race's framing of Hick's epistemology as a response to historicist criticisms, Frei's criticism of relationalism and perspectivism shows how pluralism's approach to proving the congruence and universality of transcendent encounter yields an interpretation of history which minimizes the significance of historical contingency and renders suspect the status of human freedom in belief and unbelief.

Epistemological Monophysitism and the Disregard for Jesus' Historical Life

Frei discerns a different apologetic epistemology in Barth's early thought, though one that is similar to relationalism in its antagonism to the *sensus literalis*, that Frei called "epistemological monophysitism."[107] Interestingly, Frei applies this criticism not just to Barth but also to Bultmann and Tillich (once again showing his inclination toward heuristic categories that admit a wide variety of examples), though he suggests it is only a *risk* in Barth's early theology while an *actual* transgression of Bultmann and Tillich. For all three, a theological devaluation of history's particularity appears to be the price of faith. Although those who fall in this camp do not "deny the full, historical humanity" of Jesus, "the situation is quite different with

---

[107]   Hans Frei, "The Theology of H. Richard Niebuhr," in Ramsey, *Faith and Ethics*, 106, 111; Higton, *Christ, Providence and History*, 54–59.

regard to their suggestions about our *knowledge* of Jesus Christ."[108] For they put forward what Frei sees as an epistemological permutation of the monophysite claim, in their failure to affirm that "the Christ present in revelation, or the one who confronts us existentially is . . . significant for our knowledge of Jesus of Nazareth, or vice versa."[109]

In their rush to affirm the ontic fact of Christ, however diverse their understandings of it, they risk losing sight of the humanity of Jesus.[110] Thus, not only is the significance of the history of Jesus the human undermined, but so too is our own historical existence emptied of importance in the reception of revelation. Under such an emphasis on the ontic fact of Christ as the source and focus of human faith, it appears as if our own reception of revelation relates neither to the historical details of Jesus' life nor to the events and occurrences within our own historical lives. As Frei describes it,

> as a human, historical figure [Jesus] is simply "there," but neither his life nor his teaching seems to have much connection with his personhood or with the historical-revelatory person's connection with us. The historical figure of Jesus is not significantly illumined in "revelation." Rather, it is the meaning of the course of history that is illumined, and the application of critical-historical estimates of the historical witness in the Gospels is productive of only minimal positive theological results for the interpretation of revelation.[111]

For these theologians, affirmation of the ontic fact of the incarnation, whether this is understood in a Barthian or Bultmannian fashion, takes precedence over its historical, human expression in Jesus of Nazareth.[112]

For Bultmann, Frei argues that Jesus the man "is lost sight of and Christology becomes merely a particular perspective on the human historical situation."[113] For Barth, the emphasis on the ontic fact of the incarnation risks obscuring the historical features of Jesus' embodiment of that

---

[108] Frei, "Theology of H. Richard Niebuhr," 106.

[109] Frei, "Theology of H. Richard Niebuhr," 106.

[110] As Higton describes it, "that the Word took flesh is relevant, supremely so. What flesh the Word took is not." Higton, *Christ, Providence and History*, 55.

[111] Frei, "Theology of H. Richard Niebuhr," 106.

[112] As Higton summarizes Frei's take on the early Barth, "attacking relationalism head on, [Barth] gets dangerously close to setting up a competition between God and humankind, with God's freedom only being asserted by means of denials about human faith." Higton, *Christ, Providence and History*, 46–47.

[113] Frei, "Theology of H. Richard Niebuhr," 106.

ontic fact. Moreover, the great chasm that the early Barth sees dividing this ontic fact from our normal mode of experience and the knowledge acquired therein, also means that the *faith* which responds to the unfathomable gift of God's grace in Christ is itself equally unfathomable and *entirely* independent of human agency and the historical context in which it is carried out.

Frei expressed these issues in relation to Barth's early theology, and through closer consideration of Barth's emphasis on figural interpretation in his biblical exegesis, Frei would come to a greater appreciation of the possibilities in Barth's work for a positive theological account of the particular features and events of the life of Jesus (and our own).[114] Yet the concerns Frei voiced regarding epistemological monophysitism still serve as an indication of just how important it was for him that rejecting historicism and historical criticism as gatekeepers of theologically viability not exclude the possibility of a positive engagement between history and Christian faith.

Epistemology and the Escape from History:
Different Responses, Similar Mistakes

Frei notes that, on the one hand, relationalism and epistemological monophysitism risk rather different mistakes, resulting from their diverging prioritizations of protecting human freedom or God's freedom, respectively. But they might also be viewed as making a similar mistake in their neglect of history. Both relationalists and epistemological monophysites treat history as a hurdle to be overcome, and, unsurprisingly, both fail to provide a positive account of history as theologically significant. For relationalists like Schleiermacher, upholding the diversity and individuality of each historical event and person while still situating the entirety of history within some common, transcendental scheme means history becomes a façade, behind which lies something more ultimate. Inversely, Frei sees that for theologians like Barth the overwhelming focus on affirming the ontic fact of the incarnation and of Christ as the eternal Word of God can lead to a similar obscuring of the details of the historical life of the person in whom the Father has become incarnate: Jesus of Nazareth.[115] It

---

[114]   Higton, *Christ, Providence and History*, 63, n. 64, 155–74; see Hans Frei, "Scripture as Realistic Narrative," in *Reading Faithfully*, 1:49–63.

[115]   Hans Frei, "The Doctrine of Revelation in the Thought of Karl Barth, 1909–1922: The Nature of Barth's Break with Liberalism" (Ph.D. diss., Yale University, 1956), 571; cf. Higton, *Christ, Providence and History*, 54–59.

is worth restating that Frei observes similarities between Schleiermacher and Barth which he finds praiseworthy, such as their shared Christocentrism. Yet he also finds deficits in their thought which emerge for different reasons but which point to a similar danger—the risk of undermining a positive theological perspective on history and historical contingency as part and parcel of God's providential plan for humanity.[116]

Frei finds that the risk of epistemological monophysitism in Barth's dialectical theology is ultimately mitigated by an increased emphasis on a doctrine of reconciliation, itself grounded in an Anselmian doctrine of the analogical relationship between God and creation.[117] Following Barth, especially his *Anselm: Fides Quaerens Intellectum*, Frei will affirm that it is the Chalcedonian definition, with its juxtaposition of the infinite with the finite in the person of Jesus, that grounds the affirmation of an analogical correspondence among history, humans, and God.[118] It is this correspondence that provides for the possibility of a positive, *descriptive* account of our knowledge of God and its relation to history in all its contingency. This is not a justification of the epistemic rationality of Christian faith, but a meditation on how Christian faith relates to our knowledge and experience of the world itself. This analogical correspondence between the transcendence of God's being and our history-bound descriptions and experiences of God's immanence is in one sense thoroughly epistemological in that it is not, at least primarily, an analogy of ontological correspondence, the *analogia entis*. At the same time, Frei suggests that Barth follows Anselm in affirming an *analogia relationis*, which grounds any analogy between God's existence and that of humanity as "co-existence . . . an extrinsic analogy [for humanity], an analogy to God that takes place only in relation between human being and human being . . . intrinsic only to God, not to man."[119]

On this view, the relationship between humanity and God narrated in scripture and especially the Gospels is not determined by epistemology but is that which undergirds the "epistemology" of Christian faith itself. This is an epistemology preceded by an affirmation of an analogical relationship between humanity and God, revealed and made possible in the

---

[116]   Hans Frei, "Barth and Schleiermacher: Divergence and Convergence," in *Theology and Narrative*, 183–97.

[117]   Frei, "Barth and Schleiermacher," 184.

[118]   Karl Barth, *Anselm: Fides Quaerens Intellectum* (Eugene, Ore.: Pickwick, 1960).

[119]   Hans Frei, "Analogy and the Spirit in the Theology of Karl Barth," in *Reading Faithfully*, 2:202.

life, death, and resurrection of Jesus Christ. Yet it is for this very reason that Christian faith demands an interpretation of history and its contingent occurrences in analogical relation to the witness of scripture and the life of the church. It is this analogical, historical correspondence that grounds the figural interpretation of the Bible as God's Word both past and present, narrating historical events which serve as figures through which contemporary happenings can be theologically construed. Frei's figural hermeneutic will be discussed at length in the next section. First, we will look at Frei's analogical epistemology as a descriptive account of Christian faith that proceeds from, and is implicit in, the incarnation itself.

Epistemology, the Order of Belief, the Analogy of Faith, and the Prioritization of Hermeneutics

Frei held Barth's theoretical, epistemological exposition of the analogy of faith to be insufficient without being both directly tied to the details of the life of Jesus Christ as depicted in scripture (not only the "fact" of Jesus Christ) and the events and persons comprising the contemporary historical world.[120] In other words, Frei saw any epistemological theory of Christian faith as inadequate unless it emerged in the light of, and was provided with content by, the narrated life, death, and resurrection of Jesus. Second, and contrary to accusations like N. T. Wright's that Frei reduces Christian epistemology to an unquestioning affirmation of the resurrection, Frei indicates that any Christian epistemology would be insufficient that did not also connect its exegesis of scripture to the contemporary world outside scripture and the church. This is not an extraneous step added by Frei in response to accusations of fideism. Rather, the epistemic connection between the past, as narrated in scripture, and the present, both within and without the church, is for Frei grounded in a faith in the incarnation and resurrection of Jesus Christ and the promise of history's providential culmination in the future.

For Frei, then, the epistemology of Christian faith not only addresses the question of what it means for us to know God in relation to narrated events of scripture. It also concerns the question of how, knowing God to be present in those narrated events, we come to know God's presence within the history of the world at large and the lives of those beyond the church's confines. Because the resurrection implies that Jesus is both alive and present across time and space, any Christian epistemology needs to

---

[120]   Higton, *Christ, Providence and History*, 54, 156.

take both the historical and contemporary (and to some extent, future) aspects of revelation into account.[121] Describing *how* we gain knowledge of Jesus' presence in relation to the history-like narratives of his life in the Gospels, is, for Frei, a task proper to Christian epistemology. He insists that "when the Christian theologian speaks about sacred history and its relation to secular, universal history, his or her first duty is to avoid the historicist or perspectivist reduction. Whatever his or her way of going about it, he or she is discerning a *public* pattern in which humankind is seen as united in destiny, albeit in a dialectic of sacred and profane history."[122]

This emphasis on discerning a public pattern implies that hermeneutics, for Barth and Frei, precedes epistemology but does not dismiss it. Race's prioritization of historicism leads him to the apologetic adoption of Hick's epistemology and to a hermeneutic rooted in Smith's phenomenological analysis of religious communities around the world as the only plausible justification of transcendent revelation. Barth and Frei, refusing to cede to philosophy the power to determine the limits of God's freedom, believe the Christian affirmation of the reality of divine revelation is justified simply in its being grounded in the Gospel narratives and celebrated in the life of the church. This reversal yields an epistemology and a view of history which, Frei argues, share numerous, though ad hoc, resemblances with those arrived at by philosophers unconcerned with religious apologetics.[123] So Frei came to see that for Barth and for his own theology, the epistemology appropriate to both our faith in Jesus Christ and the experiences comprising our daily lives both clarifies and is subsumed as a corollary of biblical exegesis.[124]

Faith and Philosophy

As noted above, for Frei, the basic mistake of modern theology has been its apologetic aim in response to and in reliance upon *wissenschaftlich* discourses like historicism and epistemology.[125] This is neither to say that Frei believes Christian theology can take place without philosophical input, nor is it to suggest that Frei sees apologetics as impermissible for Christian theology. Rather, for Frei, as for Barth, it is largely a question of the order of operations.

[121] Cf. Frei, *Identity of Jesus Christ*, 66.
[122] Frei, "Salvation-History," 156.
[123] Frei, "Salvation-History," 152ff.
[124] Frei, "Salvation-History," 157–58.
[125] Frei, "Remarks," 28.

As mentioned earlier, Frei works out the implications of different configurations of theology along these lines in his *Types of Christian Theology*. And although he there outlines five types, these are variations of a more fundamental divide between two basic theological approaches. On one side are those who view philosophy as a foundational discipline, providing "us with the criteria of meaning and certainty, coherence as well as truth, in any arena of human reflection" and who therefore view theology "as a prime candidate for philosophical scrutiny."[126] On the other side are those who see Christianity not as a phenomenon of some universal, organic relationship with the divine, but rather as "a specific religion among many others, a religious community called after its founder, whose name, Jesus of Nazareth, is linked to the title embodying the claim his followers made on his behalf that he was Christ."[127] Within this second approach, Frei delineates three orders of Christian theology:

> First-order theology . . . is Christian witness, including the confession of specific beliefs (for example, the creeds) that seem on the face of them to be talking about acknowledging a state of affairs that holds true whether one believes it or not . . . Second, there is what we have just called the logic, or grammar, of the faith, which may well have bearing on the first-order statements, an endeavor to bring out the rules implicit in first-order statements. And third, there is a kind of quasi-philosophical or philosophical activity involved even in this kind of theologizing, which consists of trying to tell others, perhaps outsiders, how these rules compare and contrast with their kinds of ruled discourse.[128]

This schematization helps to explain why Frei approaches epistemological questions as secondary not only to straightforward Christian confessional statements and creedal affirmations, but also even to other second-order considerations such as hermeneutics. It also shows why Frei himself should not be seen as advancing a simple fideistic epistemology, despite the assertions of those like Wright. Though Frei does affirm the priority of first-order theology such as Christian confession, he still acknowledges the inextricable connection between first- and third-order theology which consists in explication and comparison concerning the relation between Christian theology and alternative discourses. As Frei

---

[126]   Frei, *Types of Christian Theology*, 20.
[127]   Frei, *Types of Christian Theology*, 20.
[128]   Frei, *Types of Christian Theology*, 20–21.

writes in his response to Carl Henry: "I indeed can't do without some philosophical equivalent to natural theology, some philosophical equivalent to epistemology, let's say, but I have to piece it together eclectically and provisionally."[129]

It is also important to note Frei's caveat in the final sentence of the passage quoted above: "trying to tell others, *perhaps outsiders*, how these rules compare and contrast with their kinds of ruled discourse." For Frei sees the importance of third-order theology in relation to life both *within* the church and *without* it. These other discourses and their rules are not, as Frei understands them, only held by non-Christians. We too, within the church, participate in discourses that originate outside it and which follow their own rules. Frei himself affirms his inclination toward an empiricism like Popper's in "analyzing the shape of human existence" while still rejecting such empiricism in mounting arguments in favor of the plausibility of Christian truths.[130] Frei is able to hold these views which, though not necessarily in conflict, are not fully integrated into his theology because he believes that "[a]s long as two alternative descriptions do not conflict, there is really no need that one maintain a connection between them."[131] Rather, Frei believes that "for any proper theology, faith is a coherence of knowledge with acknowledgement and obedience. More than that cannot and need not be said."[132]

Frei designates this three-ordered approach to theology as "critical or normed Christian self-description."[133] For self-description as understood by Frei is not *simply* a retelling of scripture and creedal affirmations, although it does start there. Rather, self-description seeks to identify the norms of Christian scripture as interpreted in the church and, alongside its own introspective analysis, pursues a better account of how such norms relate to those of other discourses: hermeneutical, historical, epistemological, and beyond. Moreover, for Frei, Christian self-description, i.e., Christian theology, should also include the aforementioned features of Barth's theology: dialectical description and analogy.[134] In other words, Frei's approach to theology as self-description eschews the kinds of historicist and epistemological prolegomena that Hick, Race and others see as

---

129 Frei, "Response to 'Narrative Theology,'" 210.
130 Frei, "Remarks," 30; cf. idem, "Accounts of Jesus' Death," 61–62.
131 Frei, "Accounts of Jesus' Death," 62.
132 Frei, "Barth and Schleiermacher," 185.
133 Frei, *Types of Christian Theology*, 21.
134 Frei, "Accounts of Jesus' Death," 61.

necessary. Yet Frei insists that theology must remain attentive to philosophy, particularly as it helps us to uncover the differences and similarities between the comprehensive and normative vision of human life implicit in the "first-order statements" of Christian scripture and those visions put forward by others, whether that is secular philosophy or the theology of other religions.

Herein lies the answer to the question put forward by Frei at the start of *Identity*: "How shall we speak of Christ's presence?"[135] Of course, this question reflects a concern shared by Frei and Race. For as Race makes clear, even Christian pluralism's affirmation of the universal perceptibility of God depends upon a rejection of Christ's actual universal presence alongside an affirmation of other ways in which Christ might still be *conceived* as present (mythically, ethically, symbolically, etc.). Whereas Race pursues such questions of the "presence" of Christ in *opposition* to the historically particular identity of Jesus, Frei will take the reverse approach, prioritizing Jesus' identity as the grounds upon which his presence must be construed. For Frei, the matter of Christ's presence, even outside of scripture and the life of the church, is a hermeneutical one.

The Identity and Presence of Jesus Christ:
Frei on the *Sensus Literalis*, Figural Interpretation, and Providence

Frei rejects approaches to Christian theology that rely upon philosophical prolegomena. At the same time, he shares some of the concerns that motivate the mediating theologians' turning to such philosophical preludes. But Frei addresses these concerns not in his theological methodology or in an appeal to some alternative philosophical defense, but in his emphasis on theology's rootedness in the realistic sense of Christian scripture itself. For Frei, the meaningfulness of the history-like accounts of Jesus' resurrection is a function of faith, not the fruit of any metaphysical or epistemological principles. But it is also in eschewing appeals to such general theories as bases of its meaningfulness that this faith in Jesus' resurrection that underscores an emphasis on historical particularity, one that is more similar to the historicism of Strauss and Troeltsch than theologies that turn to the idealism of perspectivism.

So while he refuses to let the legitimacy and character of Christian faith be determined by historicism or the philosophical claims upon which it is based, Frei also rejects theological distortions of philosophy for apologetic

---

[135]   Frei, *Identity of Jesus Christ*, 65.

purposes. In his very insistence upon the distinctiveness of faith and philosophy, Frei provides an account of Christian theology that allows, and even hopes for, the possibility of reciprocity and overlap, even if such overlap can only ever be discerned provisionally and encountered ad hoc and figurally—a framing that honors both the vastness of the horizon of providential consummation and the irreducible particularity of history and all historical creatures. Similarly, though Frei rejects an approach to Christian faith on which its legitimacy is founded on its conformity to the dictates of a neo-Kantian epistemology, he finds in Barth's retrieval of Anselm's doctrine of analogy an account of Christian knowledge that provides the *possibility* for discerning connections between our ways of knowing God and our ways of knowing the world.

It will be argued that Frei's upholding of the possibility of identifying ad hoc reciprocity between theology and philosophy results from his scriptural hermeneutic and its prioritization of the *sensus literalis*. Convicted by Troeltsch's historicism and inspired by Hick's epistemology, Race turns to Smith's phenomenology as the hermeneutical foundation of a philosophically tenable account of faith. Inversely, Frei begins with a hermeneutical prioritization of the plain sense of scripture, only subsequently identifying particular, if provisional, points of reciprocity between Christian faith and philosophy.

More importantly, it will be shown that this reciprocity is not limited to theology and philosophy but extends into the church's reenactment and encounter of Jesus Christ's identity and presence in the world itself. Where Smith's phenomenology, and Race's typology, set in opposition a faith in Jesus' particular identity as savior of the world and a faith in the universality of his presence, thereby rendering universal salvation as a *certainty*, Frei's theology takes a very different approach. Grounded in what Erich Auerbach called *figural interpretation* and guided by faith in God's providential plan for the world, Frei suggests that the strange amalgamation of the particular identity and universal presence of Jesus Christ leads Christians into an engagement with the world in which they are both reenacting and encountering afresh the public patterns of Christ's saving presence. And in this hermeneutical possibility of discerning the presence of Jesus Christ in the lives of non-Christians—"a *public* pattern in which humankind is seen as united in destiny"—Frei finds a strongly held *hope* for the universal salvation of humankind.[136]

---

[136]   Frei, "Salvation-History," 156.

The *Sensus Literalis*

To affirm the universality of God's salvific presence in the world, Wilfred Cantwell Smith insists that faith and tradition must be differentiated. The human experience of faith takes precedence as the source of tradition and the basis for a phenomenological analysis, which can provide empirical evidence supporting the existence of, and universal access to, the transcendent. Thus, tradition or scripture must be read through this phenomenological lens, universalizing and mythologizing those aspects that run afoul of the anthropological account of faith. Smith's phenomenology, while oriented away from scripture, is inherently a biblical hermeneutic.

Frei notes that one problem with such phenomenological interpretation is that it is at odds with an interpretive consensus that has long prevailed within the Christian tradition. To start, Frei points out that, in Protestant and Catholic theology (at least), there has been agreement that "the central persuasion of Christian theology . . . is that Jesus Christ is the presence of God in the Church to the world."[137] For Smith, Jesus is best described phenomenologically, as an example of transcendent presence but not a source of God's presence: "I do not say that God was revealed in Jesus Christ, just like that, absolutely, impersonally; and I suggest that it is not a good thing to say. I do say that God has been revealed to me in Jesus Christ and has been to many millions of people throughout history . . ."[138] And again: "Christianity, I would suggest, is not true absolutely, impersonally, statically; rather, it can *become* true, if and as you or I appropriate it to ourselves and interiorize it, insofar as we live it out from day to day. It becomes true as we take it off the shelf and personalize it in actual existence."[139] On a phenomenological interpretation of scripture, Jesus' theological value is symbolic. He is a "*locus* of transcendent vision and human transformation . . . a figure of universal significance, but not unsurpassably [sic] or indispensably so."[140]

Smith's phenomenological hermeneutic implies that scripture is more about those reading it than the persons or events narrated therein.[141] The

---

[137]   Frei, *Types of Christian Theology*, 8.

[138]   W. C. Smith, *Towards a World Theology* (Basingstoke, UK: Macmillan, 1981), 174.

[139]   W. C. Smith, *Questions of Religious Truth* (New York: Charles Scribner's Sons, 1967), 67–68.

[140]   Race, *Christians and Religious Pluralism*, 136.

[141]   W. C. Smith, "Idolatry: In Comparative Perspective," in *The Myth of Christian Uniqueness*, ed. John Hick and Paul Knitter (Eugene, Ore.: Wipf & Stock, 1987), 61.

possibility of transcendent presence represented in the stories of Jesus' life is prioritized over, and often against, the actual events and actions of that life and identity. Yet, across the history of Christian theology in the West, Frei notes that, "in the interpretation of Scripture, especially the New Testament, the literal sense has priority over other legitimate readings, be they allegorical, moral, or critical," and furthermore, that this consensus extends to the acceptance of "a strong interconnection (which may even indicate derivation) between this priority of the literal sense and its application to the figure of Jesus Christ."[142] There is, Frei suggests, an interpretive consensus, traceable from the earliest days of the church and into the present day, in which Christians of all stripes have agreed "that the story of Jesus is about him, not about someone else or about nobody in particular or about all of us; that it is not two stories (most people abandoned the supernatural features of the story rather than concede two stories) or no story and so on and on." In other words, Jesus' centrality in Christian theology has been inherently tied to the interpretive prioritization of the "realistic, ascriptive sense" of the Gospels.[143]

Such a consensus *does not* equate to an assertion of a single, legitimate reading. Neither does it deny the legitimacy of the wide variety of readings to which the Gospels have been subjected, "readings in which Jesus shares the spotlight with the Kingdom of God or with universal religious experience or with some specific quality which he embodied, such as love or moral reason or faith."[144] All that the consensus suggests is the legitimacy and priority of a reading grounded in Jesus' identity and of the centrality of this identity in enduring Christian communal structures and practices.[145] It is this synthesis of the Gospels' narrative and their ecclesial celebration, or in Frei's words, the "descriptive fit between *verbum* and *res*, sense and reference, signifier and signified . . . between the narrative sequence and what it renders descriptively" and "the way the text has generally been used in the community," its "use-in-context," that Frei identifies as the *sensus literalis*.[146]

Though Frei freely admits the possible legitimacy of other hermeneutical approaches, there are some he finds broadly illegitimate, such as the

---

[142] Frei, *Types of Christian Theology*, 5.
[143] Hans Frei, "Letter to Gary Comstock," in *Reading Faithfully*, 1:39.
[144] Frei, *Types of Christian Theology*, 140.
[145] Frei, *Identity of Jesus Christ*, 21, 63.
[146] Frei, "Interpretation of Narrative," 103, 104, 110; cf. idem, *Types of Christian Theology*, 137ff.

mythological interpretation championed by Smith and Race.[147] Yet such a rejection of a mythological interpretation must not be construed as a truth claim concerning the historical reality of events narrated within the Gospels. To say the Gospel accounts of Jesus' life, death, and resurrection are misinterpreted under a mythological heading is *not* to say the accounts are historically accurate. Rather, Frei argues that, regardless of the truth or accuracy of the Gospel accounts, what they—and specifically, the passion narratives and the narrative moving from crucifixion to resurrection—are *about* is not a repeatable, idealist existential account of religious significance for humanity. Rather the "sense" of the Gospels stories concerns the description of acts and events that constitute the identity of the ascriptive subject, Jesus.[148]

Frei asserts that questions of Jesus' identity must precede questions of his presence. The question "How is Christ present?" can only be answered after the prior question, "Who is he?"[149] The readily apparent sense of this ordering is only bolstered by the fact that it is also the traditional way in which the Gospels have been used within the church. Relatedly, it appears to Frei as if this ordering is implied in the Gospel accounts themselves. So rather than beginning with a theoretical system and a set of prior commitments concerning history, epistemology, or the like, Frei begins hermeneutically, or rather, exegetically. The consensus on the *sensus literalis* leads Frei to be as suspicious of general hermeneutical systems as he is of general historical or epistemological methodologies.[150]

Yet it is also true that Frei views the literal sense's focus on Jesus' identity as inseparable from a focus on his presence. Echoing Anselm, and Barth's interpretation of his ontological argument, Frei insists that "if Jesus is really who the Bible says he is; if that is his identity; then he *cannot not be present*. If he is who the Bible says he is then, having died once, he lives; he is in some manner present, here to us—to be sure in a very unique and unrepeatable manner, and yet he is."[151] And along the same lines, "to speak of the identity of *Jesus*, in which he is affirmed by the believer to be present, is also to speak of the presence of *God*."[152] So although Frei rejects a biblical hermeneutic which relies upon philosophical prolegomena, his

---

[147]   Frei, "Accounts of Jesus' Death," 51–56; cf. idem, *Identity of Jesus Christ*, 173.
[148]   Frei, *Identity of Jesus Christ*, 61.
[149]   Frei, *Identity of Jesus Christ*, 132.
[150]   Frei, "Historical Reference," 96; cf. idem, *Identity of Jesus Christ*, 132–34.
[151]   Frei, "Interpreting the Christian Story," 83.
[152]   Frei, *Identity of Jesus Christ*, 186.

own approach ends up affirming a view of Christ's presence that in some important respects is similar to some of the philosophically driven theologies mentioned earlier. Most significantly, Frei's emphasis on prioritizing the identity of Jesus of Nazareth is the basis of a theology which, though unwavering on the centrality and unsubstitutable particularity of the life, death, and resurrection of Jesus Christ, shares a concern for the particularity and uniqueness of *all* historical events, for the communal and contextual nature of knowledge, and for the presence of God across time and space, within *and without* the church.

We will deal with these aspects of Frei's hermeneutic in turn, first considering how he conceives of the Gospels' subject matter as the description of the ascriptive subject, Jesus Christ, and second, how Jesus' unique identity implies an affirmation of his universal presence.

Subject-Alienation Identity Description

Frei's ordered prioritization of identity before presence was not his initial approach. In an early serialized piece titled "The Mystery of the Presence of Jesus Christ," Frei relied upon the notion of "presence" as "the distillate of the philosophical conceptuality under which such otherwise very different people as Hegel, Schleiermacher, Kierkegaard, and the dialectical theologians of the 1920s set forth their religious and theological proposals."[153] But he would soon change tack, becoming convinced that prioritizing the technical category of "presence" was an unnecessary philosophical imposition onto the text itself, one which inevitably skewed the results of the inquiry. For Frei came to see that countering philosophical manipulations of the Bible with alternative philosophical arguments only further obscured the real issue, which is that all "such intellectual instruments have a habit of taking charge of the materials to be described."[154] So "The Mystery of the Presence of Jesus Christ" became *The Identity of Jesus Christ*.

Of course, any inquiry concerning "identity" could easily become just as philosophically loaded as "presence," similarly risking a distortion of the Gospel stories that might closely resemble the picture painted by theologians who privilege historicism and/or perspectivism. Indeed, Frei notes the inclination of some to invoke what he calls a "subject-alienation scheme" in which the identity of a person lurks behind its public actions and engagements—what philosopher Gilbert Ryle described as a "ghost in

---

[153] Frei, *Identity of Jesus Christ*, 53.
[154] Frei, *Identity of Jesus Christ*, 101.

the machine" view of personal identity.[155] Here there is a cleavage between intention and action, such that external actions in the public world are at best separate from, and at worst distortions of, interior intentions. The significance of an individual's public and communal life in an accurate account of her identity is questionable, to say the least.[156] This view of identity is grounded in Cartesian dualism and informed by existentialist and idealist philosophy and theology.[157] For the subject-alienation account of identity posits a strong distinction between the "inner" (i.e., intention) and the "outer" (i.e., public action), such that description of a person's identity not only prioritizes the "inner-self" isolated from the outer, public self, but also sees such public acts as potentially (if not inherently) distorting.[158]

Whether or not we find this account applicable for our own identities, Frei finds a subject-alienation description of Jesus' identity deeply problematic. For in the Gospels' presentation of Jesus, and most especially in the passion narratives, he is described through "his unsubstitutable deeds, words, and sufferings."[159] Not only does such emphasis on Jesus' public and communal life appear to be constitutive of the Gospels' ascriptive identification of Jesus, but such emphases have also been constitutive of the plain sense of the Gospels as used within the church.

Intention-Action and Self-Manifestation Identity Description

Indeed, Frei observes that in the Gospel narratives, first, identity descriptions of Jesus are rooted in what he does and what is done to him, and second, that his "ongoing [sic] self-continuity" is discernible "as he acts and is acted upon in the sequence of the story's events."[160] As such, Frei turns to two symbiotic accounts of identity he borrows from Ryle, which Frei calls "intention-action" and "self-manifestation" description, respectively.[161] Here we find another helpful indication of the kind of provisional relationship between philosophy and theology Frei continuously affirmed.

---

[155]   Gilbert Ryle, *The Concept of Mind* (Whitefish, Mont.: Kessinger Legacy Reprints, 2010), 15–61.
[156]   Frei, "Accounts of Jesus' Death," 68–70.
[157]   Cf. Frei, *Identity of Jesus Christ*, 98–100; Race, *Christians and Religious Pluralism*, 117–37; Smith, "Idolatry," 66.
[158]   Frei, "Remarks," 35; Frei, "Accounts of Jesus' Death," 68; cf. Higton, *Christ, Providence and History*, 104.
[159]   Frei, *Identity of Jesus Christ*, 111; cf. Higton, *Christ, Providence and History*, 70ff.
[160]   Frei, *Identity of Jesus Christ*, 136ff.
[161]   Frei, *Identity of Jesus Christ*, 16, 17, 20, 21, 23, 137.

On the one hand, Frei makes it clear that "the identity of the Christian savior is revealed completely by the story of Jesus in the Gospels and by none other."[162] On the other hand, Frei declares that any second-order *description* of a person's identity, including Jesus', demands attention is paid to "the appropriate technical and formal categories with which to describe identity."[163] Such categories must be formal so as "to keep them from taking over the show."[164] But provided they are pursued formally, Frei insists that such philosophical categories are both helpful and unavoidable.

Unlike subject-alienation identity description, the intention-action scheme posits a nearly unified account of the relationship between intention and action.[165] Action is explicit intention and intention is implicit action.[166] As such, intention-action identity description takes public actions not as "representative" of an individual identity but as *embodying* that identity.[167]

If intention-action is the means we employ to describe an individual's identity time and again over the course of their life, self-manifestation description builds on this vision to answer the summary question, "Who is she?" Here, Frei notes that the tension between inner and outer upon which the subject-alienation scheme is fixated is to some degree real: "Because the subject-self is elusive and cannot be a direct commentary on that performance which is itself, the unity between the self's identity and the *manifestation* of that identity in the person's use of his name or of other words is bound to remain mysterious and indirect for any description."[168] But that this mystery has neither rendered us paralyzed in the face of the question "Who am I?" or "Who is she?" nor has it paralyzed the church in its account of Jesus in response to the question "Who is He?" indicates that self-alienation has over-extended the gap and overemphasized the tension.

Instead, Frei recommends a self-manifestation scheme, through which a person's identity is described as a cumulative function of verbal and embodied acts. Whereas intention-action is focused on a particular event or set of events, self-manifestation "tries to point to the continuity of a person's identity throughout the transitions brought about by his acts and

---

162 Frei, *Identity of Jesus Christ*, 133.
163 Frei, *Identity of Jesus Christ*, 134.
164 Frei, *Identity of Jesus Christ*, 134; cf. Higton, *Christ, Providence and History*, 94ff.
165 Frei, *Eclipse of Biblical Narrative*, 281, quoting Ryle, *Concept of Mind*, 40.
166 Cf. Higton, *Christ, Providence and History*, 102; Frei, "Accounts of Jesus' Death," 62–64.
167 Frei, *Identity of Jesus Christ*, 140; cf. Springs, *Generous Orthodoxy*, 34.
168 Frei, *Identity of Jesus Christ*, 140.

life's events."[169] On the one hand, this affirms that our identities are not based simply on what we say and what we do at any single point in time. Rather, such particular intentions and actions speak to "a certain elusive and unfinished, but also persistent, quality"—a quality that is evinced over "the whole scope or stretch of a person's life."[170] On the other hand, then, such a lifelong scope allows for the possibility not only that some of those things we say and do will be "out of character," but also that some things might be utterly in character, clearly manifesting our identity.

Frei argues both that Jesus' identity has generally been acknowledged to be the subject of the Gospels and the focus of the church's use of them, and that it is in his portrayal in the crucifixion-resurrection passages that this identity is most fully manifested.[171] While Smith's phenomenology purports to be a response to historicist concerns with Chalcedonian Christology, its implicit reliance upon a self-alienation identity scheme ends up devaluing the significance of historical events and public actions. Frei argues that intention-action and self-manifestation schemes are the most appropriate for those of us who take public engagement, verbal and embodied, to be of primary significance in identity description. But more importantly, Frei argues that such public engagement is the focus of the Gospels, particularly in the passion accounts and in their use within the church in answering the question "Who is Jesus?"

Jesus' Non-mythological, "Chalcedonian" Identity and the Limits of Dogma

With the above exegetically grounded, philosophically formal identity description of Jesus in hand, Frei forcefully rejects a mythical interpretation of the Gospels and, particularly, the resurrection of Jesus. Whether the events of Jesus' life occurred in history as they are depicted in the Gospels, Frei's argument indicates that his life is not presented in ways amenable to the idealism of mythological interpretation:

> It is evident that in the story Jesus' true being is not mysteriously hidden behind the action or within a supposedly distorted, "objectified," or "mythological" self-manifestation. No. He is what he appeared to be—the Savior Jesus from Nazareth, who underwent "all these

---

[169]   Frei, *Identity of Jesus Christ*, 165.
[170]   Frei, *Identity of Jesus Christ*, 165.
[171]   Frei, "Remarks," 37. For similar remarks but made in reference to the church's use and interpretation of the Gospels, see idem, "'Literal Reading,'" 120ff.

things" and who is truly manifest as Jesus, the risen Christ. Such, it appears, is the story of Jesus in the Gospels.[172]

Again, this is not to say that a prioritization of the *sensus literalis* precludes all other interpretations of scripture in general or of Jesus. It is simply to say that it does preclude some, and the mythological interpretation of phenomenologists like Smith is one of them.

Frei notes that "the simple fruit of identity analysis of the New Testament narrative" is a "high Christology," where Jesus "is who he is by what he does and undergoes, and chiefly we must say that he is Jesus crucified and raised"—a historical and individual human who is, mysteriously, the presence of God.[173] But even as it echoes the dogmatic language of Chalcedon, Frei's emphasis on the priority of Jesus' identity retains the power to reshape the categories at work within such dogmatic formulations, thereby rendering it secondary in importance to the *sensus literalis*. For Frei believes that our "understanding of a text is often far greater than our understanding of how we can understand it."[174] As such, the uniqueness of Jesus' identity and the suitability of the descriptive schemes of intention-action and self-manifestation become clear only in exegetical engagement with the Gospel narrative.

Frei's point is that although our interpretation of the Gospels should not allow philosophy *or* dogma to lead it by the nose, an interpretation that prioritizes the *sensus literalis* provides room for the influence and criticism of both. Smith and Race insist that anything short of a phenomenological and mythical reading of scripture perpetuates an interpretive feedback loop, relying upon (and inevitably reaffirming) the a priori beliefs upon which the interpretation was initially based. Yet Frei's prioritization of the literal sense is what leads to his affirmation of the multiplicity of interpretive options for scripture. He writes:

> The proof of the pudding is in the eating, not in any printed recipe. The task of the redescription [sic] of Jesus will remain unfinished as long as history lasts, but that is *not at all* to claim that the conceptual bond of re-description woven by the very linguistic continuity of the community pledged to him cannot adopt for itself the culturally relative forms of that history. There is no contradiction in principle between the hermeneutical procedures of ascriptive literalism in

---

172   Frei, *Identity of Jesus Christ*, 173.
173   Frei, "Remarks," 32; cf. idem, *Identity of Jesus Christ*, 164.
174   Frei, "Remarks," 41.

Christology and the methods of other subdisciplines [sic] that produce specific cultural articulations that enter into the statement and restatement of Christology.[175]

The particular ecclesial tradition of putting the Gospels' narration of Jesus' life first, though it has been shunned by some modern theology, is what opens the Bible up to a myriad of hermeneutical options. The particular narrative of Jesus' life, death, and resurrection can thus be seen as meaningful for everyone, everywhere, while *also* an *incomplete* and even *ambiguous* clue for the search for meaning in the rest of scripture and the experience of history.[176]

Similarly, the interrelation between Jesus and God, including but not limited to the resurrection as the central event in Jesus' self-manifested identity, cannot be abstractly addressed, at least exclusively or primarily, but rather must be narrated. By virtue of the "irreducibly complex pattern of interrelation between God's action and that of Jesus," Frei suggests that such interrelation cannot be explained but only *described*.[177] So while the intention-action and subject-manifestation schemes appear to be the best formal, philosophical tools to that end, they must be readily abandoned when either their justification becomes prioritized over their application to the story or when a more apt account is elsewhere discerned. Yet, again, Frei suggests that these limits on philosophical identity schemes also apply to dogmas like the Chalcedonian definition, for the "nature of the narrative . . . imposes a limit on theological comment."[178] Though Frei insists this should not discourage us from seeking philosophical and dogmatic clarity—for the quest for a more full and clear account of Jesus' identity is forever unfinished—he argues that it should force us to acknowledge this kind of thought as speculative and revisable. Like certain philosophical schemes, dogmas like the Chalcedonian definition might be helpful and even necessary as *description*, but "they cannot provide *explanatory* theories for the narrative's claims and for the various patterns of meaning inherent in it."[179]

The long-standing ecclesial prioritization of the *sensus literalis* leads Frei to conclude that both intention-action and self-manifestation identity descriptions are the best *formal* means of describing the identity of

[175]   Frei, *Types of Christian Theology*, 146.
[176]   Cf. Frei, "Remarks," 41.
[177]   Frei, *Identity of Jesus Christ*, 161f.
[178]   Frei, *Identity of Jesus Christ*, 163.
[179]   Frei, *Identity of Jesus Christ*, 163.

Jesus of Nazareth. In the Gospel narratives, Jesus is the one who is perfectly obedient to God, the Son of God who lives, is crucified, dies, and is resurrected. This identity, although it evokes a Chalcedonian Christology and appears to be well *described* by this dogmatic formulation, is not governed by it or any other dogma. Indeed, Frei argues that the *sensus literalis* allows for and encourages ceaseless attempts to redescribe Jesus' identity, both philosophically and dogmatically. As such, Frei's account of the *sensus literalis* and its portrayal of Jesus' identity is opposite to that provided by the mythological bend of pluralism's phenomenological hermeneutic. With its phenomenological interpretation of the resurrection as an existential paradigm, pluralism eschews dogma altogether and engages with philosophy only insofar as it critically determines and apologetically overcomes the intellectual hurdles of faith's contemporary viability.[180] Similarly, it is also contrary to exclusivism as Race depicts it, with its dogmatic ring-fencing and (supposed) exclusion of philosophical concerns.

In this way, we can see the extent of the descriptive deficiencies inherent in Race's typology and its reliance upon Smith's phenomenology. Frei's theology has no home in Race's typology. But we can also see the limitations of Race's insistence upon the oppositional relationship between Jesus' particular identity and God's universal presence. Race insists upholding one comes at the expense of the other. But for Frei, the very possibility of the universal existential import of Jesus' identity, i.e., his presence, is itself determined by its very particularity. Frei writes:

> If, the writers seem to tell us, this one has a genuine identity so that we know who he is, how can we possibly say that human destiny is loss of identity or alienation, or even that alienation and identity are mysteriously and finally identical in the mythical savior-man figure? For it is he and none other, Jesus the Son of God, who is the representative man, the second Adam, representative of human identity and not alienated in his very singularity. Because he has an identity, mankind has identity, each man in his particularity as the adopted brother of Jesus.[181]

---

[180]   Frei, *Identity of Jesus Christ,* 173.

[181]   Frei, "Accounts of Jesus' Death," 81. Mike Higton has suggested that Frei's identification of Jesus with all of humanity is a later development in his career, citing his 1987 "Humanities Council Lectures" printed in Frei, *Types of Christian Theology,* 137. But the above passage, coming from an article he wrote in 1966, perhaps suggests this was a long-standing feature of Frei's Christology. Cf. Higton, *Christ, Providence and History,* 234.

In other words, by focusing first on Jesus' particular identity, Frei concludes that we are led to affirm the possibility of his universal presence, not *in spite* of the historical particularity that shapes all human experience and identity, but *through* it. This brings us to Frei's "figural" account of Jesus' presence.

From Identity to Presence (and Back Again): Frei's Figural Interpretation

Frei's hermeneutical prioritization of the *sensus literalis* and its emphasis on Jesus' identity does not exclude the possibility of external influences or considerations in biblical interpretation and Christian theology. Frei believes that our descriptions of Jesus' identity can be enriched and even reshaped by external sources, provided they are approached unsystematically and applied provisionally. He does not just think that the world outside the church *might* serve as a site of theological development for Christians in their pursuit of a fuller account of Jesus' identity and an experience of his presence. Indeed, for all the emphasis Frei places on the adequacy of scripture and the church's use of it, his qualification of it as only "adequate" is significant. As with any identity, but *especially* the identity of Jesus Christ, bound up as it is with unique and incomparable events like the resurrection and the irreducibly complex relationship between God and Jesus displayed in it, any textual or verbal account of it will be limited. Frei concludes that "a Christian case can be made that we have not met the textual Jesus until we have also met him, as Søren Kierkegaard said, in forgetfulness of himself or incognito in a crowd."[182] The cognitive link between our encounters with Jesus' textual identity and his public presence is, for Frei, rooted in figural interpretation.

Christian figural interpretation involves discerning a connection between two historically real and causally independent events or individuals, such that the connection is construed in the context of God's providence and centered on God's act in Jesus Christ. It is an attempt to identify the patterns of Jesus' presence both in the Hebrew Bible and in human history. Again, Frei sees the possibility of discerning the patterns of Jesus' identity in the world not in spite of the unsubstitutability of his identity but because of it. Not only does Jesus' identity demand affirmation of his presence, but the inexhaustibleness of this identity also leaves open the possibility that subsequent accounts of Jesus' presence might alter our descriptions of his identity. Just as figural interpretation

---

182   Frei, *Types of Christian Theology*, 136.

provides a way of discerning the presence of the person with that particular identity, Jesus of Nazareth, beyond the confines of his earthly, historical life, so too does it provide a way of describing that identity *afresh* in light of the particular historical encounters with Jesus' presence and the patterns discernible across them.

In other words, Frei sees that figural interpretation not only allows for a description of Jesus' contemporary and historical presence that is inextricably tied to his particular identity, but also points toward external discourses and events outside the Bible and church as *essential* sources for furthering the task of describing Jesus' identity and his presence. In this sense, then, while rejecting an approach to Christian theology that considered Jesus primarily in terms of presence, in his endorsement of figural interpretation Frei acknowledges that "presence," if initially grounded in Jesus' identity, can end up providing the grounds for new perspectives on that identity.

Frei's account of figural interpretation was greatly influenced by the work of Auerbach and Barth. Both Barth and Auerbach, in their respective ways, emphasized the centrality of figural reading within Christianity. Auerbach portrayed figural interpretation as a natural extension of the realism of Judeo-Christian scripture itself and as a basic ingredient in Hebrew and Christian scripture and its interpretation.[183] He highlighted figural interpretation as a feature of the realism of much of the Old and New Testament narrative, used within the early church and applied in relation to both the Old Testament and the New, as well as between the New Testament, the present and the future Kingdom of God. In both cases, the same dynamic applies:

> Figural interpretation establishes a connection between two events or persons, the first of which signifies not only itself but also the second, while the second encompasses or fulfils the first. The two poles of the figure are separate in time, but both, being real events or figures, are within time, within the stream of historical life. Only the understanding of the two persons or events is a spiritual act, but this spiritual act deals with concrete events whether past, present,

---

[183]   Cf. Karl Barth, *Church Dogmatics*, II.2, trans. G. W. Bromiley et al. (Edinburgh: T&T Clark, 1957), 340–409; Erich Auerbach, "Figura," in *Scenes from the Drama of European Literature*, ed. Wlad Godzich and Jochen Schulte-Sasse, trans. Ralph Manheim, Theory and History of Literature 9 (Manchester: Manchester University Press, 1984), 28–60; idem, *Mimesis: The Representation of Reality in Western Literature*, trans. Willard R. Trask (Princeton, N.J.: Princeton University Press, 2013), 7–23.

or future, and not with concepts or abstractions; these are quite secondary, since promise and fulfilment are real historical events, which have either happened in the incarnation of the Word, or will happen in the second coming.[184]

The figural connection is neither primarily historical, linking the events in terms of causation, nor ideological, connecting the events only in relation to what they represent ideally. Rather, "*figura* is something real and historical which announces something else that is also real and historical. The relation between the two events is revealed by an accord or similarity."[185] And although Auerbach describes the second event as a fulfillment, it is also incomplete, in the sense described earlier in regard to Frei's account of the adequacy of the Gospels' narrative accounts of Jesus' identity, in light of its providential hope in the second coming and the eschatological consummation of creation, where the spiritual relations between independent historical events will be realized.[186]

While such an interpretation does not abandon the possibility of allegorical meaning, it does limit its scope and prevent it from taking precedence.[187] Freed of the burden of heeding historical intricacies, allegorical interpretation supports a tidy interpretation both of scripture and of the historical world. But the figural view, for all the weight placed on Jesus Christ as the interpretive clue of God's providential plan, insists upon a historical world that defies complete explanation and, therefore, on an interpretation of this world which remains partial and subject to future amendment.

Figural Interpretation: Analogy and Providence

The search for Jesus' presence in the world as Frei describes it has a pronounced moral aspect, in keeping with the vision of figural interpretation and the *sensus literalis*. Figural interpretation's realism forsakes an abstract or propositional account of Jesus' presence. The presence of Jesus of Nazareth must be approached and described in ways that privilege the real world as the site of such an encounter. In other words, Jesus' presence figurally understood is discernible within embodied enactments—those of others and our own—that are real and historical apart from the discern-

---

[184]   Auerbach, "Figura," 53; cf. idem, *Mimesis*, 73; Frei, *Eclipse of Biblical Narrative*, 28f.; idem, "Karl Barth: Theologian," in *Theology and Narrative*, 168–69; idem, "Accounts of Jesus' Death," 51, 91, n. 1; idem, "Interpretation of Narrative," 111.
[185]   Auerbach, "Figura," 29.
[186]   Frei, *Identity of Jesus Christ*, 194.
[187]   Auerbach, "Figura," 41–43.

ment of his presence. The strange amalgamation of the particular identity and universal presence of Jesus Christ leads Christians into an engagement with the world in which they are both reenacting and encountering afresh the public patterns of Christ's saving presence.

Of course, this account of Jesus' figural presence also echoes the Anselmian epistemology and the *analogia relationis* Frei found championed in Barth. In keeping with Barth's rejection of an *analogia entis*, Frei maintains that we should only posit any such analogy hermeneutically and not ontologically. So, Frei approvingly notes of Barth's theology, "all Christian language is self-involving, existential; that whether it is directed toward God or the neighbor, it is the learning and exercising of concepts in a performative manner."[188] While Christians themselves live their lives in pursuit of a kind of Christological mimesis, there is nothing intrinsic in their words or actions that connects to Jesus. Similarly, Christians can neither systematically deny nor assert that non-Christians are so connected, as in Race's inclusivism.[189] And again, following Auerbach, Frei stresses that in light of the realism underlying figural interpretation, *"only the understanding of the two persons or events is a spiritual act."*[190] The figural hermeneutics of Christ's presence, then, has a moral, existential, but not ontological, thrust. Frei describes it as aesthetic, echoing an aspect of Troeltsch's interpretation of religion that Frei commended. As Frei reads him, even Troeltsch rejected an organic and explanatory account of God's presence across history, preferring a more descriptive, less metaphysically burdened approach.[191]

While Troeltsch's aestheticism is a function of his historicism, for Frei it is more closely tied to the notion of the *analogia relationis* and the doctrine of providence. Frei describes providence as the belief that "God sustains his creatures, non-human as well as human, whom he has called into being, one creation in two realms, cosmos and history, the revealed unity of their administration being not the collapse of either into the other but Jesus Christ as the all-governing providence of God."[192] A faith in God's providence both *calls for* and *constrains* figural interpretation in the quest for Christ's presence, insisting that all things are ordered in Jesus Christ while

---

[188]   Frei, *Types of Christian Theology*, 42.
[189]   Cf. Frei, "Remarks," 30.
[190]   Frei, "Salvation-History," 159, quoting Auerbach, "Figura," 43; cf. Frei, *Eclipse of Biblical Narrative*, 28; idem, "Karl Barth," 168–69; idem, "Religious Sensibility," 147.
[191]   Frei, "Remarks," 43.
[192]   Frei, "Salvation-History," 153.

cautioning against any cumulative or definitive assessments of the relationship between Christ and particular historical events or individuals.[193]
Viewed in this way, figural interpretation is an appropriate, even inevitable,
mode of interpreting the world in the light of Christian faith, and for this
reason, a practice that must also be carried out with the utmost caution.[194]
The peculiarity of this juxtaposition is "precisely because understanding the
teleological connection between the events is a judgment that is at once historical, moral, and, yes, aesthetic," resulting in an interpretive situation in
which "one cannot escape elements that are odd."[195]

In other words, Frei argues that in light of the *sensus literalis*, the *analogia fidei*, and the doctrine of providence, our figural interpretation of
the world posits connections between events in scripture and those historical events outside of scripture in which the teleological connection is
"expressed by the temporal lapse or transition, perhaps even by the risk of
being wrong in the juxtaposition."[196] So while faith in God's providence
means that we "now have to regard the whole of human history as the
enactment of a complex design . . . the *character* of the pattern is not clear
in history at large but rather in salvation history."[197] Analogy and providence, then, both fortify and temper figural interpretation, yielding an
acknowledgment that "the design is cumulative," and therefore beyond
our ken, while at the same time affirming that between gospel and world,
"at least proleptically, the unity of its pattern is also manifest."[198]

Figural Interpretation and the Theology of Religions

Frei's figural approach to discerning Christ's presence and the significance
of the doctrine of providence points to another aspect of figural interpretation that Frei inherited from Barth—the coincidence of faith and what
Frei calls skepticism. If the grace of God's election pertains first and foremost to Jesus, and is an inner work of God, the doctrine of providence
pertains to creation.[199] Barth's affirmation, echoed by Frei, that our election is not an inherent existential quality, but is given in God's act in Jesus
Christ and offered to all humanity whether they are aware of it or not,

[193] Frei, *Identity of Jesus Christ*, 193.
[194] Cf. Higton, *Christ, Providence and History*, 86.
[195] Frei, "Salvation-History," 159.
[196] Frei, "Salvation-History," 159.
[197] Frei, "Salvation-History," 156.
[198] Frei, "Salvation-History," 159.
[199] Matthias Grebe, *Election, Atonement, and the Holy Spirit* (Cambridge: James
Clarke, 2015), 15f., 103–6.

parallels Frei's account of Jesus' presence as universal and yet impossible to approach systematically. In this sense, the dynamic between election and providence—affirming a direct relationship between Christ and every human life while also curtailing and cautioning against a systematic account of how this relationship is demonstrated, discerned, or finally realized—anticipates and orients the relationship outlined between analogy and providence.

Soteriologically, this tension yields a view for non-Christians that is both hopeful and humble. It is always *possible* to discern Jesus' saving presence in the lives of those outside the church. But this very affirmation depends upon another, held with equal force, that those lives and events might *not* reflect the presence of Jesus. Neither a Calvinist doctrine of double predestination nor a doctrine of universal salvation can be put forward with any certainty. It simultaneously supports two opposite figural possibilities: one positive, the other negative. Frei summarizes it nicely:

> It is not only the case, I believe, that Barth took pleasure in the vast variety of this indefinitely expansive human experience in this vast natural context—not only that he affirmed every part of it, at once in and for itself and for its potentiality as a *figura* of God's fulfilling work. Additionally, I believe, he looked with a long, cool skepticism at that scene and every part of it because he believed that none of it shows that figural potentiality by any inherent qualities or signs of its own—either positive or negative. I believe that there was in Barth a self-conscious secularity of sensibility far, far beyond that shown by any of those modern Christian apologists who would make theological hay out of this very state of affairs.[200]

For Barth, and for Frei, the nature of God's reconciling of creation through Jesus means that to affirm it is also to grant each individual the possibility of *not* reflecting this reconciliation. This is a luxury not afforded humans in Smith's phenomenology or Race's pluralism, where the universal human capacity for transcendent encounter with the divine presence is a certainty (provided it conforms to the requisite philosophical dictates laid out in the last chapter).

This points to a possible explanation of Frei's apparent reluctance in addressing questions concerning the so-called Christian theology of religions. For if the Christian faith and its theological description revolves

[200]   Frei, "Karl Barth," 172.

around the figured presence of a particular person, Jesus Christ, it can only be pursued ad hoc and provisionally outside the Gospels. Searching for God's presence with the aid of an additional interpretive system skews the inquiry, imposing an interpretive framework that undermines the particularity of this identity, something Frei discerned of his own work "The Mystery of the Presence of Jesus Christ" and its reliance upon the category of "presence." Moreover, and equally problematic, systematically searching for God's presence, particularly in the manner advanced by Smith and Race, risks making an unnecessary imposition onto the particular, historical lives of non-Christians. "Fear not . . . you're *not* tone-deaf . . . (you couldn't be if you tried)."[201]

Frei's figural hermeneutic also implies that even a theology of religions committed to rendering different religious traditions as intrinsically morally synonymous—or as fundamentally morally incongruous—would not fit alongside the *sensus literalis*.[202] As discussed above, there is, for Frei as for Barth, a faithful prioritization of "ontic fact" which precedes ethical and metaphysical concerns in the interpretation of scripture's plain sense. Yet even while distinguishing between ontic fact and morality in his theological prioritization, Frei also suggests they are inseparable, though the connection must be attended to with care:

> When treated univocally across the board, moral virtues become distortions, instruments of paralysis or else irrelevant platitudes, which is not to say that they are any of these, only that their application demands the delicacy of imaginative moral artistry, both when we inquire about ourselves and analogously when we inquire about God. Moral and theological virtues have constantly to be plucked from the stony cracks of doctrinaire sloganeering.[203]

Nonetheless, a quest for Christ's presence that prioritizes his identity might be best described in moral terms because, in light of the inherently self-involving and existential nature of Christian language, to search for Jesus' presence, embodied and real, is not only to search for enacted analogies or patterns of his identity, but also to participate oneself in its enactment. "At its apex," Frei writes, the quest for the presence of Christ

---

[201]   Frei, "Religious Sensibility," 145.

[202]   E.g., Paul Knitter, *No Other Name? A Critical Survey of Christian Attitudes toward the World Religions* (London: SCM Press, 1977).

[203]   Hans Frei, "God's Patience and Our Work," in *Reading Faithfully*, 1:165.

"becomes mysteriously turned into an enactment of the self-sacrificial authority of that presence."[204]

In other words, as Frei describes it, *the search for Jesus' saving presence itself implies our own figural reenactment of his identity in relation to our neighbors, however inherently limited such reenactment will be.* Christian theology is for the world, which inevitably brings other religions into its sphere of concern and hope. But to isolate "religion," or any other concept, risks imposing too much upon the text, obscuring the very identity of the one whose presence we seek to embody ourselves and to encounter in others—Jesus. For Frei, to pursue Christ's presence through the theology of religions would be to take a wrong turn in the quest for Christ's presence in the world.

Hope and the Moral Pattern of Christ's Saving Presence

Although the theology of religions would likely be viewed by Frei as a blind alley for Christian theology, he shares many of the concerns of its proponents, including Smith and Race. Frei is, after all, deeply concerned with the question of God's presence. For all his emphasis on the priority of Jesus' identity, the question of presence looms almost as large in Frei's theology. So it is perhaps unsurprising that, in shunning an approach to Christian theology that is determined by concern for Jesus' presence over and against that of his identity, Frei finds that Jesus' unsubstitutable identity involves an unavoidable affirmation of his universal presence, however mysterious and indeterminate our grasp of it might be.

Like Smith and Race, Frei is also keen to emphasize the existential implications and dimensions of faith. But in rejecting the subordination of tradition and scripture to experience that Smith employs, he finds in figural interpretation an unyielding affirmation of the value of historical existence without undermining it, as in Smith's phenomenology. And like Smith and Race, Frei is concerned for the postmortem salvation of those outside of the Christian faith. But in eschewing an approach that insists soteriological universality comes at the cost of the specificity or particularity of Christian faith, Frei is also rejecting the limitation of theology's interest in discerning ad hoc correlations between Christian faith and other religions—in discerning figures of Jesus' identity in public events, in the lives of non-Christians—to a function of soteriology alone. If the life and ministry of the Savior does not start at Golgotha and end with

---

[204]   Hans Frei, "Saint, Sinner, and Pilgrim," in *Reading Faithfully*, 1:135.

the empty tomb, neither is Christian love of neighbor limited to concerns with death and the afterlife. Sharing the concerns that motivate Race's theology of religions typology and pluralism, Frei nonetheless charts a very different course.

As already outlined, Frei's alternative involves the figural reenactment of, and encounter with, Jesus in the world. The quest for the presence of Christ takes place in the light of the witness of scripture *and* its existential expression, however inherently limited such expression might be. Indeed, Frei strenuously emphasizes the miraculousness of our own acts of love somehow also becoming acts of God's infinite love:

> Perhaps nothing is more miraculous than the fact that ordinary kindness and natural gentleness can be the earthly form taken by that divine love (agape) which is so utterly disproportionate to the ordinary. The enjoyment of the neighbor in her and his peculiar character, religion, lifestyle, and work—the enjoyment of just the way she or he is—may also be part of the service of Christ: Reconciliation as a form of celebrating co-humanity—or, less ornately put, loving the neighbor as oneself—seems to be what the text recommends before we come to serve God or his Christ in the specific place set up for the purpose.[205]

Frei sees the reconciling and accepting love of neighbor as the defining characteristic of the life of Christian faith. This is not an overtly soteriological statement. Indeed, Frei's remarks on soteriology are scant and tantalizing. But Frei's emphasis on the moral shape of Jesus' presence and the miracle of its reenactment and encounter has unmistakable salvific implications. After all, Jesus' identity, and the presence of this identity, is constituted by "the unique coherence . . . of two elements: unsubstitutable individuality and universal saving scope."[206] For Frei, faith in Jesus demands a limited, mysterious but real quest, like that of a pilgrim, to reenact and encounter anew his saving presence.[207]

Frei's description of the miracle of ordinary kindness sets out his vision of what reenacting Christ's presence looks like. The church and its members, as the body of Christ, are characterized by the reenactment of the pattern of Jesus' life. Such reenactment cannot be in either "total likeness

---

[205] Frei, *Types of Christian Theology*, 136.
[206] Frei, *Identity of Jesus Christ*, 123.
[207] Frei, "Saint, Sinner, and Pilgrim," 125.

or unlikeness."[208] The church is a follower "rather than a complete reiteration of its Lord," because, "unlike that of Jesus, the church's intention-action pattern—evolved in the interaction of character and circumstance, of church with humanity at large through history—is obviously not finished."[209] So the church's figural or analogical relationship to Jesus not only means that it is to be a follower of Jesus, serving its neighbors as Jesus served his. It also means that the identity of the church is determined in part by the flux of historical circumstances in which it finds itself. The church's identity—and therefore, in some sense, Christ's identity—is determined not only by its relationship to Jesus of Nazareth but also by its neighbor, which "is the human world at large, to which the church must be open in gratitude without forsaking its own mission and testimony."[210]

On the one hand, this means that our reenactment of the presence of Jesus is not merely evangelistic:

> Because of this textual Jesus' inclusion of *all* humanity, in all its variety, in himself, we have known disciples of this kind also, who love their neighbors and take a simple pleasure in them . . . for their own sake and do so not compulsively—not, as it were, hounding them with the image of Jesus—but with simple and delighted generosity. In a religion touched by such apparently contrary marks as severity and generosity and a Savior so specific yet so universal, so particular and yet irreducibly potentially exponential for almost every kind of human quality, the line between devotion in religious service and fanatical religious imperialism can be thin, but it is real and deep, and a generous unobsessive [sic] love of the neighbor marks that line.[211]

Our reenactment of Christ's love on behalf of others is for their own sake and need not involve "hounding them with the image of Jesus." Frei's emphasis on the theological prioritization of Jesus' identity does not translate into an engagement with the world marked primarily by the compulsive recounting of Jesus' identity to others. Rather, the emphasis on Jesus' particularity grounds a corresponding emphasis on the intrinsic value of the particularity that characterizes *all* human lives and relationships. The universal importance of Jesus' particular life is the foundation for the importance of all particular lives. This is not to say that evangelism or Christian witness has no

---

208   Frei, "Saint, Sinner, and Pilgrim," 125.
209   Frei, *Identity of Jesus Christ*, 190–91.
210   Frei, *Identity of Jesus Christ*, 191; cf. idem, "Resurrection of Christ," 189.
211   Frei, *Types of Christian Theology*, 136–37.

place in Frei's theology. In fact, it would appear to hold a place of central importance given the combination of Frei's firm insistence upon the universal import of the resurrection coupled with his rejection of any ontological account of Jesus' resurrection. As Frei sees it, the resurrection of Jesus matters, somehow, for all of creation across time and space. Yet precisely because its significance is enmeshed in history, because it cannot be chalked up to ushering in an ontological change in creation or, more narrowly, Christians, the resurrection of Christ is good news that must be shared. "The resurrection happened in the first place to Jesus, not to the Christian community," writes Frei.[212] But it is to say that Frei appears to delineate a noncompetitive view of the relationship between verbal evangelism and physical act—what the ecumenical movement has come to discretely describe as evangelism and mission, respectively.[213]

On the other hand, Frei's highlighting of Jesus' universal inclusion of all humanity suggests that the Christian reenactment of Christ's identity is not the only source of Jesus' presence. We also encounter Jesus—albeit mysteriously, imperfectly, and incompletely—in the world. In following Jesus, we "with some caution may speak even . . . of certain intimations or tentative reiterations of his presence."[214] Again, as this encounter is not conceived ontologically, as it is in Smith's phenomenological characterization of human faith, how and where it will occur cannot be predetermined. Frei writes: "We are saying that this presence to history means that history is neither chaotic nor fated, but providentially ordered in the life, death, and resurrection of Jesus Christ, who is Lord of the past, the present, and the future."[215] We *hope* to encounter Jesus in the world beyond Gospels and church even if we cannot anticipate when and where such an encounter will take place.

The soteriological implications of Frei's account of Jesus' presence are as unavoidable as they are unresolved.[216] Recall Frei's statement at the end of *Identity*: "A Christian case can be made that we have not met the textual Jesus until we have also met him, as Søren Kierkegaard said,

---

[212]   Frei, "Resurrection of Christ," 189.
[213]   "Mission and Evangelism: An Ecumenical Affirmation," in *You Are the Light of the World: Statements on Mission by the World Council of Churches 1980–2005*, ed. Jacques Matthey (Geneva: WCC Publications, 2005), 11, 16.
[214]   Frei, "Saint, Sinner, and Pilgrim," 125.
[215]   Frei, *Identity of Jesus Christ*, 191.
[216]   As Hunsinger notes, the "context in which the problem of [Jesus'] presence arises" in Frei's work "is essentially soteriological." George Hunsinger, "Afterword: Hans Frei as Theologian," in Frei, *Theology and Narrative*, 252.

in forgetfulness of himself or incognito in a crowd."[217] In meeting our neighbors with love, and in being loved by our neighbors, not only do we have faith that we are reenacting *and* encountering afresh the patterns of Christ's presence, but we also must consider that such encounters with Christ's presence can affect our reading and enactment of the literal sense of the Gospels. "Humanity at large is the neighbor given to the church, through whom Christ is present to the church," Frei writes. "It follows that, even though events in history, such as the imperative move toward church reunion, are important, there are other events in the history of mankind at large that may parabolically bespeak the presence of Christ in a far more significant and evident way."[218]

Frei does not touch on the salvific consequences of Christ's parabolic presence possibly being greater in world events outside of those involving Christians and the church. Given the prominence of soteriology in motivating and orienting Race's typology and his advocacy for pluralism, not to mention the many defenses of exclusivism and inclusivism that have arisen partly in response, this might strike those familiar with the theology of religions as odd, if not neglectful. To some extent, this is because Frei acutely feels the weight of the church's past dealings with the issue:

> Christians who have reflected about human historical destiny are not exactly famous for their genteel treatment of the nations when they imagine the last day . . . Pagans and the worldly within the church have had good reason to think that the rope of Christian mercy looked more like the hangman's noose than a strand to aid the drowning.[219]

Although he notes that this situation has changed in the twentieth century, with "openness" serving as something of a theological buzzword, he laments that "the openness all too often resembles that of the oyster shell under the knife."[220] But, beyond the humility and reticence born out of this historical awareness, Frei's soteriological modesty is fundamentally rooted in the central importance he places on the doctrine of providence. Christian faith in God's providential government of the world necessarily limits our knowledge of the future, as Frei sees it.

[217]   Frei, *Types of Christian Theology*, 136.
[218]   Frei, *Identity of Jesus Christ*, 192.
[219]   Frei, "Salvation-History," 150.
[220]   Frei, "Salvation-History," 151.

Far from justifying the certainty that Race attributes to exclusivism's unrelenting faith in the universal significance of Jesus' particular identity, Frei argues that the centrality of Jesus' unsubstitutable identity in our understanding God's providence provides us with a "reserve of not knowing" which we must apply even to our faith in the future presence of Jesus Christ.[221] Frei writes that, while the "believer must affirm that the future summing up will be that of God with whom Jesus Christ is one, rather than simply a recapitulation in more enormous scope of the events of the story of Jesus," this is the boundary of what we can know about the fate of the world: "Beyond this confession the believer cannot go."[222]

Frei's prioritization of the *sensus literalis* and his ensuing emphasis on the identity of Jesus and of figural reading as the means of relating the Gospels to both the larger biblical canon and the historical world not only yields a vision of Christ's universal presence—it suggests that this presence outside of the Gospels and the church, in "profane" history, might be even more pronounced and suggestive than those events in "sacred" history. While this is far from a certainty—Jesus' presence is not conceived organically or as an existential given—Frei sees this as the *hope* of Christian faith. It is a hope that is borne out in cautious or "aesthetic" interpretation, a search for public, parabolic patterns that do not infringe upon the "final and ineradicable 'thereness'" either of Jesus' death and resurrection or of all other historical events.[223] It is, inevitably, a teleological and eschatological hope, that for both the church and the world, "not only the events we find significant by the use of certain parables but *all events* will find their place" in Christ.[224]

The urge felt by Christians to offer answers and explanations regarding salvation is understandably strong, especially in the globalized and interconnected context of North America and Europe, where an increase in the experience and awareness of religious pluralism has coincided with a decrease in the numbers of self-identifying Christians.[225] Yet Frei cautions that such an urge should not succumb to the alluring temptations of idealism, making people "and cultural groups become sheer consciousnesses [sic] or minds to whom all activities, all institutions, linguistic and social structures, and the like adhere as though in secondary reflection

---

221   Frei, *Identity of Jesus Christ*, 193.
222   Frei, *Identity of Jesus Christ*, 194.
223   Frei, *Identity of Jesus Christ*, 192; cf. idem, "Salvation-History," 159.
224   Frei, *Identity of Jesus Christ*, 193.
225   David Masci, "Christianity Poised to Continue Its Shift from Europe to Africa," Pew Research Center, April 7, 2015, http://www.pewresearch.org/fact-tank/2015/04/07/christianity-is-poised-to-continue-its-southward-march/.

only."[226] Salvation is not ours to give but God's. And though we can discern the presence of Jesus—who lived, died, and rose again for the whole world—outside of the Bible and the church, our hope for the universal salvation of creation can only be that—hope.

But it is equally imperative that we acknowledge not only our *hope* for universal salvation but that this hope is possible not *despite* but *because of* the unsubstitutability of Jesus' life, death, and resurrection. Frei wrote that a "commitment to universalism concerning human destiny and a commitment to the specificity of sacred or salvation history within it are not in ultimate conflict, even if the manner of their cohesion is hidden."[227]

> We can only tell the story of our communities as part of a fragmentary yet not wholly unknown, a hidden but genuinely universal narrative, a narrative the account of which is not only sequentially but synchronically unfinished.
>
> Our story, our inquiry as observers into patterns which we as agents may act out, goes on, here in time, on the plane where God and humans meet. It is an inquiry into not only the church's but also our country's future, and an inquiry into the polarity between the two, but always under the limited contingent conditions of response for our time to the creating, judging and redeeming work of God.[228]

Conclusion

Race's typology and his support for pluralism rest upon a constellation of historical, epistemological, and hermeneutical commitments that are advanced for their supposed apologetic import—which is to say that the commitments themselves are not held for their own sake but only insofar as they provide responses to certain *concerns* that Race holds in these areas. Frei, independent of any explicit engagement with Race or with the theology of religions discourse, considers the force of each of these concerns but concludes that, while none should be construed as offering a decisive challenge to Christian faith, neither can they be shrugged off, whether by simply ignoring their force or by amending the Christian faith accordingly. The former position—that such criticisms do not necessitate the radical revision of Christian faith—is the one often associated with

---

[226]   Frei, "Religious Sensibility," 148.
[227]   Frei, "Salvation-History," 151f.
[228]   Hans Frei, "H. Richard Niebuhr on History, Church, and Nation," in *Theology and Narrative*, 219.

the so-called Yale School and postliberalism. But the latter position—that rejecting the force of such criticisms ab initio or amending Christian faith to accommodate them post hoc would be to fail to appreciate the significance of such criticisms—is just as pronounced in Frei's writing.

Frei argues that whether eschewing the potency of historical, metaphysical, or epistemological criticisms or apologetically adapting Christian faith to fit around them, both responses obscure the force of these criticisms and, in so doing, misconstrue the challenges inherent in Christian faith and the task of Christian theology. In all three areas of history, epistemology, and hermeneutics, Frei rejects responses that shield "faith" from the force of these concerns, whether this is done by those Race terms "exclusivists" in defense of the uniqueness of Christian belief, or by those Race terms "pluralists" in defense of faith as a universal feature of human life. In this sense, Frei's work can, perhaps surprisingly, be seen as echoing that of David Friedrich Strauss.[229] Strauss' rejection of those attempts at accommodating Christian faith to contemporary criticism included the realization that such accommodation made both Christianity and its criticisms weaker, yielding "the worst of both worlds—the conjunction of reduced Christology with hobbled scientific exegesis."[230] Indeed, this is the diagnosis of Race's pluralism latent in Frei's work.

Frei's refusal to accept historicism as delineating the limits of God's acting in history is in deference to the freedom of God and the particular claims of the Christian faith, but also in deference to the freedom and particularity of the historical world itself. Frei suggests that the question of historical reference and the resurrection is an unavoidable aspect of interpreting text while also secondary in some sense to the Bible's syntactical sense. This is not to say that the historical reference of the Gospels is irrelevant for Christians. But it is for Frei neither the primary question in determining the meaning of the text nor the basic condition upon which the text can retain its claim of being the Word of God.

Frei's rejection of relationalism and epistemology as the gate through which any valid faith must pass is indeed determined by his reading of scripture and its historical use and interpretation in the church. It is also a rejection of the subjugation of the order of belief, with its descriptive and existential concern, under the order of coming to believe, with its explanatory objective, an approach that renders religious faith not simply as viable

---

[229]   Strauss, *Christ of Faith*, 4f.; cf. Frei, "Strauss," 254.
[230]   Frei, "Strauss," 251.

but inescapable: "Fear not . . . you're *not* tone-deaf . . . (you couldn't be if you tried.)"[231] Frei neither believes faith in Jesus Christ requires an epistemic justification nor thinks that those experience-focused, relational, or perspectival formulations offered by the likes of Hick leave room for history *not* to be sacred.[232] Hick's attempt at outflanking those who charge transcendent faith with a lack of epistemic warrant ends up outflanking itself, requiring a defense for those who *do not* experience transcendence in the physical world.

Instead, following his interpretation of Barth's affirmation of an Anselmian doctrine of analogy as a means of describing the relationship between Christian faith and the diverse particularities of the historical world, Frei argues for an analogical epistemology. Prioritizing the "ontic fact" of the incarnation and of biblical exegesis over an apologetic epistemology that attempts to explain the plausibility of faith, Frei nonetheless emphasizes that in this analogical epistemology is found the preservation of a sense of history's contingency and distinctness alongside faith in God's freedom to act in history.

Finally, Frei eschews those hermeneutical schemes—whether in the opposing guises of historical biblical literalism or the idealistic reductionism of Smith's phenomenological approach—that arose in light of the concerns above. Instead, Frei appeals to the adequacy of the *sensus literalis*, understood as both the plain sense of the Gospels and the use-in-context within the church. Yet in upholding the literal sense of the Gospels, Frei identifies figural interpretation as the natural and traditional means of relating the Gospels to both the wider biblical canon and the historical world. Along these lines, Frei sees that prioritizing the literal sense of the Gospels, their identity description of Jesus, and figural interpretation pointed not only toward Christ's presence as constituting the ecclesial community in which the Gospels are celebrated, but also toward the presence of Christ outside the Gospels and the church as *essential* to the discernment of Jesus' identity and presence therein.

With these elements laid out, it is clear that Race's typology takes for granted a very particular relationship between philosophy and theology, one that Frei interrogates and finds problematic. Frei's own theological vision scrambles Race's types themselves, rendering suspect the descriptive breadth of exclusivism, inclusivism, pluralism—and even the

---

[231] Frei, "Religious Sensibility," 145.
[232] Frei, "Religious Sensibility," 145.

subsequently added type of particularism that was specifically intended to deal with so-called postliberals like Frei.[233]

But if Race's typology will not do, what should replace it? One way of looking at the argument presented up to this point is that it simply amounts to a call to consider what we mean by Christian theology itself before we consider the theological significance of other faiths. This would probably not lead to any more likelihood of consensus, but it would certainly help clarify and contextualize the differences between opposing positions. Only by taking into account what kind of a discourse Christian theology is, what it identifies as authoritative, and to whom or what it is responsible, can we expect to gain any clarity on how it relates to other discourses—whether those are particular philosophical traditions, academic disciplines, or religious traditions and practices. So a replacement for Race's typology should provide clarity as to the variety of construals of Christian theology and its sources of authority, which facilitate our understanding of what concerns are held in common and what gives rise to the assortment of distinct answers.

At the same time, throughout the history of Christianity, and particularly in the West throughout the twentieth century, the Christian theology of religions has been a prominent area of concern and discussion. Indeed, the ecumenical movement that coalesced around the International Missionary Council and, later, the World Council of Church's Commission on World Mission and Evangelism, made it one of their central concerns, continuously addressing the questions and exploring different theological responses throughout that century (and into the present). Yet Race's typology neither provides types that map on to the positions advocated in the assemblies' summary statements, nor does it help clarify what generated the diversity of positions advocated in successive assemblies of the same organization. Neither exclusivism, inclusivism, nor pluralism seem very apt descriptions of the theological perspectives these assemblies endorsed—an observation that calls into question the value of that typology as much if not more than the argument advanced in the first chapter. Whatever conceptual clarity a typology provides should not come at the expense of its attending to actual concepts advanced by historical persons and groups, particularly if that typology claims to be defined by its historical concern. In the case of Race's typology, the gulf between conceptual and historical possibilities proves to be wide.

[233]   Knitter, *Theologies of Religions*, 178–83; Alan Race, *Making Sense of Religious Pluralism: Shaping Theology of Religions for Our Times* (London: SPCK, 2013), 44–54.

A suitable replacement, it will be argued, is found in Frei's own typology of Christian theology, which not only better accounts for the theological differences between the ecumenical gatherings but also allows us to see important continuities between gatherings previously viewed in largely antithetical terms—in this case, Jerusalem 1928 and Tambaram 1938. Just as Frei's typology was born out of his realization of a theological proximity between Schleiermacher and Barth by virtue of their hospitality to the *sensus literalis*, so too does Frei's typology allow us to see these ecumenical gatherings, and their very different assessments of Christianity's relationship to other faiths, in more constructive and generative ways.

4

Frei's Typology and the Twentieth-Century Ecumenical Movement

Introduction

Hans Frei's Christian theology, in its very refusal to grant philosophy the first or final word on the viability of Christian beliefs and biblical interpretation, both retains the critical capacity of external discourses (such as historicism and epistemology) and presents a theological argument for the necessity of attention and sensitivity to such external discourses. On the one hand, this means that Christian faith remains vulnerable and susceptible to refutation. Locate Jesus' un-resurrected corpse, for example, and Christian faith becomes implausible. On the other hand, it is in Frei's prioritization of the *sensus literalis*, the description of Jesus' identity that emerges from it, and the tradition of figural interpretation that developed in light of it that Christians discover a description of Jesus in which it is inherent to his identity to be viewed as *present*, across time and space, inside and outside the witness of the Gospels and the life of the church.

Because this seemingly unavoidable affirmation of Jesus' presence emerges not from an epistemological or phenomenological argument, its discernment demands attention to the particularities of historical events and the lives of individuals and communities not simply as screens behind which the transcendent might be glimpsed, but as things significant in their particularity and unique place in God's providential plan. Along the pilgrimage of the Christian life, seeking both to manifest and to encounter the presence of Jesus Christ, we inevitably cross paths with those of different faiths, religious or secular, persons with visions of life and truth shaped by various discourses or disciplines beyond the Christian community and tradition. Indeed, all of us are in different ways, simply by virtue of our own particular social and historical contexts, influenced by discourses and visions of life from more than one tradition, whether political, philosophical, economic, psychological, etc. But, unburdened by any conscripted service to a religious apologetic, Frei argues that such intersections and encounters are now free to reflect both conflict and congruence. Theology and philosophy, along with any other discourse or tradition, retain the power to critique and question one another precisely because they are not conflated. And though Frei had academic disciplines largely in mind when he used the term "external discourses," we can easily extend it to include other faith traditions. Other religions are of course not external descriptions of Christian faith, but their particular descriptions of God (or ultimate reality) and flourishing human life are rightly considered as external descriptions of the central focus of Christian self-description and can be treated in like fashion.

So, where pluralists turn to philosophy to support their claim for the universal presence of *the transcendent*, it is Frei's very emphasis on the unsubstitutability of Jesus' identity that leads him to affirm that Jesus is present everywhere—including in the lives and experiences of those shaped by the traditions and theologies of other faiths. But as this presence is a function of God's grace and not of some inherent metaphysical or anthropological quality, we are called on a pilgrim's quest in search of God, following at a distance, patterning our lives in emulation of Jesus' obedience and sacrificial love of neighbor, and being prepared to discern this pattern in the lives of others and in ways that might reshape our own understanding of it.[1]

Not only is this view of Christian faith and theology precluded from Race's three main types, but it also does not fit in the subsequently added type of "particularism" alluded to above. Frei's figural view of Jesus' presence implies that Christian faith *cannot* be hermetically sealed from external discourses, which here can be understood as including the traditions and theologies of other faiths.[2] Moreover, where some have described

---

[1]   Hans Frei, "Saint, Sinner, and Pilgrim," in *Reading Faithfully: Writings from the Archives*, ed. Mike Higton and Mark Alan Bowald, 2 vols. (Eugene, Ore.: Cascade Books, 2015), 1:125.

[2]   Cf. Paul Hedges' account of particularist theology as resting on three principles: (1) religious traditions are "mutually incompatible," (2) "each religion has its own core experience, and only superficial similarities [between religious experiences] exist," and (3) religious teachings and doctrines "are given, even fixed, as part of internally

something approximating Frei's approach as a postmodern response to philosophical criticisms, Frei argued that this view was neither radically new nor a result of philosophy's prodding.[3] It has been implicit always, and explicit to varying degrees, across the history of Christianity. The reasons for its having fallen into a kind of obscurity are directly tied to theology's hermeneutical failure to take seriously the *sensus literalis*.

Indeed, Frei argues that the rising influence of empirical philosophy, Kantian epistemology and historicism obscured the *sensus literalis* and figural interpretation in modern theology.[4] *The Eclipse of Biblical Narrative* traces the history of this development, focusing particularly on the liberal prioritization of idealist and existential reference over the plain sense, but also accounting for the obverse fundamentalist prioritization of historical reference as a response to the same external criticisms. And while *Eclipse* is primarily an account of what went *wrong* in Christian theology, framed in terms of hermeneutical missteps taken in response to philosophical criticisms and the apologetic concerns they inspired, Frei's typology of Christian theology represents a more positive approach, describing not just the extreme responses of fully embracing (type 1) or rejecting (type 5) such critiques but also the intermediary positions (types 2–4) between them—all of which have been and continue to be upheld by Christians and Christian theologians.

Simply put, Frei's typology is a better heuristic tool for grasping the theological options concerning the relationship between Christian faith in Jesus' singular revelatory and salvific significance and the presence of God to those outside the Christian church. By taking one step back from Race's typology and refocusing the question away from the philosophical legitimacy or the soteriological conclusions of different types, Frei's typology allows us to see that the disputes Race posits among his types—and the disputes that have arisen over the course of twentieth-century Christian theology—are rooted in legitimate and complex disagreements on

---

coherent systems which cannot be compared"—none of which would appear to be acceptable within Frei's account of Christian theology. Paul Hedges, "Particularities: Tradition-Specific Post-modern Perspectives," in *Christian Approaches to Other Faiths*, ed. Alan Race and Paul M. Hedges (London: SCM Press, 2008), 115.

3   Hans Frei, *The Eclipse of Biblical Narrative: A Study in Eighteenth and Nineteenth Century Hermeneutics* (New Haven, Conn.: Yale University Press, 1974), 1–15; cf. Hedges, "Particularities," 112–32; Paul Knitter, *Introducing Theologies of Religions* (Maryknoll, N.Y.: Orbis, 2002), 178–83; Alan Race, *Making Sense of Religious Pluralism: Shaping Theology of Religions for Our Times* (London: SPCK, 2013), 44–54.

4   Hans Frei, *Types of Christian Theology*, ed. George Hunsinger and William C. Placher (New Haven, Conn.: Yale University Press, 1992), 14f.

theological authority and the nature of theological discourse. What is more, Frei's typology points to the possibility of an approach to Christian theology that rejects Race's zero-sum construal of the relationship between particularity and universality, where it is instead affirmation of the very particularity of Jesus Christ that demands the hopeful and humble quest for his universal presence.

A Less Partisan Typology

Right away, it must be said that this argument is not based on a claim that Frei's typology is unbiased. Indeed, Frei clearly acknowledges its distinct inclinations toward the types that affirm theology's responsibility to both the church and the plain sense of scripture *without* appealing to a kind of Wittgensteinian fideism that renders Christian theology as a completely internal discourse, absolutely separated from all external discourses.[5] But there are good reasons to view Frei's typology as both less partisan than Race's and more transparent in its partisanship. Aside from the suggestion that Frei's typology has simply identified a more basic and significant question—that of theological authority—the notion that Frei's is also less prejudiced in comparison to Race's is based largely on two of its aspects.

First, Frei's typology emerged out of a preceding historical study he had begun "on the figure of Jesus of Nazareth in England and Germany—in high culture, ecclesiastical and otherwise, as well as popular culture—since 1700."[6] Race's typology, in contrast, is a conceptual enterprise, identifying its types in relation to his implicit methodological assumption of the authoritative priority of philosophy in Christian theology, invoking historical examples only insofar as they can be made to fit within the types Race has independently designed. Relatedly, it is also an apologetic enterprise aimed at providing philosophical justification for faith in the transcendent over and against providing historically accurate descriptions, or even a theoretical exposition, of the possibilities. Frei's typology, on the other hand, is offered *in service* of his historical research.[7] It is less an argument for the verity of one theological method than it is a tool intended

---

[5]   Frei, *Types of Christian Theology*, 19, 46–55; cf. Jason Springs, *Toward a Generous Orthodoxy: Prospects for Hans Frei's Postliberal Theology* (Oxford: Oxford University Press, 2010), 132–66; Mike Higton, "Frei's Christology and Lindbeck's Cultural-Linguistic Theory," *Scottish Journal of Theology* 50, no. 1 (1997): 93.

[6]   Frei, *Types of Christian Theology*, 1.

[7]   Cf. David F. Ford, "On Being Theologically Hospitable to Jesus Christ: Hans Frei's Achievement," *Journal of Theological Studies* 46, no. 2 (1995): 536.

"to help provide conceptual orientation" for Frei's "larger historical project."[8] It was over the course of researching for this historical project that Frei discerned "two very different, often contentious, but not necessarily mutually exclusive views of Christian theology."[9] These are:

> (1) *Christian* theology is an instance of a general class or generic type and is therefore to be subsumed under general criteria of intelligibility, coherence and truth that it must share with other academic disciplines . . . (2) *Theology* is an aspect of Christianity and is therefore partly or wholly defined by its relation to the cultural or semiotic system that constitutes that religion.[10]

Between these two poles, Frei's typology depicts "five different attitudes about these two descriptions of Christian theology, first of all in general and then in the way each type focuses on the topic of the *sensus literalis* with respect to the New Testament figure of Jesus."[11]

For type 1, theology is a philosophical discipline. For type 2, philosophy retains its guiding role for theology, wherein it affirms a direct correlation between the specifically Christian and "general cultural meaning structures such as natural science or the 'spirit' of a cultural era."[12] As will be seen, so construed, type 2 includes both liberals like Bultmann and conservative theologians like Carl Henry. Type 3 similarly pursues this kind of correlation, but, significantly, does so without a "super theory or comprehensive structure for integrating them, only ad hoc procedures." Type 4 reverses type 2's ordering, such that "the practical discipline of Christian self-description governs and limits the applicability of general criteria of meaning in theology." Finally, for type 5, "Christian theology is exclusively a matter of Christian self-descriptions . . . General theory is not pertinent to Christian self-description because there really is no such thing in any grand manner in the first place."[13] That this is itself a philosophical justification, owing not to Kant as does type 1, but instead to particular interpretations of Wittgenstein, leads Frei to sardonically observe that type 5, in spite of itself, might end up mirroring type 1, rendering the typology as "a snake curled in on itself."[14] Sadly, Frei died before he could

8   Frei, *Types of Christian Theology*, 1.
9   Frei, *Types of Christian Theology*, 1f.
10   Frei, *Types of Christian Theology*, 2.
11   Frei, *Types of Christian Theology*, 2.
12   Frei, *Types of Christian Theology*, 3.
13   Frei, *Types of Christian Theology*, 5.
14   Frei, *Types of Christian Theology*, 51.

complete this historical project. Had he completed it, his historical analysis itself would surely and rightly be subject to dispute and critique. But it is in its very historical orientation that the typology's superior heuristic value can be seen.

Christian theology does not occur in a vacuum. It is a discourse that has developed alongside and in light of the myriad historical trends and events that have shaped those societies and the lives of the individuals who compose such societies. In modern times, Frei suggests that theology has been particularly influenced by its university setting and status as an academic subject alongside the physical and social sciences. Universities in the West, Frei notes, have in large part followed the example of the University of Berlin, established in 1809.[15] In Berlin, and subsequently in most Western universities, the university was held to be fundamentally accountable to the rigors of *wissenschaftlich* critique, "the inquiry into the universal, rational principles that allow us to organize any and all specific fields of inquiry into internally and mutually coherent, intelligible totalities . . . 'an inquiry into the transcendental principles justifying all systematic method and explanation.'"[16] Institutional, traditional, or communal allegiances are enemies of this free and rational inquiry and must be undermined and excised, leaving the faculty of philosophy as "the cement and the most important faculty in the university."[17]

For Christian theology to have earned a seat at the seminar table, then, the question of its authority was key.[18] In Frei's view, this question still plagues theology today, though it takes many forms. Similarly, while Frei's typology has been characterized here in reference to the question of theological authority, it can alternatively be viewed as distinguishing between views of theology's audience as either the academy or the church, as distinguishing between an apologetic and a dogmatic approach to theology, or as a typology detailing the divide between those who see theology as systematically correlated to external, philosophical discourses and those who see theology as utterly isolated from them.[19] It is important to appreciate the polyphony of Frei's typology even if it also seems fair to suggest that all of the above relate in some sense to the question of theological authority. It is therefore

[15]   Frei, *Types of Christian Theology*, 97.
[16]   Frei, *Types of Christian Theology*, 98.
[17]   Frei, *Types of Christian Theology*, 98; cf. Ford, "Theologically Hospitable," 539.
[18]   Frei, *Types of Christian Theology*, 102.
[19]   Cf. Paul DeHart, *The Trial of the Witnesses* (Oxford: Wiley-Blackwell, 2006), 195–239; Ford, "Theologically Hospitable," 536ff.

proposed that the issue of theological authority can serve as a heading that covers many, if not most, of these alternative typological orientations.

A second reason Frei's typology might be affirmed as less polemical or biased than Race's is the simple fact that Frei was unable to place himself fully within one of his own types, an indication of the seriousness with which the typology treats the tensions inherent in the relationship between faith and philosophy, particularly concerning the interpretation of Jesus Christ. Indeed, not only did Frei place himself between types 3 and 4, but he described himself as "aesthetically" participating in *all five* types.[20] In contrast, not only does Race unambiguously claim pluralism for himself, but each of his types are construed as having arrived at a final and irrevocable conclusion on the authority appropriate to theology. This could only be said about the types at the extremes of Frei's map, types 1 and 5. For the rest, the relationship between philosophy and communal self-description in Christian theology remains a question demanding continued consideration. Frei's typology takes this question as one specifically significant for Christianity. But in limiting the scope of this problem within Christianity, Frei's approach also suggests that other religions might be similarly understood in relation to a different set of concerns.

In this sense, and again contrary to the suggestion that Frei is a postliberal particularist, Frei's typology can be viewed as directly concerned with the discourse of comparative religion. Indeed, Frei says so himself, concluding the book proposal (which would posthumously serve as a preface for his *Types of Christian Theology*) with what appears to be his only recorded mention of our subject, as follows:

> I hope this book will be important not only in that it provides conceptual structure within a historical project, but also simply in its own right as a proposal to view Christianity as one religion among others—that is, as a semiotically coherent cultural system. In this way the cause of comparative religions can be served better than by interpreting Christianity (or any other religion) *exclusively* from within the matrix of its (secular or sacral) cultural setting.[21]

Frei's typology is intended to encourage us to consider not just *what* the differences are between various theological approaches but *why* and *how* those differences have emerged—and how similar dynamics, though perhaps in relation to different concerns, might be at work in other religions.

[20]   Ford, "Theologically Hospitable," 538.
[21]   Frei, *Types of Christian Theology*, 7.

This descriptive expansiveness should not be viewed as an indication of the typology's ambiguity, of a reticence on Frei's part to put his theological cards on the table, or of incoherence in his own approach to theology. Rather, it is partly a symptom of Frei's generous approach to Christian theology, such that he could describe himself as participating in all five types. It is also because the typology itself appears to be designed to compel us toward positions *between* the types, rather than toward a wholesale endorsement of *one* above all others, clearly indicated in Frei's placement of himself between types 3 and 4. Such a placement would be impossible within Race's typology, for there is no "in between" exclusivism and inclusivism, or inclusivism and pluralism.[22] More importantly, the possibility of such an intermediary placement between Frei's types indicates his marked awareness of the tensions that beset and spur Christian theology's engagement with external discourses—and the tensions inherent in affirming Jesus' unique significance for Christian faith alongside God's universal presence. The bias of Frei's typology, displayed in Frei's locating himself between types 3 and 4, is toward a view of theology that rejects philosophy's inherent prioritization even while it refuses to look away. For Frei, Christian faith in Jesus as God's resurrected son means not having to rely on philosophy for permission to make claims about reality while never abandoning the hope that such claims will one day, perhaps only eschatologically, be revealed as philosophically sound and, therein, incentivizing the continued search for such philosophical correlation today even as it also tempers its expectations.

Briefly, it should also be noted that recommending Frei's typology as a replacement for Race's in the discourse typically known as the Christian theology of religions is not a suggestion that this is the *only* useful way of parsing the differences within the discourse. For example, two type 4 theologians might well come to very different conclusions on any one of the constellations of issues—e.g., the nature of revelation or soteriology—that are subsumed under the theology of religions heading. One might identify such a dynamic in comparing Barth and Calvin,

----

[22]   Gavin D'Costa further divides Race's types up into more specific units, e.g., "structural inclusivists" and "restrictivist inclusivists," but this only further serves to underline the rigidity of Race's typology, pointing not to any ambiguity or open space between the types, but rather towards a degree of ambiguity *within* Race's types that is a function of his descriptions of them. Gavin D'Costa, *Christianity and World Religions: Disputed Questions in the Theology of Religions* (Oxford: Wiley-Blackwell, 2009), 1–53.

two theologians who are clearly type 4 but come to opposing conclusions concerning election and salvation.[23]

But this brings us back to a basic difference between Race's typology and Frei's. Whereas Race's is prescriptive, Frei's is diagnostic. Concerning Barth and Calvin, Race's typology would not only obscure any fruitful analysis of what led two such theologians, so similar in many regards, toward opposing conclusions—it would obscure the differences between their conclusions themselves, designating both Barth and Calvin exclusivists because of their shared belief in the unique significance of Jesus Christ. Using Frei's typology, on the other hand, would help us to identify the source of this discord, which afterwards might be approached using different typologies or other heuristic devices. While Frei's typology is hardly exhaustive, it might yet be seen as comprehensive.

Reformulating the Typology

There are problems with Frei's typology. Most prominent is Frei's linking of his types to individuals. Even though Frei's typology emerged as a companion piece to his historical project, he developed each type in relation to specific theologians. Type 1, the view of theology as a philosophical discipline, is tied to Immanuel Kant and Gordon Kaufman. Frei links type 2, where the specificity of Christianity is more prominently emphasized yet is itself justified by a philosophical scheme, to Rudolf Bultmann and David Tracy, among others.[24] Type 3, where correlation between theology and philosophy is similarly affirmed but the final means of their integration is left unidentified, is linked to Friedrich Schleiermacher and Paul Tillich. Type 4's prioritization of self-description as governing and limiting "the applicability of general criteria of meaning in theology, rather than vice versa" is identified with Karl Barth, John Henry Newman, and Jonathan Edwards.[25] Type 5's view of Christian theology as entirely a matter of self-description, wholly unrelated to general criteria of meaning, as is the case with all "languages' and their grammars" which only ever "function in specific contexts," is described in relation to D. Z. Philips.[26]

---

[23]   Matthias Grebe, *Election, Atonement, and the Holy Spirit* (Cambridge: James Clarke, 2015), 200–214.
[24]   Frei, *Types of Christian Theology*, 30; cf. DeHart, *Trial of the Witnesses*, 130.
[25]   Frei, *Types of Christian Theology*, 4.
[26]   Frei, *Types of Christian Theology*, 4.

The problem with this arrangement is it suggests that the types are only as apt as their application to particular theologians. Frei's designation of David Tracy as the theologian most characteristic of type 2 has come under particular scrutiny, with even Hunsinger and Placher's editorial introduction to the typology noting that, with Tracy's work following *Blessed Rage for Order* in sight, Frei might have moved him to type 3.[27] Elsewhere, Paul DeHart has argued that type 3 would be best represented by H. Richard Niebuhr, which would have the added benefit of underscoring the significance of Frei's rapprochement with his teacher.[28] In part, this simply reflects the perils of generalization that are inherent in any typology. No one example could perfectly demonstrate the general characteristics of the types and so all should be treated as imperfect representatives.

So, while our focus is primarily on identifying a better typology for the Christian theology of religions, it is also the case that in what follows, an argument is made for the reorientation of Frei's typology itself, jettisoning its individual theological exemplars and replacing them with communal or ecclesial movements. For the purposes of focusing the typology on the theology of religions, a particularly significant area for its application is the twentieth-century conciliar gatherings and statements of the ecumenical movement and its offshoots—namely the IMC, the Laymen's Foreign Missions Inquiry (LFMI), the WCC, and the Lausanne Movement's precursor, the Congress on the Church's Worldwide Mission. Moreover, the focus of Frei's unfinished social history of modern Protestant theology in relation to the impact of eighteenth-century philosophy and the nineteenth-century institutional contexts under which it was pursued, makes such twentieth-century ecumenical theology, with its combination of ecclesial and academic participants and audience, an especially fruitful context for the typology's heuristic use. By reformulating Frei's typology along these ecumenical/historical lines, we find it once again in the service of describing and analyzing particular moments in the history of modern Christian theology.

The Twentieth-Century Ecumenical Movement and
the Relationship between Christianity and Other Faiths

Frei's typology provides important insights on how twentieth-century Christians have viewed the relationship between Christian faith in Jesus' unique revelatory and salvific significance and the question of God's

---

[27]   George Hunsinger and William Placher, introduction to Frei, *Types of Christian Theology*, x.
[28]   DeHart, *Trial of the Witnesses*, 267ff.

presence to those outside the Christian church. By refocusing the question not on the philosophical viability or the soteriological conclusions of different types, but rather on the different accounts of the nature of theological discourse from which such conclusions might emerge, Frei's typology renders the twentieth-century ecumenical discussion, in all its variety, as an exchange rooted in legitimate and complex disagreements on theological authority. Used in this way, Frei's typology proves profoundly helpful in the analysis of a formative historical undertaking that has greatly influenced the ways in which Christians today discuss the relationship between Jesus and the world religions.[29]

From its first official gathering in Edinburgh 1910, a constitutive concern of the ecumenical movement has been the relationship between the traditional Christian faith in the unsubstitutability of Jesus' life, death, and resurrection and the presence of God in the lives of persons who, whether by historical accident, choice, or some combination of the two, place their faith elsewhere. Questions concerning the need for and nature of Christian evangelism to those of other religions are a large part of what led to the creation of the ecumenical movement in the first place.

Such historical application does not imply a chronological order to match the types, such that type 1 is either the earliest or latest historical example. Neither does it suggest that the examples employed here are in any way exhaustive of the possibilities. Not only could other examples from within (and beyond) the twentieth-century ecumenical movement be used in what follows, but Frei's typology could also be used to analyze movements within other religions. Indeed, even though it emerged largely out of historical and theological study specific to Christianity, Frei suggested his typology is nonexclusive in its religious application and potentially available for use in other faiths.[30]

[29]   One of Frei's guiding theological principles, evinced most clearly in his account of type 4 theology, is summarized by David Ford as follows:

> Theology reflects on the "ruled use" of the language of the Christian community understood as constituted in "complex and changing coherence" by such elements as sacred text, regulated relations between an elite and other believers, preaching, baptism, celebration of communion, common beliefs and attitudes, and an interpretive tradition.

Ford, "Theologically Hospitable," 538; cf. Frei, *Types of Christian Theology*, 21f. The ecumenical movement is an ideal site to consider the aptness of Frei's account of theology as the "ruled use" of the language of the Christian community and also of the diverse possibilities of such an approach as constituted by the "complex and changing coherence" of its elements.

[30]   Frei, *Types of Christian Theology*, 21f.

Moreover, although our focus will be on Christianity in the West represented in the early twentieth century by the predominantly Protestant IMC and today by the IMC's successor, the WCC's Commission on World Mission and Evangelism (CWME), it will include attention to two examples from the periphery of this modern ecumenical movement. Perhaps unsurprisingly, these two examples—the 1932 "Laymen's Foreign Missions Inquiry" (type 1) and the 1966 "Wheaton Declaration" (type 5)—also occupy the polar extremes of Frei's typology. Type 2 will be linked to the 1966 WCC study "The Missionary Structure of the Congregation"; type 3 is tied to the IMC assembly in Jerusalem 1928; and type 4 is attached to the IMC assembly in Tambaram 1938.

This approach has the added benefit of repositioning assemblies that are sometimes depicted in oppositional terms—Jerusalem 1928 and Tambaram 1938—instead of being seen in close proximity to each other.[31] Just as Frei's typology found a generative tension in its assigning of Schleiermacher to type 3 and Barth to type 4, so too might we find something similar here, pointing to the importance of Jerusalem 1928's affirmation of God's universal presence, including in the lives of non-Christians, alongside Tambaram 1938's emphasis on the prioritization of what Hendrik Kraemer called "biblical realism" and the notion that God's revelation in Jesus Christ is sui generis.

Type 1: Laymen's Foreign Missions Inquiry

The IMC was formed following the success of an initial gathering in Edinburgh 1910 called "The World Mission Conference."[32] Shortly thereafter the IMC was formed and subsequent assemblies were held in Jerusalem 1928, Tambaram 1938, Whitby 1947, Willingen 1952, and Accra 1958. Following Accra, the IMC became formally integrated into the WCC as

---

[31]   Stephen C. Neill, *The Unfinished Task* (London: Edinburgh House, 1957), 151f.; cf. David Bosch, *Witness to the World: The Christian Mission in Theological Perspective* (Atlanta: John Knox, 1980), 163.

[32]   The confines of space do not allow for a full discussion of the creation and development of the IMC and WCC. For this, see Rodger C. Bassham, *Mission Theology 1948–1975: Years of Worldwide Creative Tension* (Eugene, Ore.: Wipf & Stock, 2002); Jan Van Lin, *Shaking the Fundamentals: Religious Plurality and the Ecumenical Movement* (Amsterdam: Rodopi, 2002); David Bosch, *Transforming Mission: Paradigm Shifts in Theology of Mission* (Maryknoll, N.Y.: Orbis, 2011); Timothy Yates, *Christian Mission in the Twentieth Century* (Cambridge: Cambridge University Press, 1996).

the "Commission on World Mission and Evangelism" under whose auspices World Mission Conferences would continue to be held.

Outside the auspices of the IMC and WCC, a few alternative one-off meetings and long-term movements cropped up. Most notable from the latter category is the Lausanne Movement, formed after the first "International Congress on World Evangelization," held in Lausanne, Switzerland in 1974. The "Lausanne Covenant," which was endorsed by the participants of this 1974 gathering, expresses what might be called evangelical concerns for WCC's theology and approach to mission, especially the moratorium on the sending of foreign missionaries announced at the CWME assembly in Bangkok 1972–1973.[33] We will look at an important precursor to the Lausanne Movement, the so-called Wheaton Declaration of the 1966 Congress on the Church's Worldwide Mission in our consideration of type 5.

Though neither part of a larger movement nor a gathering convened in opposition to a particular movement, as in the case of Lausanne (the IMC had apparently offered its cooperation), the 1932 LFMI might nonetheless be seen in a similar light.[34] Convened by John D. Rockefeller, the LFMI was chaired by William Ernest Hocking, Alford Professor of Natural Religion, Moral Philosophy and Civil Polity at Harvard University. At the IMC meeting in Jerusalem 1928, Hocking had been one of the most outspoken advocates for an approach to mission as a global partnership of religions against secularism.[35] Of the commission's fifteen members, seven were academics: two philosophers, two medical doctors, one legal scholar, and two university presidents who had backgrounds in theology, including C. A. Barbour who was president of Brown University and a Baptist clergyman.[36] Apart from one other member of the clergy, Dr. W. Merrill of the Brick Church in New York, the rest hailed from business, education, or philanthropy.

---

[33]   John Stott, *Christian Mission in the Modern World* (Downers Grove, Ill.: IVP, 2008), 58. Stott notes that the "moratorium" was partly misunderstood, but as is demonstrated in the 1966 Wheaton Declaration, unease about the WCC's increasing emphasis on social aspects of Christian witness had been brewing for some time. Indeed, Bassham notes that the influence of the moratorium issue was not very explicit during the initial Lausanne meeting in 1974. Cf. Bosch, *Transforming Mission*, 410–18; Bassham, *Mission Theology*, 209–55.

[34]   Van Lin, *Shaking the Fundamentals*, 131.

[35]   *Report of the Jerusalem Meeting of the International Missionary Council, March 24–April 8, 1928*, vol 1, *The Christian Life and Message in Relation to Non-Christian Systems of Thought and Life* (London: IMC, 1928), 369f.

[36]   Cf. Van Lin, *Shaking the Fundamentals*, 131, n. 146.

The LFMI consisted of two parts. The first was a "factfinding" initiative of Protestant missions in India, Burma, China, and Japan, which Kenneth Scott Latourette described as "the most careful, objective study of a large cross-section of Protestant missions ever made."[37] The second part was the analyzing of this collected data and the "thorough re-appraisal of motives and methods" of Christian missionaries by the "Commission of Appraisal."[38]

Published as *Re-thinking Missions*, the Commission of Appraisal's report places itself decisively in the vein of type 1 theology. Frei captured this particular view in his account of type 1:

> In the first type that I am proposing, *theology as a philosophical discipline* in the academy takes complete priority over Christian self-description within the religious community called the Church, and Christian self-description, in its subordinate place, tends to emulate the philosophical character of academic theology by being as general as possible or as little specific about Christianity as it can be, and the distinction between external and internal description is basically unimportant.[39]

Lest this appeal to philosophical authority be misleading, Frei notes that, because type 1's notion of "God" "arises *formally* as ground and limit of the concept 'world,' and *materially* it arises out of the richness of human experience . . . the two functions of the concept 'God' thus are the relativizing and the humanizing of the world."[40] In other words, the philosophical orientation of type 1 leads it not necessarily into an abstract approach to theology but possibly to one that prioritizes the practical, material and human.[41] For type 1, "the concept 'God' is not a report on information," but rather a metaphysical limit and a phenomenologically analyzable facet of human experience:

> The images or symbols of specific religious traditions become imaginative representations whose meaning is their paraphrasing (aptly or ineptly, and in the latter case they must be reformed) of the meta-

---

[37]   Kenneth Scott Latourette, "The Laymen's Foreign Missions Inquiry: The Report of Its Commission of Appraisal," *International Review of Mission* 22, no. 2 (1933): 155.

[38]   Kenneth Scott Latourette, "Re-thinking Missions after Twenty-Five Years," *International Review of Mission* 46, no. 182 (1957): 164.

[39]   Frei, *Types of Christian Theology*, 28.

[40]   Frei, *Types of Christian Theology*, 28.

[41]   Frei, *Types of Christian Theology*, 28.

physical, conceptual master construct. The aptness or ineptness of such images depends of course in large part on the cultural situation in which they arise.[42]

Type 1 theology employs such a process not primarily for descriptive or even analytical reasons, but in service of advancing "a religious apologetic."[43] Of course, type 1 is unmistakably Race's approach to theology and where his theological pluralism would be placed.

That the LFMI aligns with this type can be discerned first in its complete disregard for localized religious traditions. Race's philosophical construal of theology is betrayed in his outlining of pluralism as focused entirely on "axial age" religions and in his ignoring indigenous, localized, and ethnoreligious groups. Similarly, the LFMI's insistence that the "questions religion deals with are not questions which admit local or national answers" implies the underlying philosophical universalism that pervades its general notion of "religion."[44]

On this view, whatever social or historical particularities a religion might have, they are wholly irrelevant to its true meaning and purpose: "Religion becomes potentially universal in range as it becomes aware of its own inner logic."[45] The very possibility of a religion's "inner logic" not being suitable for universalization is excluded ab initio. This same perspective is present in Frei's type 1, where the "'ordinary language' meaning of 'God' as a specific cultural construct . . . is ultimately indistinguishable from the general, metaphysical construct of the concept that is grounded presumably in the very structure of human nature and experience."[46] Given the operating assumption of the equivalence between "external and internal description," only those religions which might be interpreted along these lines—Hinduism, Buddhism, Confucianism, and Islam—are designated as Christianity's theological allies and interlocutors. Indeed, Hocking describes Confucianism and Buddhism as religious *advancements* upon what came before for precisely this reason: "Confucianism in Japan improved upon primitive Shinto, contributing order, rationality, social definition; Buddhism adds to both a greater cosmic depth and a more searching appeal to the motives of the heart."[47]

[42]   Frei, *Types of Christian Theology*, 29.
[43]   Frei, *Types of Christian Theology*, 29.
[44]   William Ernest Hocking, *Re-thinking Missions: A Laymen's Inquiry after One Hundred Years* (New York: Harper & Brothers, 1932), 7.
[45]   Hocking, *Re-thinking Missions*, 7.
[46]   Frei, *Types of Christian Theology*, 29.
[47]   Hocking, *Re-thinking Missions*, 37.

Second, like Race's argument for pluralism, the LFMI's philosophical subordination of Christian theology serves as an apologetic response to the threat of secularism, combining an appeal to philosophical authority with an emphasis on pragmatic objectives to reassert the viability of faith. The questions to which Christian theology, and those who participate in Christian mission, must respond are being asked *"by the turn of the times."*[48] Like Race, Hocking's report suggests that society has moved forward while Christian theology has not, calling into question its meaningfulness for modern society. In a section in the first chapter on "The Motives of Mission," Hocking states that the proper aim of Christian mission is "preparation for world unity in civilization." He continues:

> We know that to effect an understanding in religious matters is to pave the way for an understanding in other matters. The world must eventually become a moral unity: to this end, it was necessary that the apparent localism of Christianity should be broken down.[49]

In the aftermath of the devastation of the Great War and the swirling doubts about Christianity evoked by the destruction wrought by nominally Christian nations, Hocking here provides an apologetic balm, recasting theology in anthropocentric terms and advancing a reassuring view of mission as "a fundamental groping toward the moral unity of the world."[50]

Hocking's account of the "altered theological outlook" and its implications for Christian mission anticipates Race's argument for pluralism and his concern with recasting theological authority in universal, philosophical terms. Both see their approach to theology as a response to secular criticisms, appealing to religious experiences of a common, transcendent source as that which unifies the religions, a unity that also limits the particularities of all religions as "symbolic and imaginative" expressions of this transcendent, experiential, and moral unity:

> It would be a poor complement to our theological insight if a hundred years or so full of intellectual development, of advance in scientific thought and of philosophical activity, had brought no progress in the conceptions attending our religious experience. The bases of that experience belong to the eternal and unchangeable things—since it

---

[48]   Hocking, *Re-thinking Missions*, 3, emphasis added.
[49]   Hocking, *Re-thinking Missions*, 8.
[50]   Hocking, *Re-thinking Missions*, 9.

is precisely the function of religion to bring man into the presence of the everlasting and real. But since religion is not isolated from the rest of our mental life, there will be changes in every living religious system, in its symbolical and imaginative expression, and in its adjustment to the developing body of scientific truth, as the rest of our world-view changes.[51]

With this prioritization of religious experience, the LFMI concludes that it is incumbent upon Christianity to reconceive its understanding of theology and the objective of its encounters with non-Christians as a dialogue focused on "promoting world unity through the spread of the universal elements of religion."[52]

Indeed, the LFMI sees Christianity as caught in the same situation as all other religions in their confrontation with secular criticisms, all equally beset by "the same menace, the spread of the secular spirit."[53] The enemy of all religion is "materialism, secularism, naturalism."[54] Christian theology must therefore undergo "a thorough re-analysis of the purpose of missions in reference to other faiths," emphasizing the underlying unity of all in the experience of transcendence.[55] Jan Van Lin, author of one of a very detailed history of the modern ecumenical movement and its grappling with the fact of religious pluralism, describes the vision of the LFMI as follows:

> According to them, non-Christians have an inalienable intuition of the true God. For this reason they accepted the existence of a universal religion. Here Christianity was able to help the other religions to gain a better understanding of themselves and to liberate them from error and idolatry. Together they are searching for the ultimate truth in which, so to speak, the New Testament is to be found for each existing faith . . . On the way to this goal, the unique character of Christianity will be maintained *in as far as it is necessary* for the highest religious life of humankind. In coexistence, all religions will stimulate each other on the way towards the final goal: unity in the most perfect truth.[56]

---

[51]   Hocking, *Re-thinking Missions*, 18f.; cf. Van Lin, *Shaking the Fundamentals*, 133f.

[52]   Hocking, *Re-thinking Missions*, 28.

[53]   Hocking, *Re-thinking Missions*, 29.

[54]   Hocking, *Re-thinking Missions*, 29.

[55]   Hocking, *Re-thinking Missions*, 29.

[56]   Van Lin, *Shaking the Fundamentals*, 133, emphasis added.

Clearly, the LFMI echoes much of Race's account of the pluralist type, with both affirming, philosophically and phenomenologically, the underlying unity and the responsibility of mutual correction inherent in the world religions.

Unlike Race's typology, however, Frei's type 1 helps us to see what internally motivates and guides this kind of theology, particularly the apologetic impulse that accompanies an approach to theology in which "specific Christian description or self-description is not only subordinate to, but undertaken as part of, a general intellectual-cultural inquiry."[57] This is displayed in the LFMI's evident concern for appeasing secular criticisms, for viewing experience as the universal foundation of religious faith, and for the collapsing of external and internal descriptions such that any religious community's particular traditions or scriptures are viewed as "partial, culturally conditioned exemplification[s] of the universal religion."[58] As a result, there is no room in this type for the *sensus literalis* and no possibility of affirming the unique significance of the life, death, and resurrection of Jesus Christ for Christian faith. Because of its apologetic thrust, type 1 entirely subordinates the communal consensus on the plain sense of scripture to external discourses, leaving Jesus as "no more than a symbol for an independently grounded form of meaning."[59] Moreover, this excludes the possibility of any figural interpretation, leaving the LFMI with a view of history in which, ironically, its apparent prioritization results in its theological significance being undermined. Here too, history is viewed as a screen behind which the truths of universal religion flicker.

This was not lost on some theologians and missiologists at the time, although some commented more incisively than others. K. S. Latourette initially applauded the report, writing that seldom "has the philosophy of a great section of American Christian thought been stated so persuasively," and agreeing that the report "is certainly right in placing foremost the fact that philosophic presuppositions underlie missions."[60] But as David Bosch notes, although the LFMI's approach was rejected by many, few perceived the nature of the philosophical concerns that lay beneath the LFMI's particular approach, save John A.

---

[57]   Frei, *Types of Christian Theology*, 30.
[58]   Frei, *Types of Christian Theology*, 59.
[59]   Hunsinger, "Afterword: Hans Frei as Theologian," in *Theology and Narrative: Selected Essays* by Hans Frei, ed. George Hunsinger and William C. Placher (Oxford: Oxford University Press, 1993), 262.
[60]   Latourette, "Laymen's Foreign Missions Inquiry," 159, 167.

Mackay, then an employee of the YMCA and a future president of the Princeton Theological Seminary.[61]

Writing in the same 1933 issue of the *International Review of Mission* as Latourette, Mackay laments that the LFMI report has "totally ignored that a revolution has broken out in the romantic theological playground of the nineteenth century, whose spirit the Report perpetuates."[62] Bosch goes further, arguing that the LFMI "sought to substitute nineteenth century romanticism for its rationalism, little realizing that the two depended and fed upon each other."[63] This is echoed in Frei's description of type 1 theology's appeal to "a kind of rationalism in which every specific, culturally conditioned religious image is, if not equally, at least more or less grey" and his observation that in such academic theology "the concept of reason had been transformed from the rationalists' universally applicable analytical and critical instrument to the idealists' vast, universal, and unifying Absolute, ingredient at once in the world and in consciousness."[64]

With the descriptive and analytical aptitude of Frei's typology hopefully established in light of the convergence between his type 1 and the LFMI, we turn to type 2 and the WCC study project on the "The Missionary Structure of the Congregation" (MSC), the final report of which was published in 1967 just before the 1968 WCC Uppsala Assembly. This project, unlike the LFMI, did not advocate for the complete collapsing of distinctions between religions themselves or for the total unity between "religion" and "the rest of our mental life," demanding that theology always adjusts itself "to the developing body of scientific truth, as the rest of our world-view changes."[65] Nonetheless, it advocates an approach to theology in which its meaning is inherently and reciprocally correlated to universal human experience, which it terms *shalom*, as a constant locus of God's presence amidst the flux of historical change which renders the *sensus literalis*, with its grounding in historical and communal consensus within the church, an unsuitable source for discerning the meaning of Christian faith.[66]

61   Bosch, *Transforming Mission*, 333.
62   John. A. Mackay, "The Theology of the Laymen's Foreign Missions Inquiry," *International Review of Mission* 22, no. 2 (1933): 177.
63   Bosch, *Transforming Mission*, 333.
64   Frei, *Types of Christian Theology*, 34, 106.
65   Hocking, *Re-thinking Missions*, 18–19.
66   *The Church for Others and the Church for the World: A Quest for Structures for Missionary Congregations. Final Report of the Western European Working Group and North American Working Group of the Department on Studies in Evangelism* (Geneva: WCC, 1967), 14, 77ff.

Type 2: "The Missionary Structure of the Congregation" 1967 WCC Study Group

Frei describes type 2 as an approach to theology which, like type 1, priori-tizes the philosophical and external above the self-descriptive and commu-nal. But Frei posits an important distinction between the two. For type 2, theology is "a philosophical or academic discipline, but within that order-ing, the specificity of Christian religion is taken very, very seriously, in a way in which external description and self-description merge into one, and the joint product is justified by a foundational philosophical scheme."[67] Here the Christian tradition is interpreted from a philosophical framework which conceives of the particularities of Christianity—Christological, ecclesial, sacramental—as phenomena corresponding to a universal existential and/or social condition. While type 1 leaves no room for the plain sense of scrip-ture, ignoring or even deriding its significance, type 2 at least acknowledges it as a concern. But in type 2, the particularity of the Christian faith is subor-dinated to external discourses, leaving the import of the *sensus literalis* and of Jesus Christ subject to their evaluation.

This approach was on display at the WCC assembly at Uppsala 1968, which was enthusiastically described by the former general secretary of the WCC as establishing a paradigm shift in the ecumenical movement.[68] This shift included a turn from an emphasis on the church to an emphasis on the world as the locus of God's mission.[69] The impact of this change, and the sense of this new "Uppsala paradigm," is discernible in aspects of the 1973 CWME assembly in Bangkok, where the theme of "Salvation Today" was invoked to seek a comprehensive understanding of salvation that emphasized God's saving work outside the walls of the church.[70]

Both Uppsala and Bangkok, then, could be described as emphasiz-ing God's presence in the world over and against the church's celebration of God's unique identity in Jesus Christ and the unique presence this

---

67   Frei, *Types of Christian Theology*, 30.

68   Konrad Raiser, *Ecumenism in Transition: A Paradigm Shift in the Ecumenical Movement?* (Geneva: WCC, 1991); *Uppsala Report 1968: Official Report of the Fourth Assembly of the World Council of Churches, Uppsala, July 4–20, 1968*, ed. Norman Goodall (Geneva: WCC, 1968).

69   Geoffrey Wainwright, *Lesslie Newbigin: A Theological Life* (Oxford: Oxford University Press, 2000), 129.

70   *Bangkok Assembly, 1973: Minutes and Report of the Assembly of the Commis-sion on World Mission and Evangelism of the World Council of Churches, December 31, 1972 and January 9–12, 1973* (Geneva: WCC, 1973), 43, 75–78, 88–90; cf. Bassham, *Mission Theology*, 92ff.

celebration affords the church as the body of Christ. Bosch calls Uppsala 1968 "the apex of the ecumenical theology of secularization." He goes on to write the following about Bangkok 1973:

> The embarrassment with the church . . . reached crisis proportions at the Uppsala and Bangkok conferences . . . The classical Catholic adage, *extra ecclesiam nulla salus* . . . seemed to have been turned into its opposite—*inside* the church there was no salvation.[71]

Even though Uppsala and Bangkok became the most prominent examples of this kind of theology, Bosch and others have traced the source of its influence to the WCC study committee on "The Missionary Structure of the Congregation" (MSC), authorized at the 1961 WCC assembly in New Delhi and published in 1967 as *The Church for Others and The Church for the World*.[72] Indeed, the 1968 *Uppsala Report* notes the influence of MSC, and the assembly's statement, "Renewal in Mission," employs the MSC's language in its second section.[73] So while both the WCC assembly at Uppsala 1968 and the CWME assembly at Bangkok 1973 might be used as examples of type 2 theology, we will focus on the MSC and its publication, *The Church for Others and The Church for the World*, as a preceding and distilled expression of the kind of theology that prevailed in both.

It is important also to note that the "theology of religions" receives far less direct attention in the MSC and in the WCC assemblies from this period than it had in the past.[74] Nonetheless, the MSC's approach to theology is influenced by the theology of religions discussions that preceded it and the report itself emerges from and presents an approach to theology that has direct implications for how Christians understand the theological relationship between Christianity and other faiths. Indeed, the absence of such direct focus should be viewed in relation to growing concerns about secularism.[75] As I have tried to show regarding Race's typology, and as

---

[71]   Bosch, *Witness to the World*, 190; idem, *Transforming Mission*, 393f.
[72]   Bosch, *Transforming Mission*, 401; idem, *Witness to the World*, 190; cf. John G. Flett, *The Witness of God: The Trinity, Missio Dei, Karl Barth, and the Nature of Christian Community* (Grand Rapids: Eerdmans, 2010), 52–53; Bassham, *Mission Theology*, 67–91; Lesslie Newbigin, *Unfinished Agenda* (Edinburgh: St Andrew Press, 1993), 194f.; cf. Wainwright, *Lesslie Newbigin*, 175.
[73]   *Uppsala Report*, 21ff., 30ff.; cf. Bassham, *Mission Theology*, 79; Bosch, *Witness to the World*, 190ff.; idem, *Transforming Mission*, 392ff.
[74]   Van Lin, *Shaking the Fundamentals*, 220.
[75]   *Church for Others*, 8–12; cf. Bosch, *Transforming Mission*, 332–33, 392–94, 444–45; Gerald H. Anderson, "American Protestants in Pursuit of Mission: 1886–1986," *International Bulletin of Missionary Research* 12, no. 3 (1988): 109–10.

Frei's typology makes clear, concerns about theology's relationship to secular discourses can hardly be divorced from those regarding the theological relationship between Christianity and other faiths.

The MSC report is comprised of two sections. One, "The Church for Others," is the product of the Western European Working Group of the WCC's Department on Studies in Evangelism. The other, "The Church for the World," was the final report of the North American Working Group. They will be referred to here as one, under the title of the overarching study, "The Missionary Structure of the Congregation." For although they were the products of different groups, the two reports affirm the same view of Christian theology and its relation to external discourses. This view is summarized in their shared insistence that "the world must be allowed to provide the agenda for the churches."[76] Both reports argue that while the traditional view of God's relationship with the world and church can be schematized as "God—Church—World," this must be amended to "God—World—Church."[77] It was only by starting with "the world" and its concerns that the MSC believed Christian theology could be carried out meaningfully.[78]

Yet, unlike the LFMI, these studies do not focus their work primarily on religious experience, "religion," or other abstractions in service of explicating the common core underlying all human experience and religious traditions. Indeed, the MSC constantly affirms the importance of Christology in interpreting world trends and events.[79] Like the LFMI, however, the MSC assumes that there is a direct and decisive correlation between Christian theology and external discourses and experiences—one that can only be evinced by interpreting the meaning of the Christian tradition through the eyes of those outside of it.

So, although in some ways it takes the specificity of Christian faith seriously, the MSC like the LFMI suggests that its meaning can only be discerned with the aid of an external interpretive schema. This is clearly laid out on the report's very first page:

> Our work, for the past four years, has had two inseparable aspects: it has been concerned with theological investigation and, at the same time, with discovering the true face of the modern world. We are convinced that these two aspects are indivisible.

[76]   *Church for Others*, 20, 70.
[77]   *Church for Others*, 16f., 70.
[78]   *Church for Others*, 7.
[79]   *Church for Others*, 7, 20ff., 58, 63f., 70ff.

We believe that it is only by being rooted in the truths of the Gospel that we can know and face the world i.e., that we can know ourselves and accept ourselves without either optimistic or pessimistic illusions. We also believe that it is only by listening to what modern man is saying in suffering and success that theology can have any meaning.[80]

Along very similar lines, Frei describes type 2 as an approach that subsumes theology under a general philosophical framework, through which "it seeks to correlate specifically Christian with general cultural meaning structures such as natural sciences or the 'spirit' of a cultural era."[81] The correlation between these two "is made possible by the same underlying transcendental structure: for example, broadly pragmatic appeals to the character of human existence."[82] The MSC's insistence upon the indivisibility of theological and nontheological investigation, and especially its emphasis on the role of external investigation as the source of theology's meaning, make it a strikingly apt example of the theology Frei describes in type 2.

A subsequent question concerns the kind of philosophical framework that is operating in the MSC's theology. Frei orients type 2 in relation to David Tracy and his turn to Paul Ricoeur's phenomenological hermeneutics, which is itself a response to the "postmodern situation."[83] No longer is "the specificity of the Christian tradition" rendered "by *historical description*, as it was for nineteenth-century historians of dogma . . . nor by a kind of *social scientific* description, for which the Church would be the indispensable context in which the Christian symbol system alone can properly function."[84] Rather, "the specific self-description of Christianity" is here conceived as "one mode of a general description of religion, and that description is the work of phenomenology."[85]

This prioritization of general description and phenomenology is also evident in the theology of the MSC. The report strongly asserts that the only viable theology after the Enlightenment is one that embraces a historicist perspective and the related realization of the inherent instability of the historical world:

[80]   *Church for Others*, 7.
[81]   Frei, *Types of Christian Theology*, 3.
[82]   Frei, *Types of Christian Theology*, 3.
[83]   Frei, *Types of Christian Theology*, 30.
[84]   Frei, *Types of Christian Theology*, 31.
[85]   Frei, *Types of Christian Theology*, 31.

If secularization is one aspect of modern society which the churches have to understand and accept, they have also to recognize that the world is a world in transformation . . . History is now understood as the experience of change; the fluidity of contemporary society thus corresponds to modern men's experience of history as the continual transformation of the world . . . The churches have to plan for an ever-changing world, of which the only unalterable feature is permanent change.[86]

This account of history suggests that the meaning of Christian faith is located *behind* such historical phenomena, within the "specific contents of human consciousness."[87] Type 2 theology appeals to phenomenology to uncover "what we sense as meanings in the world" and how those become "internalized within us."[88]

Similarly, the report was commissioned to "arrive at a true understanding of the world today and of the Church's place in it . . . help[ing] the Church to become aware of the fact that the forms of its life are conditioned by history and that they are therefore relative and diverse."[89] Amidst this diversity, the report insists, we can uncover a stable account of Christian meaning, but only by surveying the world outside the church or scripture—a blend of historicism and phenomenology that echoes Cantwell Smith. Crucially, and unlike that blend advocated by Race and type 1, both type 2 and the MSC suggest that its view of theology is not at odds with the Christian tradition but is *native to it*. Indeed, Frei describes type 2 theology as first imposing a philosophical framework upon theology and then finding, "to nobody's particular surprise," this framework is intrinsic to Christianity.[90] To wit, the MSC asserts its historicism, or "secularization," as an imperative interpretive lens for Christianity, only to subsequently discover that this "constant process of change should not surprise the Christian; indeed, on the basis of the gospel, he should accept and welcome it."[91] Prioritizing external discourses, the MSC "discovers" the conclusions reached therein are identical to those arrived at in Christian faith and scripture. The meaning of scripture is no longer tethered to the *sensus literalis* or the particular identity of Jesus Christ,

---

86   *Church for Others*, 12f.
87   Frei, *Types of Christian Theology*, 31.
88   Frei, *Types of Christian Theology*, 31.
89   *Church for Others*, 7.
90   Frei, *Types of Christian Theology*, 33.
91   *Church for Others*, 13.

but instead rests upon a more abstract or symbolic interpretation related to the general features of human experience.[92] "Meaning, as the internal experience of selves, and religious experience in particular," Frei writes, "is the glue that allows external and internal description to be one, and Christian description or self-description is one instance of the general class 'religious meaningfulness' . . . a universal anthropological phenomenon, philosophically grounded."[93]

Though Frei criticizes type 2 theology for rejecting a kind of thick, social scientific description of Christianity that takes its ecclesial context as one vital ingredient in its description of Christian theology, the MSC insists that theology's natural and essential partner is sociology.[94] But this is really just a semantic discrepancy, as the MSC invokes sociological study as a means of both *chastening* theology's inclination to uphold the church as a stable and indispensable context for Christian theology and refocusing this attention on "the world" as the site of God's unfolding presence.[95]

Frei takes type 2 to conceive of Christian theology as "one mode of a general description of religion, and that description is the work of phenomenology . . . the technical, reflective analysis, as it were from within, of the structure of distinctively human experience—in other words, of specific contents of human consciousness."[96] On the one hand, the MSC's designation of sociology as theology's correlate might appear to be a rebuke of phenomenology's idealist prioritization of the internal condition of humanity. But its emphasis on sociality leads the MSC towards a different way of making a similar argument for the universality of God's presence in "the structure of distinctively human experience."[97] So while Frei's type 2 theology is framed in relation to phenomenology and the MSC's theology is linked to sociology, both correlate the meaning of Christian faith with universal human experiences.

Both European and North American wings of the MSC included sociologists as permanent members in their study groups. The Western European study's report goes so far as to propose at the outset of the report that sociology provides a necessary and needed correction to theology's focus on the eternal above the finite, even suggesting that

[92]   Hans Frei, "The 'Literal Reading' of Biblical Narrative," in *Theology and Narrative*, 145.
[93]   Frei, *Types of Christian Theology*, 33.
[94]   Frei, *Types of Christian Theology*, 31, 33; *Church for Others*, 7f.
[95]   *Church for Others*, 7ff.
[96]   Frei, *Types of Christian Theology*, 31.
[97]   *Church for Others*, 31.

sociology is in some ways better suited to scriptural interpretation than theology:

> In our attempt to arrive at a true understanding of the world today and of the Church's place in it, we have been greatly assisted by specialists in sociology. We are convinced that sociologists can help the Church to become aware of the fact that the forms of its life are conditioned by history and that they are therefore relative and diverse . . . Sociologists have often appreciated the dynamism and the historical basis of the Scriptures better than many theologians, who have concentrated instead upon the nature of eternal truth rather than upon the constant risk that God is prepared to run as he involves himself in each new adventure of human living.[98]

In line with Frei's account of type 2 theology, the MSC here invokes history's dynamism and relativism, as viewed by sociology, as the universal structure that conditions all human experience and provides the common existential condition requisite for phenomenological analysis of transcendent experience. In fact, the North American study group's report notes that sociologists were explicitly included in the study "to guide the search for 'structure.'"[99]

The North American study group's report goes even farther in its emphasis on the necessity of sociology for Christian theology. Noting the fears some of its members had concerning the danger of "sociological reductionism"—"a reduction of theology to the categories of sociology"—it criticizes the view that theology "provides the norms" while "sociology's world is the scene for the application of the norms."[100] Instead, the study group insists on the mutual dependence between theology and sociology and their roles in taking "seriously the historical character of Christian revelation." The report continues:

> Because the Christian faith is *historical*, the forms of this faith and life are open to change and because God is faithful to his purpose, there is continuity in the midst of that change. It is this dual characteristic that makes the dialogue between "theology" and "sociology" which lies at the heart of a study such as this both possible and desirable . . .[101]

[98]   *Church for Others*, 7f.
[99]   *Church for Others*, 59.
[100]   *Church for Others*, 64f.
[101]   *Church for Others*, 65.

This passage echoes Smith's distinction between historical tradition and internal faith. As the championed slogan of "God—World—Church" makes clear, the MSC's conviction is that, in a world of historical flux, the meaning of Christian faith itself is only truly discernible when one prioritizes a survey of the world *outside* the confines of the Christian tradition, a process which ensures the contemporary relevance, and therefore the abiding meaning, of Christian faith. Importantly, this process is not conceived as undermining the meaning of Christianity conveyed in scripture or tradition. Rather, like type 2's discovery that the extrinsic framework is in fact intrinsic to Christian faith, this sociological/phenomenological survey reveals the true character of God's purpose as communicated within the tradition. For both the MSC and type 2, "the Church as the necessary context for the use of Christian concepts and language plays no part ... *Experience* is its substitute."[102]

The MSC's assertion of the mutual dependence of theology and sociology is derived from its emphasis on the relativity and dynamism of history, where this is also understood as the primary context of God's revelation. Importantly, this also reflects the order in which the case is made: sociology and other academic disciplines reveal history to be relative and dynamic, demoting in relative significance, and perhaps even invalidating, theological appeals to the church or communal practices of biblical interpretation in the search for the meaning of Christian faith. Happily (and unsurprisingly), it turns out that this view is discernible in scripture, revealing the inherent and systematic correlation between theology and sociology. The passage cited earlier that references sociologists' greater appreciation of the "dynamism and the historical basis of the Scriptures" attests to this. So too does the MSC's argument that this dynamism and impermanence *should not* be surprising for Christian theology, even as they make the case that it has been, for it is present in the gospel itself:

This constant process of change should not surprise the Christian; indeed, on the basis of the gospel, he should accept and welcome it. According to the New Testament, the mission of the Son of God produces a very specific kind of change ... This change has two aspects; it has *already* taken place ... and it is *still* taking place—history is experienced as change, of which Jesus is the initiator and final goal.

---

[102]   Frei, *Types of Christian Theology*, 33; cf. idem, "'Literal Reading,'" 130f.

So far then from resisting change, the Christian is required to see in it the hand of God.[103]

What differentiates type 1 from type 2 theology is precisely this kind of correlative approach and appeal to generalized themes. Type 1 conceives of Christian theology entirely as a philosophical discipline, where its specificity and prior interpretations are undermined, after which it is acknowledged that its meaning can only be discerned through "a general intellectual-cultural inquiry."[104] Type 2, as in the passages above, identifies a framework outside theology such that it "is subject to judgment and evaluation by certain basic general criteria" while at the same time arguing that such a process reveals them to have been already present and entirely compatible with the Christian tradition.[105]

In his description of type 2, Frei repeatedly argues that it can apply to both liberal and conservative theologies. If the liberal side is represented by Tracy, Frei sees the conservative side as illustrated in the work of Carl Henry. But he is particularly critical of its liberal expressions, perhaps because he sees them as more undermining of the viability of the *sensus literalis*. So Frei writes: "Type 2 tries to have it both ways, especially in its liberal expressions: the meaning of the stories is at once a re-presentation of a (general or at least repeatable) experience or mode-of-being-in-the-world, but it is also the specific person Jesus of Nazareth."[106] Frei suggests that the theological model of type 2 can be stated as follows: "Contemporary Christian theology is best understood as philosophical reflection upon the meanings present in common human experience and the meanings present in the Christian tradition."[107]

This approach becomes more pronounced in light of the MSC's designation of *shalom* and *humanization*—used by the European and North American study groups respectively and, for our purposes, interchangeably—as the "goal towards which God is working."[108] After arguing that the *missio Dei* should be interpreted to mean that "the primary context of mission is history ... [that] it is [God's] concern to be present in the actual life situation of every man," the MSC describes the phenomenon and telos of God's

---

103   *Church for Others*, 12f.
104   Frei, *Types of Christian Theology*, 30.
105   Frei, *Types of Christian Theology*, 30f.
106   Frei, *Types of Christian Theology*, 5f.
107   David Tracy, *Blessed Rage for Order* (New York: Seabury, 1976), 34, cited in Frei, *Types of Christian Theology*, 30.
108   *Church for Others*, 15.

presence as *shalom*—a concept it portrays not only as one that is found both in scripture and independent of it, but also as a concept to which the *whole Christian faith* and Jesus Christ himself can be reduced to:

> This single word summarizes all the gifts of the messianic age; even the name of the Messiah can simply be *shalom* . . . The Gospel is a Gospel of *shalom* . . . and the God proclaimed in this Gospel can often be called the God of *shalom* . . .

Shalom is not just the meaning and purpose of God's mission, it is the very essence of God's identity, "the name of the Messiah." Yet because this designation is derived independently of Christian scripture and tradition, the MSC believes it can also identify *shalom* as the meaning and purpose of all other societies. It is therefore the church's *sole* task, aided by sociology, "to recognize and point" to its already established native presence outside the Christian faith. As Frei describes type 2, the external analysis that supports and orients its view of Christian theology "supposes constant kinds of experience, even if their positive contents have to be articulated in all varying cultural terms . . . Meaning . . . and religious experience in particular, is the glue that allows external and internal description to be one, and Christian description or self-description is one instance of the general class 'religious meaningfulness.'"[109]

Type 2 theology as Frei conceives it is a fitting account for the theology of the MSC. Both share an insistence upon the necessity of external frameworks in discerning a meaning that is revealed to be inherent in Christian theology. A passage from the end of the North American study section of the MSC communicates this shared sensibility well:

> Questioning has become the "piety" of thinking. Nothing remains outside the act of questioning. Even the fundamental datum and presupposition of our theology, God, is no longer self-evident, and certainly no longer taken for granted. This openness very often reflects the discovery of the *world* with all its perplexities as the arena of God's action and therefore the authentic locus of *theology*.[110]

Like type 2 theology, the MSC is emphatic on the priority of the world before the church or tradition in determining the meaning and nature of God's presence. For despite its apparent insistence on the importance of

---

[109] Frei, *Types of Christian Theology*, 33.
[110] *Church for Others*, 91.

the particularities of Christianity, in the end, this correlation approach to Christian theology "is a matter of subsuming the specifically Christian under the general, experiential religious, as one 'regional' aspect."[111]

At this point, it bears repeating that Frei suggested he participated *aesthetically* in each of the five types. One way of interpreting this is to say that he empathized with the concerns operating behind each type. For the MSC and type 2 theologians more broadly, these concerns appear to be twofold, motivating them, on the one hand, to "claim the unsurpassability of the New Testament narratives' ascriptive reference to Jesus, so that they do not become exoteric or carnal shadows, in principle surpassable by a later and fuller spiritual 'reference' or 'disclosure,' but on the other to deny that this unsurpassability involves the invidious distinction between insiders and outsiders to the truth."[112] Of course, Frei too is concerned with the tension between Jesus' historical particularity and the question of God's universal presence. But he suggests that the approach of type 2 theology relies upon "an uneasy alliance of conflicting hermeneutical aims," collapsing under its own weight, and stretching the tradition of literal reading to the breaking point.[113] "It may well be an eminently worthy goal to have a theology that is at once Christian and liberal," Frei writes, "but founding it on this general hermeneutical theory is not a good means for achieving this aim."[114]

The type 2 approach to theology as represented in the MSC sets up a theology of religions in which Christ is interpreted through a "general context-invariant criteriology" which serves as a systematic framework through which Christ's presence in other faiths can be neatly worked out—a presence that is already assured in the initial adoption of the criteriology of correlation.[115] Race's "inclusivism" would be the closest analog to type 2 and the MSC. But the key difference between analyzing the MSC as an example of type 2 theology and analyzing it as "inclusivism" is that Frei's typology calls our attention not simply to the Christological component of the MSC but also the apologetic concerns that undergird it and the methodological assumptions, commitments, and conditions to which it appeals in response. Moreover, and as the MSC shows, such an approach to theology need not be formulated in direct response to

[111]   Frei, *Types of Christian Theology*, 34.
[112]   Frei, "'Literal Reading,'" 129f.
[113]   Frei, "'Literal Reading,'" 130.
[114]   Frei, "'Literal Reading,'" 130.
[115]   Frei, *Types of Christian Theology*, 45.

questions concerning other faiths. Frei's typology not only provides us with a means of analyzing Christian theology that is equally attentive to the way theological discourse is *formulated* as it is with its *conclusions*, but also allows us to see how particular versions of the theology of religions might emerge from or at least relate to wider discussions about theology itself.

We will turn now to Frei's type 3, which represents the heart of the typology in multiple ways. It is here that he sets out his interpretation of the theology of Friedrich Schleiermacher and his realization of its proximity to the theology of Karl Barth, representative of type 4—a development in Frei's reading of Schleiermacher that inspired Frei to develop the typology in the first place.[116] It will be argued that type 3 is represented in the IMC assembly of Jerusalem 1928. Although this assembly has been maligned as an example of the ecumenical movement's syncretistic susceptibility, as many of the continental delegates expressed at the time, this is an uncharitable assessment.[117] Frei's description of type 3 theology allows us to view Jerusalem and appreciate its complexity, with its emphasis on Christianity as a practical, rather than theoretical, discourse that is rooted in its ecclesial context *alongside* an appeal to the correlation between Christianity and other faiths and ideologies. Importantly, this correlation is established *not* by appeal to an overarching philosophical framework that undermines the *sensus literalis* and the unsubstitutability of Jesus Christ, as in type 2, but by a loose and even vague affirmation of "a great yearning" for meaning and moral guidance common to all of humanity—like Schleiermacher's "feeling of absolute dependence."[118]

Type 3: IMC Assembly of Jerusalem 1928

Following the World Mission Conference of Edinburgh 1910, Jerusalem 1928 was the first official assembly of the IMC (formed in 1921). Between Edinburgh and Jerusalem was the trauma of the Great War, which David Bosch describes as having "shattered to pieces the confidence that was an indispensable ingredient of the Social Gospel movement."[119] Bosch sees the later LFMI of 1932 as a response to this loss of optimism, particularly

---

[116]   Frei, *Types of Christian Theology*, 70.
[117]   Van Lin, *Shaking the Fundamentals*, 95–97; cf. P. Hutchinson, "Jerusalem 1928," *Christian Century*, December 6, 1928, 1490–91.
[118]   "The Christian Message," in *Report of the Jerusalem Meeting*, 1:401.
[119]   Bosch, *Transforming Mission*, 333.

in its redefining of mission as "preparation for world unity in civilization."[120] Jerusalem 1928 might then be viewed as a transitional moment.

For some, Jerusalem 1928 represents an attempt to combat a rising tide of secularism through its approach to mission as a view of the world religions as partners in the fight against unbelief, alongside an affirmation of Christianity's primacy and particularity.[121] But a closer look at the assembly report reveals that the deeper concern occupying the assembly was not secularism. Rather it was the relationship between the particularity of Jesus Christ's life, death, resurrection, and the remembrance of these events in the Gospels and church life, on the one hand, and the universality of Jesus—and not just his significance, but also the possibility of the universality of human desire for Jesus—on the other.

To the extent that Jerusalem 1928 did focus on secularism, and on a related appeal to syncretism as a defense against it, this is primarily found in Jerusalem 1928's "preparatory papers." These were a series of seven studies on different religions (and one on secularism) that were sent to all anticipated delegates to inform their discussions in Jerusalem and which would then be offered up before the assembly for its approval. These papers were much maligned before the assembly was even convened and were repudiated by many during the assembly itself.

Indeed, prior to the Jerusalem assembly, a number of IMC delegates from Continental Europe met in Cairo and issued a statement relaying their concerns that "the papers were drifting on the dangerous waters of syncretism and insufficiently worked out the essential difference and absolute uniqueness of Christianity."[122] Many felt that for this reason, in the Jerusalem meeting "the Apostolic obligation of the Church was not taken seriously, the givenness [sic] of the Message was not emphasized, the dangers of Syncretism were not heeded, and the need for conversion and regeneration was not stressed."[123] Echoing this assessment, Bishop Stephen Neill, who played a prominent role in the IMC, CWME, and WCC more broadly, went so far as to call Jerusalem 1928 "the nadir of the modern missionary movement ... the moment at which liberal theology exercised its most fatal influence on missionary thinking, the lowest valley out of which the missionary

---

[120]   Hocking, Re-thinking Missions, 8; cf. Bosch, Transforming Mission, 333.
[121]   Cf. Origen Vasantha Jathanna, The Decisiveness of the Christ Event and the Universality of Christianity in a World of Religious Plurality (Berne: Peter Lang, 1981), 496; Bosch, Transforming Mission, 491.
[122]   Report of the Jerusalem Meeting, 1:348.
[123]   Jathanna, Decisiveness of the Christ Event, 497.

movement has ever since been trying to make its way."[124] Such criticisms were not limited to Europeans, but were also leveled by IMC study groups in China and Japan, who faulted the preparatory studies for failing to depict the revelation of God in Christ as *sui generis*, stating: "No comparison with any other 'system' or profession is possible."[125]

Indeed, the preparatory papers tend to emphasize correlation as the key to understanding the relationship between Christianity and other faiths.[126] There is something common to human feeling that is discernible in all religions. In this sense, Christianity is an example of this feeling's expression, alongside other faiths. But Christianity, and more specifically Jesus Christ, is also held within these papers to explain the reason for this feeling's existence in the first place and to satisfy it uniquely and superlatively. With this tension underlying them, it is no surprise that the papers were both strongly criticized and endorsed during the assembly. One of their biggest critics was Hendrik Kraemer, who would play a central role in the IMC assembly in Tambaram 1938, where the "discontinuity" between Christianity and other faiths was emphasized instead. One of their most vociferous supporters was W. E. Hocking.[127]

In the midst of this discord, it fell to the future archbishop of Canterbury, William Temple, to produce a summary statement acceptable to all, titled "The Christian Message." It reads, in part:

> We rejoice to think that just because in Jesus Christ the light that lighteth every man shone forth in its full splendor, we find rays of that same light where He is unknown or even is rejected. We welcome every noble quality in non-Christian persons or systems as further proof that the Father, who sent His Son into the world, has nowhere left Himself without witness . . . *Thus, merely to give illustration, and making no attempt to estimate the spiritual value of other religions to their adherents*, we recognize as part of the one Truth that sense of the Majesty of God and the consequent reverence in worship, which are conspicuous in Islam; the deep sympathy for the world's sorrow and unselfish search for the way of escape, which

---

[124]   Neill, *Unfinished Task*, 151.

[125]   G. W. Sheppard, *Comments upon the Jerusalem Conference, Topic I. The Christian Life and Message in Relation to Non-Christian Systems*, WCC Archives, quoted in Van Lin, *Fundamentals*, 78.

[126]   A notable exception to this is W. H. T. Gairdner's paper on "Christianity and Islam," in *Report of the Jerusalem Meeting*, 1:191–229.

[127]   Bosch, *Transforming Mission*, 491.

are at the heart of Buddhism; the desire for contact with Ultimate Reality conceived as spiritual, which is prominent in Hinduism; the belief in a moral order of the universe and consequent insistence on moral conduct, which are inculcated by Confucianism; the disinterested pursuit of truth and of human welfare which are often found in those who stand for secular civilization but do not accept Christ as their Lord and Savior.[128]

The statement directly links aspects of Christian faith to those of other faiths. But it does so in an ad hoc way, affirming an underlying faith in the correlation between Christianity and other faiths and secular ideologies *not* by imposing a systematic account of this correlation and the reasons for it, as in the MSC and type 2 theology, but through a piecemeal interpretation of those external discourses and their resonance with the Christian tradition.

Temple goes on to make a distinction that speaks directly to the difference between its approach and that of the MSC. Where the MSC prefers to talk about *shalom* when discussing God's presence in the world, Jerusalem focuses on Jesus:

> Jesus Christ, as the crucified and the living One, as Savior and Lord, is also the center of the world-wide Gospel of the Apostles and the Church. Because He Himself is the Gospel, the Gospel is the message of the Church to the world. *It is more than a philosophical theory, more than a theological system; more than a program for material betterment.* The Gospel is rather the gift of a new world from God to this old world of sin and death; still more, it is the victory over sin and death, the revelation of eternal life in Him *who has knit together the whole family in heaven and on earth in the communion of saints, united in the fellowship of service, of prayer, and of praise.*[129]

Like Frei's type 3, then, it is important to underline that Jerusalem's approach to theology upholds a vision of Christian theology as self-description, a second-order account of first-order language particular to the Christian tradition and community.[130] But also like Frei's type 3, Jerusalem 1928's con-

---

[128]   *Report of the Jerusalem Meeting*, 1:410f., emphasis added.

[129]   *Report of the Jerusalem Meeting*, 1:403, emphasis added. This is a passage from a statement issued by World Conference on Faith and Order's August 1927 meeting in Lausanne, which the Jerusalem Assembly adopted as its "formulation of the Christian message."

[130]   Frei, *Types of Christian Theology*, 3, 35.

ception of Christian theology is one that, like type 2, is inherently correlated to other accounts of truth or criteria.[131] Unlike type 2, type 3 approaches this correlation without appeal to an overarching philosophical system for justification. Rather, for type 3 correlation between Christian theology and external discourses "meant at one and the same time the autonomy of two independent factors as well as their direct reciprocity, not their common coherence under an explanatory system."[132]

Type 3 theology takes external discourses to be correlated to internal descriptions of Christianity. In other words, philosophy and other *wissenschaftlich* disciplines are assumed to be in harmony with Christian faith. At the same time, it insists that these external discourses cannot be foundational for Christian theology and that our ability to work out the underlying nature of this correlation therefore remains fragmentary and ongoing. The MSC invokes the dynamic relativism of history in its designation of *shalom*—which indicates "all aspects of human life" and the essence of God's identity—as the criterion for identifying God's presence in the world, such that this external presence has descriptive *priority* over church, scripture, or the like. Type 3 theology rejects this approach.[133]

This is not to say that type 3 theology lacks a systematic principle of correlation, but that this principle is neither derived from a philosophical framework nor seen as immutable by virtue of a philosophical foundation. Frei writes of type 3:

> The systematic principle, that of immediate self-consciousness or "feeling," is the principle of correlation between the distinctively religious mode (including the Christian mode faith, as Schleiermacher calls it) and the general character of human being and human meaning . . . General criteria for meaning on the one side, the specificity of Christian faith and language on the other, and an ad hoc conceptual instrument for bringing them together—distinctiveness and reciprocity together. (But certainly no confusion between Christian doctrine and philosophical ideas about God!)[134]

Type 3 theology conceives of Christian theology as a kind of formal deliberation on something that is specific to a unique and historical tradition and culture while also being an expression of some universal human

---

[131]   Cf. *Report of the Jerusalem Meeting*, 1:290–91.
[132]   Frei, *Types of Christian Theology*, 67.
[133]   *Church for Others*, 14; Frei, *Types of Christian Theology*, 67.
[134]   Frei, *Types of Christian Theology*, 71.

condition—for Schleiermacher, the feeling of absolute dependence. This condition, however, is one that remains loosely defined. The order in which this line of thought proceeds is crucial, as Frei points out that Schleiermacher does *not* say: "From the feeling of absolute dependence I make the inferential move to the presence of God—no, the feeling itself is the relation; God is co-present in *that* specific mediation of my presence to myself."[135] There is a clear difference between this line of thought and Hick's, who does precisely what Frei suggests Schleiermacher does not: establish the epistemic validity of religious experience and from that infer the universal presence and experience of *the Real*.

Jerusalem 1928 neither approaches Christianity's relation to other religions and ideologies from a systematic philosophical foundation, nor does it cast this correlation as one suitable for an exhaustive explanation. Instead, it appeals to a loosely defined notion of the human tendency to view life as meaningful and to search for sources of support and guidance in identifying this meaning and in encouraging actions in service of it. We might describe Jerusalem's approach to correlation, framed in terms of a universal human search for meaning, as one that did not offer an interpretation without a remainder, but rather one "where a surd or problem of reading always remains . . . resist[ing] being totally resolved by any hermeneutical solvent applied to it."[136] Jerusalem 1928 describes this search for meaning in an ad hoc fashion, pointing out specific points of apparent correlation with specific traditions, emphasizing not *how* this correlation can be derived outside Christian theology, but simply that *there is* some kind of correlation.

Again, this ad hoc identification of specific correlates is supported by what Frei describes as a "systematic principle" that links "the distinctively religious mode . . . and the general character of human being and human meaning."[137] But as it was for Schleiermacher and type 3, this systematic principle does not depend on any foregoing system, philosophical or otherwise, but requires only a "low level of intellectual force . . . 'A little introspection,' rather like common sense—nothing high-powered here!"[138]

For Jerusalem 1928 just as for type 3, theology is not primarily an academic or philosophical discipline, though it is very much also legitimate territory for philosophy and academic investigation. Neither is theology

135   Frei, *Types of Christian Theology*, 71.
136   Hans Frei, "Conflicts in Interpretation," in *Theology and Narrative*, 165.
137   Frei, *Types of Christian Theology*, 71.
138   Frei, *Types of Christian Theology*, 71.

primarily an undertaking in dogmatics, though the communal, ecclesial context of Christian self-description is both the ground and the goal of theology. Frei observes that for type 3, "phenomenology and doctrinal content are correlated, but to talk of their identity would be inappropriate."[139] Like type 3, Jerusalem 1928 represents an approach to theology in which a correlation between the philosophical and the self-descriptive is affirmed such that it stipulates the reciprocal autonomy of these two sides. Frei summarizes this approach as follows:

> Theology as academic enterprise and as Christian self-description in the Church must be correlated. Philosophy and theology must be correlated. External and self-description of Christianity must be correlated, and in each case, two factors are autonomous yet reciprocally related, but that reciprocity and mutual autonomy is not explained by any more basic structure of thought under which the two factors would be included . . . General criteria for meaning on the one side, the specificity of Christian faith and language on the other, and an ad hoc conceptual instrument for bringing them together—distinctiveness and reciprocity together.[140]

Jerusalem 1928 has been decried by some as a failed assembly, lambasted even before it began for its preparatory papers' apparent turn to syncretism to repel the rise of secularism. But just as Frei's description of type 3 suggests that an interpretation of Schleiermacher as arch-liberal theologian is misleading and superficial, so does it suggest the same for Jerusalem 1928. Frei's account of type 3 suggests that our attention should focus not on the affirmation of correlation between Christianity and non-Christian discourses itself. Indeed, Frei sees some affirmation of this correlation as inevitably proceeding from a reading of the Gospels that prioritizes the *sensus literalis* and the identity of Jesus Christ. Rather, Frei's typology in general, and his revised interpretation of Schleiermacher in particular, points out that our attention should focus instead on the basis upon which this correlation is discerned.

More broadly, this is to say that the fundamental issue addressed by Frei's typology is not *whether* Christianity is correlated to external discourses—philosophical, theological, and otherwise—but *how* this correlation is conceived. Type 3 theology, with its low-flying and conceptually sparse appeal to a universal *feeling* or the like, represents for Frei a

[139]   Frei, *Types of Christian Theology*, 37.
[140]   Frei, *Types of Christian Theology*, 38, 71.

viable path to affirming this correlation without abandoning the *sensus literalis* or the unique significance of Jesus' life, death, and resurrection. In an address delivered at the Jerusalem assembly, Canon Oliver Chase Quick describes the same concerns and their expression at the assembly:

> The problem appeared to be that of reconciling the uniqueness of the Christian Gospel with its universality. In the preliminary papers the uniqueness had not been sufficiently brought out. The whole point was that the Christian Gospel was not one aspect of truth among others, because it was not ours at all. It was based on God's revelation of Himself to us. Our Gospel was based on the great act of God in Christ, and we could only make progress by going back to the great act of God in Christ. It was not even a question of the teaching of Christ being the fundamental thing. It was Christ Himself, and that included His teaching. They could not compare the teaching of Jesus with the teaching of Buddha and arrive at the uniqueness in that way.
>
> On the other hand there was the universality of the Gospel. The Gospel was like a strong light which was so strong that it found reflection of itself everywhere. Christ was the light that lighted every man. It was no cause for surprise to the Christian to find Him at work in lives outside organized Christianity.[141]

Quick, like Frei, suggests that there were dangers to be found on both sides of this question. An overly strong emphasis on universality leads to relativism. An overly strong emphasis on uniqueness leads to "what Marcion did with the Old Testament," describing the way in which an emphasis on Jesus' particularity can quickly become yet another hermeneutical system that inevitably disfigures the very figure it is supposedly oriented around, ironically obscuring the Jewishness of Jesus in its appeal to his particularity.[142]

Quick goes on to remind the conference that it must be able to see Christ as coming from both *Nazareth and Bethlehem*, where Nazareth represents "all the unexpected places out of which He came."[143] Quick argued that in evangelism, the gospel must always be presented in terms of non-Christian thought, for "a man found a new thing in Christianity, only because he also recognized it as something for which

---

[141]   *Report of the Jerusalem Meeting*, 1:290–91.
[142]   *Report of the Jerusalem Meeting*, 1:291.
[143]   *Report of the Jerusalem Meeting*, 1:291.

he had already been seeking."[144] But this cannot come at the expense of the uniqueness and particularity of Christian revelation—not because of the risk of syncretism, but because such uniqueness and particularity are constitutive of the irreducible particularity of God's self-revelation in Jesus Christ. Quick emphasizes that this revelation is not something we can domesticate anthropologically or phenomenologically, because it is an act of God's and because of the irreducibility of the human form in which this act of revelation occurs. Jesus is neither a composite of theological truths and ethical dictums, nor simply an exemplar or model of human faith and relation to the transcendent. On the one hand, this undermines any reductive or philosophically systematic approach to understanding the theological relationship between Christianity and other faiths. But on the other, Quick argues, this undergirds both the universality of Christ's presence and the inevitability of his presence outside Christian tradition—which Quick locates in embodied acts of non-Christians—impacting Christian faith itself. In Quick's terms, Jerusalem 1928, like type 3, tried to balance an interpretation of Jesus coming from both Nazareth and Bethlehem, affirming their correlation and congruence without reducing it to a philosophical principle.

Type 3 thus might be described as "a genuine if ambiguous counterpart" of the hospitality to the *sensus literalis* available in type 4.[145] There is indeed room here for a full-throated affirmation of the interpretive tradition centered on the prioritization of the plain sense and its acknowledgment of the revelatory uniqueness and decisiveness of Jesus Christ. But though this position is not derived from a philosophical or external discourse, as in type 2, it is held to be fully compatible with and correlated to such discourses. Christian faith is not viewed as one member of the general class of religions, and neither is Jesus' significance interpreted symbolically. But there is an abiding faith that the truths of Christianity correspond to those affirmed in other traditions, even if the nature of this correspondence remains mysterious. It is an emphasis on Jesus coming from Bethlehem, on the irreducible particularity of Jesus' life, death, and resurrection as narrated in the Gospels, that is prioritized, such that any ensuing correlation remains possible but uncertain.

---

[144]   *Report of the Jerusalem Meeting*, 1:291.
[145]   Hunsinger, "Hans Frei as Theologian," 263.

Type 4: IMC Assembly of Tambaram 1938

Type 4 theology affirms that while theology cannot proceed in isolation, it is from the church and scripture—the communal consensus that constitutes the *sensus literalis*—that theology receives its unique calling and directs its descriptive efforts.[146] As such, whatever correlation exists between Christian faith and external discourses or other faiths is entirely ad hoc, including even the very possibility of such correlation in the first place. At the start of one account of type 4 theology, Frei quotes a passage from Barth's *Church Dogmatics*: "As a theological discipline dogmatics is the scientific test to which the Christian church puts herself regarding the language about God which is peculiar to her."[147] Frei breaks this down as follows:

> (1) Theology involves a critical task, a "scientific" or *wissenschaft-lich* test. (2) What is done theologically is done within a religious *community*, the Church; it is the communal self-description of the community, rather than the individual creed of an individual person, even if he or she is Christian. (3) Theology constitutes an inquiry into the specific language peculiar to, in fact constitutive of, the specific semiotic community called the Christian Church or churches.[148]

Points two and three indicate that for type 4, theology is *not* approached from some preceding philosophical framework, but instead starts with the *sensus literalis*—i.e., the plain sense of scripture and the tradition of its communal interpretation and celebration. Point one affirms that this task is itself "critical" and subject to constraints—not imposed by some general or universal standard of consistency or coherence, but of *self*-consistency. And what constitutes self-consistency for theology is not provided by "a philosophy of reason based on some theory of a unitary human nature" but is determined by the particular "conceptual referent"—God—"within a specific conceptual or cultural-linguistic structure"—the *sensus literalis* of the Gospels and the church's engagement with it.[149]

While Frei emphasizes type 4's prioritization of the *sensus literalis* rather than Christology, it is this ordering that aids us in understanding both the areas of significant agreement and areas of diverse opinions in

---

[146]   Hunsinger, "Hans Frei as Theologian," 263.
[147]   Karl Barth, *Church Dogmatics*, I/1, trans. G. T. Thomson (Edinburgh: T&T Clark, 1936), 1, quoted in Frei, *Types of Christian Theology*, 78.
[148]   Frei, *Types of Christian Theology*, 78.
[149]   Frei, *Types of Christian Theology*, 79–80.

the history of Christology.[150] Broadly speaking, this Christological consensus includes assigning to Jesus "an irreducibly unique and unsurpassable place in relation to salvation," such that "salvation here and now" is "dependent on one person then and there."[151] Type 4's prioritization of the literal sense means that Jesus' significance is not derived from a general theory, even one as low flying as Schleiermacher's. Rather, it is "the particularity of Jesus, enacted in and inseparable from history, that makes him significant for salvation and provides the criteria for what the criteria for such significance are."[152]

This kind of approach is clearly discernible in the IMC's third assembly, held in Tambaram 1938. Following the frustrations surrounding Jerusalem 1928 and its widely disparaged preparatory papers, Tambaram was conceived differently from the start. In advance of the meeting, the IMC requested that Hendrik Kraemer—who had impressed many at Jerusalem 1928 as chair of the section on Islam—write a book on evangelism in the modern world, with special reference to the non-Christian religions.[153] Significantly, the IMC requested that the book identify "the biblical method of approaching the great non-Christian religions."[154] If this assignment was not imposing enough, the final invitation went even farther, identifying Kraemer's task as follows: "To state the fundamental position of the Christian church as a witness-bearing body in the modern world, relating this to conflicting views of the attitude to be taken by Christians towards other faiths and dealing in detail with the evangelistic approach to the great non-Christian faiths"—a charge Kraemer recognized as "impossible" to fulfill.[155]

What he eventually produced—*The Christian Message in a Non-Christian World*—was a lengthy treatise, employing theological terminology of sufficient complexity to have received complaints from the IMC leadership.[156] Yet, as in Frei's type 4 theology, the critical complexity of Kraemer's approach was not tied to a general theory of explanation, derived independently of the Christian tradition and put in service

[150]   Hunsinger, "Hans Frei as Theologian," 263.

[151]   Frei, *Types of Christian Theology*, 63, 62; cf. Hunsinger, "Hans Frei as Theologian," 263.

[152]   Frei, *Types of Christian Theology*, 88.

[153]   Carl F. Hallencreutz, *Kraemer towards Tambaram: A Study in Hendrik Kraemer's Missionary Approach* (Lund: Gleerup, 1966), 263.

[154]   Van Lin, *Shaking the Fundamentals*, 158.

[155]   International Missionary Council Ad Interim Committee Minutes, Old Jordans 1936, cited in Yates, *Christian Mission*, 108; Hendrik Kraemer, *The Christian Message in a Non-Christian World* (London: Edinburgh House Press, 1938), v.

[156]   Van Lin, *Shaking the Fundamentals*, 160; Kraemer, *Christian Message*, v.

of attending to the relationship between Christianity and other faiths. Rather, the rigor of Kraemer's approach was in service of his argument for the necessity of returning to the Gospels in attempts to articulate the motivation and practice of Christian mission.[157]

Kraemer's contribution was by no means universally appreciated at Tambaram 1938.[158] The unease that some had with his account of Christian theology and the theology of religions is alluded to in one of the assembly's summary statements, where it was noted that, on the question of "whether the non-Christian religions as total systems of thought and life may be regarded as in some sense or to some degree manifesting God's revelation, Christians are not agreed."[159] Nonetheless, Kraemer's work served to reframe the discussion in enormously important ways, particularly in its emphasis on the priority of acknowledging Jesus' unique significance for Christian faith in light of the church's traditional interpretation of scripture—an emphasis that would remain intact within the ecumenical movement up to the MSC of 1967. And although Kraemer has been cast as the paragon of ecumenical exclusivism and champion of an emphasis on the *discontinuity* between Christianity and other faiths, this is mostly caricature, somewhat akin to those foisted upon Barth and even Frei, based partly on a misreading of Kraemer's intended *methodological* criticism of the fulfillment and social-gospel strains of Christian theology championed at previous IMC assemblies.[160] So although we are here focusing on Tambaram 1938 as a whole and not Kraemer's contribution alone, it is impossible to do this without first considering Kraemer's impact.

Kraemer rejected the divide that had sprung up within the ecumenical movement, prominently displayed at Jerusalem 1928, between continental Europeans and others on the theology of religions. Where continental European Christians tended to appeal to dogma in arguing for a separation between Christianity and other faiths, others, most prominently Anglo-Americans, typically advocated for an approach that emphasized experience, values, or other general frameworks that suggested a basic

---

[157]   Van Lin, *Shaking the Fundamentals*, 160; cf. Bassham, *Mission Theology*, 22–26.

[158]   Van Lin, *Shaking the Fundamentals*, 159–211; Bassham, *Mission Theology*, 25f.

[159]   "The Witness of the Church in Relation to the Non-Christian Religions, The New Paganisms and the Cultural Heritage of the Nations," in *The Tambaram Series: The Authority of the Faith*, vol. 1 (London: Oxford University Press, 1939), 211.

[160]   *Tambaram Series*, 1:1–23; cf. Alan Race, *Christians and Religious Pluralism: Patterns in the Christian Theology of Religions* (London: SCM Press, 1993), 16–24.

commonality between Christianity and other faiths.[161] As a later commentator described it, in terms similar to those that Frei might have used, the nature of his approach "meant that Kraemer was fighting on two fronts: against a liberalism which threatened to make Christian belief a form of religious idealism; and against an orthodoxy which made of it a set of revealed truths."[162] Kraemer insisted that both sides of this debate were indefensible, being equally "determined by cultural and psychological considerations, very valuable in themselves, but of secondary importance."[163] Frei sounded a similar note when responding to Carl Henry: "I am looking for a way that looks for a relation between Christian theology and philosophy that disagrees with a view of certainty and knowledge which liberals and evangelicals hold in common."[164]

Kraemer argued that the "missionary has to rise above these attitudes by letting himself be inspired by motives, sprung from the essence of the gospel; he must try to define the real religious issue, that transcends all cultural and psychological issues."[165] Like Frei's account of type 4 theology, Kraemer was concerned with the inclination among his peers to substitute external disciplines for scripture as the cornerstone of Christian theology. As in type 4, Kraemer saw this as a result of modern theology's insistent search for "a so-called wider and more inclusive standpoint from which to probe and determine the significance and meaning of the religious dream of mankind."[166] Echoing Frei's own account of type 4 theology, Kraemer argues that this "simply means that there is another ultimate standard than Christ, a so-called general religious a priori by which even Christ, who upsets all human standards, is measured."[167] Where Frei uses the term *sensus literalis* to refer to type 4's "ruled use" of scripture, grounded in the church's tradition of prioritizing the literal or *realistic* sense, Kraemer appeals to "biblical realism."[168]

---

[161]   Van Lin, *Shaking the Fundamentals*, 160.
[162]   Evert Jansen Schoonhoven, "Tambaram 1938," *International Review of Mission* 67, no. 267 (1978): 310.
[163]   "Outline of Book by Dr. Kraemer," 2, WCC Archives, quoted in Van Lin, *Shaking the Fundamentals*, 160.
[164]   Frei, "Response to 'Narrative Theology: An Evangelical Appraisal,'" in *Theology and Narrative*, 211.
[165]   "Outline of Book by Dr. Kraemer," 2, WCC Archives, quoted in Van Lin, *Shaking the Fundamentals*, 160.
[166]   *Tambaram Series*, 1:9.
[167]   *Tambaram Series*, 1:9.
[168]   Kraemer, *Christian Message*, vi–vii.

This is to say that Kraemer's take on Christian theology, the IMC's selection of him as the central interlocutor for the sections on Christian mission and other faiths, and the request that he focus his attention on the Christian message, led Tambaram to take a different approach than that of Jerusalem 1928. Whereas Jerusalem had begun its deliberations by commissioning papers on other traditions in relation to Christianity, at Tambaram, the IMC began with an account of Christian faith grounded in scripture and the church, attempting to describe the Christian message and its view on other faiths. Some have portrayed this as a dogmatic, exclusionary, and unnecessarily narrow focus, but this misplaced accusation obscures that it was partly offered in response to the growing inclination toward dogmatism that Kraemer believed was a misguided response to the threat of secularism.[169]

Indeed, at Jerusalem 1928 Kraemer had been a prominent critic of the tendency to blame secularism alone for the decline in Christian adherence, arguing that the problem was just as much European Christianity's lack of a coherent view of life and its misplaced focus on "a set of detached dogmas."[170] This is not an accusation of dogmatic liberalism, but of a more general over-reliance on dogma. It was, in Kraemer's opinion, not secular society but Christian churches and missionaries that had failed to provide a comprehensive, "Christian view of life, of the world, and of God."[171] "The representatives of religion themselves, because of their own diluted conception of religion," Kraemer wrote, "have contributed to this rise of the notion of God's irrelevancy."[172] For this and other reasons, Kraemer argued it was not to dogma, but to Jesus, as revealed in scripture and celebrated in the church, where our attention should be first directed.

Having said that, Kraemer also found fault with theological liberalism itself. Kraemer criticized Jerusalem's preparatory papers not by attacking their objective but their method, arguing that although their approach was emblematic of the aforementioned incoherent view of life and the diluted conception of Christianity, it was indeed crucial for Christian evangelists to have "an intense longing to discover the spiritual values in other religions."[173] What he resisted was *not* the possibility of correla-

---

169   Cf. Stanley J. Samartha, "Mission in a Religiously Plural World: Looking beyond Tambaram 1938," *International Review of Mission* 77, no. 306 (1988): 312; Race, *Christians and Religious Pluralism*, 16–24.

170   *Report of the Jerusalem Meeting*, 1:283.

171   *Report of the Jerusalem Meeting*, 1:283.

172   Kraemer, *Christian Message*, 14.

173   *Report of the Jerusalem Meeting*, 1:349.

tion between Christianity and non-Christian traditions, but rather the systematic imposition of such correlation, and the preparatory papers' pursuit of this by appealing to sources or frameworks external to Christianity. Again, confronting the suggestion that comparative religion had cemented within Christianity a longing to discover "spiritual values" in other faiths, Kraemer does not discount the possibility of discerning God's presence in other religions but laments that it "was a matter for reproach" for Christians "that the science of comparative religion had been the first to give this to us."[174]

In other words, Kraemer's emphasis on discontinuity between Christianity and other faiths is more methodological criticism than dogmatic affirmation. It was a wholesale rejection neither of the existence of good elements in other faith traditions nor of the possibility of discerning God's presence outside the confines of Christian faith. Rather, it expressed Kraemer's belief that "theologically speaking, 'nature', 'reason' and 'history' do not, if we want to think stringently, afford preambles, avenues or lines of development towards the realm of grace and truth as manifest in Jesus Christ."[175] At the same time, something similar could be said for even the most scrupulous prioritization of Christian dogma. For this reason, Kraemer suggested that the relationship between Christianity and the world beyond it must be premised upon neither dogma nor philosophy, but instead on a hermeneutic he called "biblical realism," which emerges from the church's traditional embrace of "the apostolic urgency of gladly witnessing to God and his saving and redeeming Power through Christ."[176] In other words, Kraemer argued for the primacy of the *sensus literalis* of the Gospels and for the centrality of the church as its community of use.[177] This is also to say that Kraemer fits well in type 4 theology, alongside Frei's selection of Karl Barth as its quintessential representative.[178]

---

[174] *Report of the Jerusalem Meeting*, 1:349.

[175] *Tambaram Series*, 1:2f.

[176] Kraemer, *Christian Message*, vi–vii.

[177] Frei, "'Literal Reading,'" 146.

[178] Some suggest Kraemer's theology falls closer to that of Brunner than to Barth, considering *Kraemer's own* endorsement of Brunner's affirmation of "points of contact" between God and humanity. Frei's interpretation of Barth suggests this distinction, including its presence in Kraemer's own thought, misconstrues the methodological nature of Barth and Brunner's divergence. Kraemer, *Christian Message*, 130–41; Hans Frei, "Niebuhr's Theological Background," in *Faith and Ethics: The Theology of H. Richard Niebuhr*, ed. Paul Ramsey (New York: Harper & Row, 1957), 43f.; Race, *Christians and Religious Pluralism*, 16ff.; Van Lin, *Shaking the Fundamentals*, 180–81; Yates, *Christian Mission*, 113.

It is here worth emphasizing an important difference between type 3 and type 4 theology concerning the reciprocity between theology and other discourses that is easily misunderstood. While insisting upon the communal and practical nature of Christian theology, type 3 also assumes there is a correlation between "general experience, God-consciousness, and the specific figure of Jesus of Nazareth."[179] Type 4, while sharing type 3's emphasis on theology's practical concern and its ecclesial context, rejects not only any "context-invariant criteriology" as prolegomena to Christian dogmatic theology, but also any principled affirmation of such correlation.

Rather, type 4 seeks "to exhibit the rules or fragments of rules implicit in the ruled use of language which is the sign system of the sociolinguistic community called the Church."[180] But this should not be construed as opposition to the possibility of correlation. For type 4 maintains a hopeful faith in the *possibility* of correlation of Christian theology to external discourses while refusing to approach it systematically. Frei explains:

> One can therefore designate no relationship *in principle* between external descriptions of Christianity and Christian self-description, but one must not exclude as a matter of principle the possibility of overlap at specific, possibly even mutually contradictable, points of actual investigation . . . The relationship between internal self-description and external description thus remains ad hoc, with freedom for each side, possible family resemblance, and obedience to the criterion of the priority of Christian self-description as the task of the Church.[181]

This is not a rejection of correlation itself, but a refusal to premise Christian theology upon its principled affirmation. Writing specifically about Barth, Frei suggests that the "problem was that of *overcoming* (rather than either denying or affirming) a theological method whose basic tenet and constant factor is 'relationality,' 'religion,' 'the condition of man' or any other anthropological datum."[182]

The difference between type 3 and type 4 is therefore not rooted in a divide concerning the possibility of correlation itself. Rather, it is more a difference in theological sensibility concerning how such correlation might be conceived. This is contrary to Race's depiction of Barth and Kraemer as rejecting the theological significance of philosophy or other faiths—not to

---

[179]   Frei, *Types of Christian Theology*, 82.
[180]   Frei, *Types of Christian Theology*, 45.
[181]   Frei, *Types of Christian Theology*, 45f.
[182]   Frei, "Niebuhr's Theological Background," 44.

mention his absurd characterization of their theology as dealing "with the mystery of God and man's relationship to him in so hasty a manner."[183] The *Church Dogmatics* is many things, but hasty it is not.

For type 4, "first, theology is not philosophically founded, and, second, what makes theology an orderly and systematic procedure . . . [is] not a set of universal, formal criteria which are certain and all-fields-encompassing and can therefore be stated apart from the context of specific application."[184] Rather, "fundamental theology . . . is internal to, part of, the dogmatic enterprise. It is not a procedure for correlating theology to other disciplines in the academic spectrum."[185] In other words, type 4 represents a view of theology in which priority is given to scripture's plain sense and to the church's ruled use-in-context over any external or philosophical concerns.

This reveals two very different but equally important aspects of type 4 theology. On the one hand, the rejection of philosophy or other external discourses as providing theology with an interpretive framework is so thorough that even the most noncontroversial postulates of reason like the law of noncontradiction "is acceptable in theology only within limits," as, for example, in the Chalcedonian formula, which John Hick has compared to saying that a "circle drawn with a pencil on paper is also a square."[186] With this, Frei notes that one might take type 4 theology as actually occupying the extreme end of Frei's typological spectrum, wholly insulating itself from even the most basic and seemingly noncontroversial external frameworks.

On the other hand, the rejection of an external framework for Christian theological inquiry itself allows type 4 to affirm the possibility of discerning overlap in the present, and even of affirming the possibility of ultimate coherence in the future, between theology and other discourses. This is to say that type 4's rejection of external frameworks is so consistently applied that this very rejection itself cannot be a "*principled* priority choice" but rather "a *pragmatic* priority choice."[187] Type 4 theology subordinates any "rules to the actual use of the language [so] that one will not be tempted to prescribe rules for it but allow the rules to be fragmentary if that is what the proper and consistent use of the language seems to imply."[188]

---

[183]   Race, *Christians and Religious Pluralism*, 25.
[184]   Frei, *Types of Christian Theology*, 39.
[185]   Frei, *Types of Christian Theology*, 39.
[186]   Frei, *Types of Christian Theology*, 45; John Hick, "Jesus and the World Religions," in *The Myth of God Incarnate*, ed. John Hick (London: SCM Press, 1977), 178.
[187]   Frei, *Types of Christian Theology*, 42f.
[188]   Frei, *Types of Christian Theology*, 42. Cf. Frei, "Niebuhr's Theological Background," 43f.

In other words, type 4 theology cannot appeal to a principle of non-correlation between Christianity and other discourses and faith traditions, because *to do so would be to invoke an external framework*.[189] What is more, Frei argues that Barth and type 4 affirm that external and internal modes of discourse "belong together fully" even if we lack the means of conceiving the true nature of this unity, much less the apparatus for its systematic identification. So, similar to type 3, there is even in type 4 an underlying faith in the reciprocity between theology and other discourses. But unlike type 3, the nature of this reciprocity is not subject to a principled formulation, even one as broad as Schleiermacher's feeling of absolute dependence. It is instead left to be encountered in an ad hoc and piecemeal fashion: "do not call it a paradox, a principled violation of the criterion of noncontradiction [sic] supposedly acceptable on a loftier plane. No, the internal coherence of the two modes of discourse is fragmentary; its fullness as the logos or rationale of faith, hidden but not absent."[190]

As with Kraemer's prioritization of "biblical realism"—a hermeneutical approach that like Barth's is less systematic than *ruled*, based on its centrality in the communal tradition of Christian biblical interpretation—type 4's emphasis on the literal sense of scripture does not exclude the influence of external discourses or the possibility of reciprocity between Christian theology and other traditions.[191] In fact, for type 4, the prioritization of the literal sense means its interpretation is best conceived as *redescription*, a rather low-key designation in comparison to the interpretive possibilities affirmed in types 1 and 2. In redescription of the literal sense of scripture, correlation operates as an "article of faith" and not a systematized objective that might bend the plain sense of the text itself as necessary to that end:

> The text means what it says, and so the reader's redescription [sic] is just that, a redescription and not the discovery of the text as symbolic representation of something else more profound. But in the *process* of redescription we can—and indeed cannot do other than—employ our own thought structures, experiences, conceptual schemes; there is neither an explicit mode for showing how to *correlate* these things with the job of redescription, nor is there a fundamental conflict between them. Without knowing success or lack of

---

[189]   DeHart suggests that this is also a key difference between Frei and Lindbeck, undermining the view of Frei as a "post-modern particularist." DeHart, *Trial of the Witnesses*, 149–239.
[190]   Frei, *Types of Christian Theology*, 43.
[191]   Frei, *Types of Christian Theology*, 45.

it in any given case beforehand, it is an article of faith that it *can* be done; it *is* done.[192]

Type 4 theology's prioritization of the *sensus literalis* and its rejection of an antecedent and independent interpretive framework for Christian theology sits alongside an abiding faith in correlation while also casting both the correlation itself and its identification as fragmentary and *ongoing*. In this sense, type 4 calls for an unceasing engagement between theology and other traditions, one that refuses to determine the extent or object of their reciprocity without abandoning a faith in this reciprocity, however presently restrained its account of such reciprocity might be.

Having focused on Kraemer's own foundational work for Tambaram 1938, we turn now to the wider assembly and its summary statement. Though the delegates at Tambaram 1938 were hardly united behind Kraemer's vision, his influence is easily discerned in the summary statement issued at the assembly's conclusion.

It is worth noting that Kraemer himself was deeply disappointed with the depth of the discussion on his work and the account of Christian theology he had laid out before the assembly.[193] In a synopsis of his *Christian Message* published in the assembly report issued after the assembly, he lamented:

> As regards the problem of how to relate the Christian revelation and Christianity as a historical religion with the non-Christian religions . . . The amount of agreement and mutual understanding *in regard to this problem*, reached at Tambaram, has been so appallingly small that we in the first place stand in need of a patient endeavor to understand and probe each other's presuppositions and starting-points.[194]

Yet, the very thing that Kraemer bemoans as being absent from Tambaram—a methodological awareness of "each other's presuppositions and starting-points"—might in retrospect be counted as his most significant contribution to the ecumenical discussion on Christianity and other faiths, insofar as he provided the assembly with an account of his own. Moreover, it might be said that the hope for mutual understanding Kraemer expresses here is precisely what Frei's typology offers.

---

192   Frei, *Types of Christian Theology*, 44.
193   *Tambaram Series*, 1:7; Van Lin, *Shaking the Fundamentals*, 193.
194   *Tambaram Series*, 1:7.

At the Edinburgh 1910 IMC assembly, and, to a lesser degree Jerusalem 1928, the focus had been largely on *non-Christian* faiths, the possibilities of identifying a systematic framework for conceiving their relationship to Christianity, and the subsequent cataloging and interpretation of specific points of contact. For some twenty-five years following Tambaram, however, the IMC and later the CWME and WCC would shift their approach, exploring the theological underpinnings of Christian mission rather than mining other faiths for Christian content.[195] Tambaram 1938 was an important turning point for the ecumenical discussion not just on the relationship between Christianity and other faiths but also on reasserting the place of scripture and church in the prolegomena to mission theology and the theology of religions.

And although such a shift might imply a static vision of Christian faith, isolated from external discourses or traditions and exulting in its superiority, Tambaram's summary statement takes an approach echoing that of type 4. To start, Kraemer's insistence upon the priority of scripture's plain sense and of the church as the community responding to and interpreting it, is first invoked not in a spirit of ecclesial triumphalism but of judgment on the church:

> It is in and to this world that the Church must conduct its mission, seeking to repossess and proclaim its God-given message in all its truth and power . . . but we see also His judgment upon our churches . . . We must come too in deep humility, knowing that no merely human deed or word of ours will suffice to meet humanity's need. God's words and deeds alone are the healing of its sickness. Yet it is still His will to utter and accomplish them through His Church. His promise is still that His strength shall be made manifest in our weakness.[196]

Echoes of the central question for type 4 theology as framed by Frei— "Does Christian discourse come from [God] and move toward him, and is it in accordance with him?"—are conspicuous here.[197] So too is the notion of theology as "specific and critical Christian self-description and self-examination by the Church of its language."[198] In Tambaram's summary statement, affirmations of the primacy of scripture and church, and indeed of the uniqueness and unsubstitutability of Jesus Christ, are cast

---

195   Cf. Bassham, *Mission Theology*, 23–67.
196   *Tambaram Series*, 1:187–88.
197   Frei, *Types of Christian Theology*, 39.
198   Frei, *Types of Christian Theology*, 40.

not so much to invoke judgments against other faiths as to highlight the shortcomings of Christians themselves.

In its direct reflections on non-Christian religions, Tambaram charts a course that altogether avoids assessing other faiths for their salvific potential or ethical value, a pronounced difference from the IMC assemblies that preceded it. Tambaram identifies no *system* or *method* that governs the analysis of other faiths, independently or in terms of their relation to Christianity. Instead, the section of the Tambaram statement on non-Christian religions begins simply by affirming: "Our message is that God was in Christ reconciling the world unto Himself."[199] On the one hand, this is interpreted to mean that "we do not think that God has left Himself without a witness in the world at any time."[200] On the other hand, "all religious insight and experience have to be fully tested before God in Christ; and we see that this is true as well within as outside the Christian Church."[201] There is a tension here that the Tambaram statement refuses to resolve—a key aspect of type 4 theology. Types 1 and 2 erase any tension through the subordination of self-description to philosophy, type 3 acknowledges the tension but seeks a dialectical resolution.[202] On the other side, the isolation of Christian theology of type 5 rejects even the possibility of tension. Type 4, in contrast, acknowledges the friction between theology and external discourses, refusing to obliterate it while also affirming its faith in the possibility of correlation and refusing to systematize it.

Tambaram's summary statement goes on to list three consequences for the Christian approach to those of other faiths that result from its formulation of Christian theology. These three outcomes are tied to three principles put forward by Kraemer, and those characteristics Frei associates with type 4. When Kraemer explains that, for him, theology's standpoint must be *within* the realm of Christian revelation," the assembly's statement suggests that *for this reason* "witnesses for Christ must have a deep and sincere interest in the religious life of those among whom they are sent . . . for Christ's sake and for the sake of those people."[203] Care for and attention to the specific beliefs, traditions and practices of other faith communities is an essential component of a Christian encounter with such communities and the search for God's presence therein *because* Christian theologians approach Christianity from "within" the realm of the *sensus*

---

[199] *Tambaram Series*, 1:200.
[200] *Tambaram Series*, 1:200.
[201] *Tambaram Series*, 1:201.
[202] Frei, *Types of Christian Theology*, 30ff., 65ff.
[203] *Tambaram Series*, 1:7, 201.

literalis, without an overarching philosophical or anthropological system accounting for religious phenomena in general.

Kraemer's second principle "is that a persistent and attentive listening to the Bible is essential," rejecting "the tendency to live with the Bible as far as religious edification is concerned, but not to take it seriously as the valid and normative guide for our theological thinking."[204] By framing an interpretation that takes the Bible "seriously" and "normatively" in opposition to one that centers on religious edification, Kraemer implies that the Bible must not be made to fit into any preconceived interpretive system. It must instead be allowed to continuously challenge and reconstruct our views of God and the world. Similarly, the Tambaram assembly's second principle involves a rejection of fulfillment theology and the idea "that the Scriptures of these religions could take the place of the Old Testament as introductions to the Christian Gospel."[205]

Centered on a rejection of any procedure for interpreting the Bible that yields a complete and final answer without remainder, both Kraemer and the Tambaram statement echo type 4's wariness of domesticating scripture.[206] Without reflective and critical attention to our own "various ideologies, resulting from and molded by the stream of Christian tradition and experience and by various currents of ancient or modern thought," Kraemer argues that we risk treating the Bible as "an interesting and highly important piece of religious literature, but not a unique book with a standard of its own, as containing the apostolic witness to God's dealing with mankind, the Word of God."[207]

Though obviously different in important respects, fulfillment theology represents one way of interpreting the Bible that neither treats critically the incentives and assumptions underlying its appeal and application, nor grants the Bible the prioritized power to constantly reshape and challenge our own interpretation of it. Instead, the method underpinning fulfillment theology becomes the lens through which we interpret scripture. In the terms Frei uses to describe type 4, in rejecting fulfillment theology, Tambaram affirms "that the text or *the* meaning of the text is regarded as simply autonomous . . . a semiotic world of its own, regardless of its reception."[208] Likewise, Kraemer warns that the "discrepancy between the

---

204   *Tambaram Series*, 1:9.
205   *Tambaram Series*, 1:201.
206   Frei, "Conflicts in Interpretation," 165.
207   *Tambaram Series*, 1:9–10.
208   Frei, *Types of Christian Theology*, 85.

religious (or edificatory) and theological application of the Bible is . . . a secret poison that subtly undermines the sincerity and strength of our theological thinking."[209]

Kraemer's third principle is that "the results of the so-called comparative study of religion" must be given "their due weight and influence . . . to try to understand [other faiths]—not in the logical or intellectual sense of the word, but in that of sympathetic understanding of their essential nature and function—according to the *intention* that animates them and gives them their peculiar life and attitude."[210] Similarly, the summary statement's third and final principle declares that Christian churches in traditionally non-Christian societies should be rooted in "the Christian heritage and fellowship of the Church Universal . . . But they should also be rooted in the soil of their own country."[211] This is an affirmation that churches in majority non-Christian countries should be informed by the local cultures and traditions—external discourses, in Frei's terms. Similarly, Kraemer insists on empathetic, patient, and unceasing study of the world religions, while pointing out that this "must never become our authoritative guide."[212] So construed, Kraemer suggests that comparative religion can help Christians to adopt attitudes of both "downright intrepidity and radical humility" toward the world religions.[213]

In other words, Kraemer points out that Christians cannot be faithful without attending to the historical or secular complexities and particularities that shape their own lives and the lives of non-Christians. The summary statement extends this significantly by emphasizing that such attention will inevitably and rightly influence our interpretation and celebration of scripture: "The Gospel should be expressed and interpreted in indigenous forms, and . . . in methods of worship, institutions, literature, architecture, etc., the spiritual heritage of the nation and country should be taken into use."[214] Both comparative religion and an approach to Christian worship that attends to the resonances and tensions between the "Church Universal" and the local community are framed as opportunities to acquire an "intrepidity and radical humility" befitting the tension

---

[209]   Frei, *Types of Christian Theology*, 10.
[210]   Frei, *Types of Christian Theology*, 10–11.
[211]   Frei, *Types of Christian Theology*, 202.
[212]   Frei, *Types of Christian Theology*, 11.
[213]   Frei, *Types of Christian Theology*, 12.
[214]   Frei, *Types of Christian Theology*, 202.

upheld in type 4 between the mystery of God's presence in the world and the particular unsubstitutability of the identity of Jesus Christ.[215]

As mentioned above, Kraemer left Tambaram bitterly disappointed in the lack of consensus achieved there. But with the benefit of hindsight, we can affirm the decades-long influence Tambaram had over the ecumenical discussion on the theology of religions. Despite, or perhaps *because* of, the disputes that accompanied the reception of Kraemer's theology at Tambaram, we find here a general approach to Christian theology that reflects Frei's description of type 4. Tambaram prodded the ecumenical movement to eschew systematic accounts of the theological significance of other faiths, and to embrace an approach to Christian theology that prioritized the realistic sense of Christian scripture and its communal use. Jesus is not a symbol, a principle, or a constellation of truths that can be detected in the scriptures of other texts. By abandoning this systematic approach and centering its hermeneutic on "the rules or fragments of rules implicit in the ruled use of language which is the sign system of the sociolinguistic community called the Church," Tambaram can be seen as advancing a type 4 approach to Christian theology that remains hospitable to the figure of Jesus as the center of Christian continuity and communal self-description.[216]

This yields a view of Christianity's theological relationship to other faiths that allows for both hope in their correlation and the acknowledgment that they might not be compatible. For all the primacy type 4 affords the communal rules of scriptural interpretation, Frei makes clear that they remain piecemeal and ambiguous in any appeal to, or rejection of, correlation to external discourses. For they are *rules* and not a *method*. Frei explained the difference between the methodological systems that characterize other types and the *ruled use* that distinguishes type 4's approach to biblical interpretation:

> To that we might well reply, "That's all very well, but now tell us *how* to apply these rules." But there's the rub, and the rub is the point. If he could tell us how, the rule would no longer be a rule but a method, a systematic and general theory for *how* to read. "Subordination" of a scheme to the scriptural text means inescapably taking a real risk, in the confidence that in, with, and under our identical or very different, indispensable auxiliary philosophical tools we may be able to

[215]   Frei, *Types of Christian Theology*, 12.
[216]   Frei, *Types of Christian Theology*, 45; DeHart, *Trial of the Witnesses*, 139.

reach agreement or at least mutually understanding disagreement in the reading of crucial biblical texts.[217]

Contrary to the disappointment of Kraemer and the Tambaram assembly at their failure to reach a final consensus on the theology of religions, from the perspective of type 4, this is a salutary and inevitable result of Tambaram's "ruled" approach to Christian theology.[218] With Kraemer's writings and the summary statements of Tambaram, Frei's type 4 represents an approach to Christian theology and its relation to other discourses and traditions that is both fixed and flexible at the same time, and where the flexibility comes *in light of* and not *in spite of* its fixed or *ruled* aspects.

Type 5 theology will place an even greater emphasis on the significance of rules in Christian theology. Frei describes type 4's conception of rules as "the formal or, more likely, informal rules that the members of the community follow with regard to the reading of the sacred text . . . learned in or by application." In other words, type 4 treats such rules not as absolutes but as "guides or signposts for orientation."[219] The fifth and final type in Frei's typology, however, is characterized by its unwavering emphasis on the rule differentiating internal and external discourses—a rule so resolutely and universally applied that Frei will argue it operates more like the philosophical methodology of type 1 than type 4. We turn now to type 5 and the 1966 Congress on the Church's Worldwide Mission statement, the "Wheaton Declaration."

Type 5: Wheaton Declaration of 1966

Frei's account of type 5 poses some challenges in applying it to the history of twentieth-century ecumenical discussion. This is largely a result of Frei's selection of the philosopher of religion D. Z. Phillips as its representative. By centering his description of type 5 around a philosopher, Frei points out the perils of a view of Christian theology that supplants Kant for Wittgenstein in the name of particularity, an approach he depicts as invoking an external, universal, and absolute rule to justify an entirely internal and particular approach to Christian theology. But in using a philosopher instead of a theologian to ground his account of a radical isolationist approach to Christian faith, Frei's typology of Christian theology risks obfuscating the relationship between type 5 and theology.

---

[217]   Frei, *Types of Christian Theology*, 86.
[218]   *Tambaram Series*, 1:211.
[219]   Frei, *Types of Christian Theology*, 48.

That said, type 5 *does* depict a vision of Christian theology similar to the kind demonstrated by some evangelicals.[220] Indeed, an evangelical gathering at Wheaton College in 1966 appears to advance a vision of Christian theology very much in line with that of Frei's type 5. Such theology will not include overt Wittgensteinian pronouncements akin to Phillips' "philosophy can claim justifiably to show what is meaningful in religion only if it is prepared to examine religious concepts in the contexts from which they derive their meaning."[221] But, even absent any appeals to Wittgenstein, Wheaton 1966 still represents an approach to Christian theology akin to Frei's type 5, in which theology is viewed entirely as self-description, eschewing any hint of correlation or reciprocity with external discourses.

For eight days in April 1966, nearly a thousand delegates from over seventy countries convened at Wheaton College in Wheaton, Illinois for the "Congress on the Church's Worldwide Mission," sponsored by the Evangelical Foreign Missions Association and the Interdenominational Foreign Missions Association. In the conference announcement, it was made clear that the impetus came primarily from pervasive evangelical discontent with the mission theology propounded by the ecumenical movement, particularly in the wake of the 1961 merger of the IMC and WCC.[222] Perhaps the most pressing concern regarding WCC mission theology was over the influence of syncretism, universalism, and secularism in the WCC's approach to Christian theology in relation to other faiths and, relatedly, its increasingly prominent tendency to subordinate evangelism to social action in the name of the "social gospel."[223] A WCC representative present at Wheaton 1966, Eugene L. Smith, wrote afterwards that "the most frequent charges against us were theological liberalism, loss of evangelical conviction, universalism in theology, substitution of social action for evangelism, and the search for unity at the expense of biblical truth."[224]

Wheaton 1966 was held to be an important opportunity for "evangelical leadership to make plain to the world their theory, strategy, and practice

---

[220]   Cf. Ford, "Theologically Hospitable," 537.

[221]   D. Z. Phillips, *Faith and Philosophical Enquiry* (New York: Schocken Books, 1979), 17, quoted in Frei, *Types of Christian Theology*, 47.

[222]   Bassham, *Mission Theology*, 210.

[223]   Harold Lindsell, ed., *The Church's Worldwide Mission: Proceedings of the Congress on the Church's Worldwide Mission, 9–16 April 1966 at Wheaton College, Wheaton, Illinois* (Waco, Tex.: Word, 1966), 225.

[224]   Eugene L. Smith, "The Wheaton Congress in the Eyes of an Ecumenical Observer," *International Review of Mission* 55, no. 220 (1966): 481.

of the church's universal mission."[225] The proximity in timing between Wheaton 1966 and the 1967 MSC underscores the growing divide within the ecumenical movement. This oppositional attitude colored much of the proceedings and is easily discernible in the summary statement, the "Wheaton Declaration" (WD).[226]

The defining feature of Frei's type 5 is its total isolation of Christian theology from external descriptions and discourses. Frei describes this as "Christian self-description with no holds barred."[227] For type 5, "the rule of inside and outside talk concerning religion is absolute, and theology is strictly inside talk."[228] On the one hand, there is an evident affinity between type 4 and type 5, insofar as both reject the imposition of some universal standard for theological adjudication.[229] On the other hand, unlike type 4, type 5's absolute isolation of self-description from external analysis undermines the very notion of self-description itself, supplanting *description* with *repetition*.[230]

For type 4, although the focus is on first- and second-order Christian discourse, the productive indeterminacy that characterizes the relationship between them is itself a function of the ad hoc application of third-order, external discourses. For type 4,

the heart of theological discourse [is] in the constant transition between first-order Christian statements, especially biblical confession and exegesis, and their second-order redescription, in which description as internal dogmatic description makes use of third-order free, unsystematic, and constant reference to conceptual patterns of a non-Christian, non-theological kind—including phenomenology, conceptual analysis, Hegelian philosophy, analyses of culture, and so on.[231]

Importantly, Frei notes that the direction of this dynamic is governed by the prioritization of first- and second-order discourse, meaning that the *sensus literalis* of scripture "regulates" this engagement. More than that,

---

225   Lindsell, *Church's Worldwide Mission*, 4; cf. Bassham, *Mission Theology*, 210.
226   Cf. Lindsell, *Church's Worldwide Mission*, 2–4, 10–11, 27, 68–72, 89, 91, 97, 109, 114, 116, 118, 140, 149, 163, 166–70, 179–80, 220, 231, 241, 243; cf. Smith, "Wheaton Congress," 480.
227   Frei, *Types of Christian Theology*, 46.
228   Frei, *Types of Christian Theology*, 48.
229   Frei, *Types of Christian Theology*, 51.
230   Frei, *Types of Christian Theology*, 55.
231   Frei, *Types of Christian Theology*, 43.

type 4's prioritization of the literal sense—the basis for its hermeneutical emphasis on *redescription*—appears to *demand* engagement with external discourses. Yet Frei sees this not so much as a principled choice as a pragmatic one, for "in the *process* of redescription we can—and indeed cannot do other than—employ our own thought structures, experiences, conceptual schemes."[232] Type 4 therefore reflects an acknowledgment of our being located in specific contexts and a faith in the relevance of correlating these contexts to our scriptural interpretation—"without knowing success or lack of it in any given case beforehand, it is an article of faith that it *can* be done; it *is* done."[233]

In contrast, type 5 takes an entirely hostile view of the influence of contemporary context in scriptural interpretation and Christian theology. Eschewing any reference to external discourses, type 5 sunders the unceasing transition between first-order Christian statements and their second-order redescription, facilitated by "unsystematic and constant reference to conceptual patterns of a non-Christian, non-theological kind," affirmed in type 4. With no distinction between first- and second-order discourse, doctrinal formulations are indistinguishable from the literal sense of scripture, leaving type 5 with a view on the *sensus literalis* as a "negative criteriology" for Christian theology, absent its generative capacity embraced in type 4:

> In matters of doctrinal statement, pure self-confinement to Christian self-description means no self-description. To the extent that this situation is a product of making theology purely internal to the religion, its result is a theology of total silence when one cannot simply and uncritically parrot biblical and traditional formulae. To the extent that this absence of doctrinal self-description is the result of absolutizing and rigidifying the warranted, indeed essential, distinction between religious statements and statements about religion, it is a function of the dominance of a philosophical theory or negative criteriology over theology as Christian self-description. The sensus literalis here is logically equivalent to sheer repetition of the same words. That is hardly how it has functioned in the Christian interpretive tradition.[234]

On this basis, type 5 is clearly differentiated from type 4 theology not simply in relation to their different positions concerning the influence of

---

[232]   Frei, *Types of Christian Theology*, 44.
[233]   Frei, *Types of Christian Theology*, 44.
[234]   Frei, *Types of Christian Theology*, 55.

external discourses, but also in relation to how this difference relates to their different views on the *sensus literalis*.

Type 5 theology is readily discernible in the WD, with its stark divide between the internally derived "validity of biblical affirmations" and the "disturbing secular forces . . . at work in the hearts of Christians eroding their commitment to Christ and His growing missionary purpose."[235] And while there is no obvious "dominant philosophical theory" operating behind this position, as with type 5's lopsided approach to the literal sense as a theological constraint, the WD contains a clear "negative criteriology" tied to its emphasis on biblical inerrancy and the incontrovertible authority of Christian doctrine. In a thinly veiled allusion to the WCC, the WD appears to sarcastically dismiss the concern for church unity, rejecting it out of concern for doctrinal purity:

> Today many voices call for organizational church union at the expense of doctrine and practice . . . Christians having been regenerated by the Holy Spirit and who agree on the basic evangelical doctrines can experience a genuine biblical oneness even if they belong to different denominations. *Such genuine biblical oneness cannot exist among those who have not been regenerated or among those who disagree on the basic evangelical doctrines even if they belong to the same denomination.*[236]

It is here worth reiterating that Frei's typology was largely generated by his realization that despite the profound differences, doctrinal and otherwise, between Barth and Schleiermacher, both pursued Christian theology in ways congenial to the plain sense of scripture and hospitable to Jesus' unique and unsubstitutable significance for Christian faith. In contrast, the WD renders *doctrinal accord* as the only lens through which the relations between Christian theologies can be conceived. In so doing, the WD presents a picture of Christian theology in which, as in type 5, not only is third-order analysis excluded but first- and second-order language are collapsed. There is no difference between the reading or interpretation of scripture and its doctrinal redescription. As Frei says of type 5, in the WD, "the sensus literalis here is logically equivalent to sheer repetition of the same words."[237]

---

[235]   Lindsell, *Church's Worldwide Mission*, 218.
[236]   Lindsell, *Church's Worldwide Mission*, 231, emphasis added.
[237]   Frei, *Types of Christian Theology*, 55.

This is not to say that type 4 theology employs a more sophisticated or externally influenced hermeneutic, but that the approach to biblical interpretation in type 5 and the WD is more ideologically loaded than it acknowledges. Whereas in Frei's account of type 5 this is the product of Phillips' Wittgensteinian philosophy of language, in the WD it is a result of their principle of inerrancy. In a brief section on "Our Authority," the WD invokes "apostolic precedent" to insist that the Bible must be read as "the inspired, the only authoritative, *inerrant Word of God . . . our final rule of faith and practice.*"[238]

Here, not only is the inerrancy of scripture called upon by appeal to its supposed foundation within the Christian community from its inception, but the Bible itself is described, singularly, as a "rule." Not to be confused with Frei's description of type 4's ruled use approach to theology, this designation of the Bible as a rule is a far cry from Frei's conception of the *sensus literalis*, the practice of figural interpretation founded upon it, and the recognition of God's providence that undergirds it. Similarly, the WD insists that what justifies the isolation of Christian faith and theology from all other disciplines and traditions is the "revealed" status of the Bible—a designation that is formed outside the Bible itself and applied to biblical interpretation: "Biblical faith is unique because it is revealed. To add to it or to change it is to pervert it."[239] As with the description of the Bible as a rule, the reference to it as revealed here is also linked to an assessment of scripture in which its meaning is perfectly transparent and fixed.

This brings up another important parallel between type 5 and the WD concerning the arbitration of interpretive disputes. The configuration of type 4 theology, where first-, second-, and third-order levels of Christian discourse remain distinct yet mutually informative, means that discordant interpretations of scripture have recourse to extra-scriptural discourses, such that doctrines are firmly held but *potentially* susceptible to reformulation, not despite but *in light of* the plain sense. Type 4's emphasis on the incarnation of Jesus Christ as *incompletely* but *adequately* described in the Gospels leads it to affirm and constructively engage the inevitable and ambiguous influence of our social contexts and the philosophical or cultural discourses that accompany them in scriptural interpretation. This is most evident in its view of doctrines as *redescription* of the plain sense of scripture, held tightly given both their apparent appropriateness

---

[238]   Lindsell, *Church's Worldwide Mission*, 221, emphasis added.
[239]   Lindsell, *Church's Worldwide Mission*, 223.

in describing this plain sense and the continued communal endorsement of this appropriateness.

But in type 5, and in the WD, doctrines are permanent and absolute, in line with the fixed nature of scripture that follows from the principle of inerrancy. Doctrines are not descriptions so much as recapitulations of scripture, which is not an analogically adequate but a *complete* account of salvation history. As such, doctrines can shape the interpretation of scripture but not the other way around, as the doctrines themselves are viewed as perfect distillations of the Bible's indisputable and immutable meaning—even when the doctrine itself is drawn from outside of scripture, as in the case of inerrancy.

As such, type 5 theology leaves little if any room for the arbitration of disputes *within* Christianity, much less for any meaningful engagement between Christianity and other faiths. The same is true of the WD. As Frei suggests, Phillips "*seems* to be saying, 'If you don't agree with me, you don't understand what I'm saying, you're confused.'"[240] Echoing this is the WD's vilification of the secular and non-Christian, and its audacious assertion of the authority of its particular construal of the Christian faith: "We ask only that those of like faith ponder our words in the light of Scripture, and thereby ascertain their truthfulness."[241]

For type 5, all alternative theological proposals are viewed as resulting "from the philosophical craving for generality, 'That what constitutes an intelligible move in one context must constitute an intelligible move in *all* contexts.'"[242] Similarly, Wheaton 1966 blames the context of globalization accompanying the twentieth century, where, "with all human affairs moving toward an age of universality never previously witnessed, many voices call for a religion that has universal validity."[243] In response, both type 5 and the WD completely isolate Christian theology from all other discourses and faith traditions, insisting not just that what constitutes an intelligible move in one particular context *need only* be intelligible therein, but that it *can only* be intelligible within that community. For the WD, this means both that the doctrinal encapsulation of scripture is the only recourse to resolving interpretive disputes, and that any correlation or reciprocity between Christian faith and other discourses or traditions is ruled out ab initio.

---

[240] Frei, *Types of Christian Theology*, 50.
[241] Lindsell, *Church's Worldwide Mission*, 221.
[242] Frei, *Types of Christian Theology*, 50.
[243] Lindsell, *Church's Worldwide Mission*, 222.

For Wheaton 1966 and type 5, external elements are not simply depicted as unrelated to Christian faith, but as hostile and deceptive influences on the legitimacy of Christian theology. Though type 5 purportedly ignores external discourses, it finds the inclination toward granting them any kind of influence over Christian theology to be deeply threatening. As quoted above, Frei describes the confrontation of disagreement within type 5 as inevitably being attributed to the "philosophical craving for generality," an urge that undermines the cogency of Christian faith. The WD similarly frames the radical isolation of Christian theology as an inevitable result of the necessary rejection of "syncretism" and "universalism," thereby excluding the possibility of any correlation or reciprocity due to the world's intrinsic and total hostility to Christian faith.

The WD posits a radical hostility between Christian faith and the world, "intensified by the rise of atheistic communism, extreme nationalism, resurgent ethnic religions, secularism, and corrupted forms of Christianity."[244] This is the work of Satan, "the 'Prince of this world.'"[245] Given that the world is now Satan's domain, Christian faith can only take shape in utter isolation from its influence and in total opposition to it. The WD's definition of syncretism is fittingly broad, consisting simply in "the attempt to unite or reconcile biblically revealed Christian truth with the diverse or opposing tenets and practices of non-Christian religions or other systems of thought that deny it."[246] To even suggest similarity, much less agreement, between Christianity and another philosophy or religious tradition is to deny "the uniqueness and finality of Christian truth."[247]

Similarly, to acknowledge the possibility of salvation of non-Christians is to commit heresy. The WD takes the absolute divide between inside and outside talk in religion of type 5 theology to have clear soteriological implications. There can be no surprises when it comes to salvation, regardless of the WD's emphasis on God's sovereignty.[248] Universalism, which here includes even the hope for the salvation of anyone, much less everyone, outside the Christian faith, is rejected because it "proclaims the essential and final unity of the human race, which will never be

---

[244]   Lindsell, *Church's Worldwide Mission*, 235.
[245]   Lindsell, *Church's Worldwide Mission*, 235.
[246]   Lindsell, *Church's Worldwide Mission*, 222. The addition of "diverse" alongside "opposing" indicates that the "denial of Christian truth" is not dependent upon an explicit rejection of Christianity or any specific aspect of Christianity, but is simply to *not be* Christian.
[247]   Lindsell, *Church's Worldwide Mission*, 222.
[248]   Lindsell, *Church's Worldwide Mission*, 219, 236.

broken—now or in the future—by God or by man."[249] In its place, the WD affirms the binary division of the human race as an inviolable principle that even God cannot contravene: "Although God's claims are universal and His triumph will be universal, yet His saving grace is effective only in those who believe in Christ (John 1:12)."[250] Here again, the WD suggests this view is the result of a strictly internal approach to Christian theology: "Scripture, however, must explain Scripture."[251] But, as Frei's account of type 5 helps to uncover, this approach itself is premised upon a combination of hermeneutical principles derived outside of scripture and justified by their being the "internalized concepts" of the Christian community, alongside a negative criteriology that is here centered on the Bible's sole status as *divine revelation*. It is by virtue of the isolated *status* of revelation, not, significantly, by the content or literal sense of scripture, that all other discourses are viewed as not simply void of God's presence but hostile to it, manifestations of the Prince of the world, Satan.[252] As the WD's final section, "Mission and a Hostile World," concludes, "the world is hostile to the church because it is hostile to God. His Church is at war, not at rest."[253]

Conclusion

Race argues that it is a focus on history that separates his typology and the theological pluralism it champions from other approaches. Yet looking at the ecumenical movement in the twentieth century, it appears this typology is ill suited to analyzing and accounting for the different approaches to the theology of religions advanced there. In contrast, I have argued in this chapter that Frei's typology shows itself to be very well suited to an analysis of the ecumenical debate in general and specifically as it concerns the theology of religions. More than that, Frei's typology reveals surprising similarities among Christian movements and assemblies, such as the proximity between Jerusalem 1928 and Tambaram 1938 or between the LFMI and Wheaton 1966. Such insights into the relations between these approaches to the theology of religions are excluded from Race's typology, with its polemical preference for pluralism orienting its framing of the types from the start. Furthermore, I have tried to show in this chapter how Frei's own theological approach, though he did not engage the theology

---

[249]   Lindsell, *Church's Worldwide Mission*, 223f.
[250]   Lindsell, *Church's Worldwide Mission*, 224.
[251]   Lindsell, *Church's Worldwide Mission*, 224.
[252]   Frei, *Types of Christian Theology*, 48.
[253]   Lindsell, *Church's Worldwide Mission*, 235.

of religions, is reflected in the ecumenical movement (most notably in Jerusalem 1928 and Tambaram 1938), that this approach represents a way of configuring the relationship between Jesus' uniqueness and universality that acknowledges the tensions between them without asserting that they are mutually exclusive, and yet that an approach like this is excluded ab initio from Race's typological framework.

We saw how the WD view that contemporary questions concerning biblical interpretation reflect uncertainty "about the *validity* of biblical affirmations in this age of change" echoes the type 1 theology of the LFMI, which expressed equal alarm over the plausibility of religious meaning and the relationship between inside and outside religious discourse.[254] For type 1, a valid Christian faith is accountable to the dictates of universal *wissenschaftlich* discourses. For type 5, the plausibility of Christian faith is only subject to the terms of an internal, social structure of validity. Their results might be different, but they are configured in much the same way—an observation in keeping with Frei's suggestion that type 1 and type 5 are more alike than might first be apparent.

In the totalizing logic of both type 1 and type 5, there is no room for the *sensus literalis*, much less for the practice of figural interpretation in a historical world, providentially ordered, if often inscrutably so, and capable of surprise. Both are therefore also inhospitable to Jesus, whose unique identity is both particular and universal, familiar and foreign. Both are also most closely related to Race's types of pluralism and exclusivism. This is an important point. For, as it has been argued that Race's typology possesses little descriptive capacity in an engagement the history of the theology of religions discourse in key contexts like the twentieth-century ecumenical movement, the suggestion that the LFMI and the WC would serve as fitting examples of the exclusivist and pluralist theologies Race's typology sets out might seem to contradict this claim. In response, one need only point out that while these two examples are accommodated, the question of where the MSC, Jerusalem 1928, and Tambaram 1938 could fit within Race's typology is much less clear. Race himself cites Tambaram 1938 as an example of exclusivism, a claim which obscures the massive difference between the types of Christian theology at work in these two contexts—differences which Frei's typology, on the other hand, accounts for with a remarkable clarity.

On the other hand, it should also be acknowledged that the matter of historical description is related to, but distinct from, the matter of the provi-

---

[254]   Lindsell, *Church's Worldwide Mission*, 217, emphasis added.

sion of helpful analysis in exploring how and why these historical examples took shape in the ways they did. For while the LFMI and WC would seem to fit within Race's typology in pluralism and exclusivism, the simple fact that such positions *exist* is a different question than how to organize and understand why these positions emerge and what views on the nature of theological discourse and Christian faith itself undergird them. Race's initial narrowing of the analytical or explanatory logic of his typology, exploring the extent to which his types conform to certain alethic-philosophical (to use Paul Eddy's term) dogmas is unjustified and unhelpful, not because it omits the possibility of articulating types of the theology of religion that find real-world expression, but because it demands those positions be understood entirely on Race's own philosophical terms.

To use Eddy's terms again, Race's alethic-philosophical commitments and their place as organizing principles in Race's typology lead Race to infer an inherent connection between philosophical truth claims and alethic-religious and soteric truth claims. If you affirm the utter uniqueness of Jesus' incarnation, in defiance of Troeltsch's historicism and/or Hick's epistemology, no matter what *meaning* you take the belief in Jesus' unique incarnation to have (including but not limited to the soteric), Race's typology demands you conceive of yourself as an exclusivist. But as has been shown in this chapter, this is akin to saying that there is no meaningful difference between the account of the meaning of the incarnation operative in Jerusalem 1928 and that of the Wheaton Declaration. So while even certain examples explored in this chapter like the LFMI and the WD might fit within Race's typology, it is also the case that a broken clock is right twice a day, and that such overlap between real-world examples or articulations of theology of religions positions and Race's types is as much incidental as intentional, a function not of the descriptive and analytical scope of the typology but of these two (rather extreme) examples conforming to the narrowness of Race's account.

Opposite to this is type 3 and 4's congeniality to the literal sense and the uniqueness of Jesus, whereby it becomes clear that to affirm his specific and historical identity is also to affirm his universal presence—which by virtue of its universality is also inherently capable of surprising us, even drawing us into redescriptions of scripture that perhaps alter, but always add to, rather than subtract from, our reading of the *sensus literalis*. There is indeed a tension here, but one that Frei thinks is appropriate to the *ruled* use of scripture, an approach that eschews the interpretation without remainder characteristic of those theologies that employ various hermeneutical methods toward systematically apologetic ends. "That's all very well, but tell us how to apply these rules," Frei imagines someone asking Barth. "But there's the rub, and the rub's the point. If he could tell us how, the rule would no longer be a rule but a method."[255]

The same can be said for a Christian theology of religions that honors the tension between the particular and the universal, wherein an affirmation of the uniqueness of Christ and the Gospel accounts of his life, death, and resurrection *demand* some theological acknowledgment of the possibility of surprising encounters with him. Though this cannot come at the expense of the *sensus literalis* and the unique status afforded Jesus in the tradition of Christian faith, it also cannot exclude the possibility of meeting Jesus in the lives and even traditions of non-Christians. To suggest otherwise, in whatever way, is to misconstrue the unique complexity of Jesus Christ's identity and to illegitimately constrain God's sovereignty and providential ordering of the world.

[255]   Frei, *Types of Christian Theology*, 86.

5

Conclusion

Unique Faith and the Hope of Universal Belonging

In the preface, I outlined the very personal reasons that led me to this study. The preceding analysis has provided me with the critical capacity to see for the first time the ways in which Race's framework had constrained my attempts at understanding the situation of my own Jewish/Christian family. On the one hand, Race's typology is constructed in such a way that it is inhospitable to the particular questions that arise concerning the relationship between Judaism and Christianity. On the other hand, and as a result of the way in which the typology obscures this matter, I came to find that my own questions had been transformed. The binary or, to use the Jewish philosopher of religion Peter Ochs' term, *dyadic* framing of Race's typology between the supposedly opposing embraces of particularity and universality eschews questions concerning the particularities of my own Jewish-Christian context in favor of those concerning religious pluralism in general.[1]

---

[1]   Peter Ochs, *Another Reformation: Postliberal Christianity and the Jews* (Grand Rapids: Baker Academic, 2011), 9. Ochs differentiates between binary logics, which are appropriately applied "when the lived situation calls for a dichotomous logic," and *dyadic* logics, which are instances "when binary logics are employed inappropriately." An example of the appropriately binary is the individual experience of suffering, which presents itself in binary logic of being "*in* suffering or *out* of it, either this pain or its cessation" (8). For Ochs, the segregating of "human" and "divine" discourse, as in Smith's distinction between scripture/beliefs and transcendent experience/faith, is an example of the dyadic.

That said, for all of the problems and inadequacies I discern in Race's typology and theological pluralism, I understand our interests and objectives to be significantly aligned. While I take issue with Race's insistence that religious faith needs to adopt the standards of modern academic legitimacy if it is to survive, and that the embrace of theological pluralism is the inevitable outcome of such a rescue mission, the end goal or hope that Race envisions for this process is *belonging*—even if his typology does not contribute to this goal.

Certainly any account of the Christian theology of religions worth our attention has this as its defining hope and concern, an acknowledgment and affirmation of Christianity's power "to imagine and enact connection and belonging," as Willie Jennings puts it.[2] The Christian theology of religions is a discourse that is irrevocably social and relational—an inquiry into the God to which (and/or in whom) we all belong and what that relationship of belonging means for all of our other relationships—or it is not Christian theology at all.

For all of its faults, and though it accompanies other apologetic concerns regarding the rationality of religious faith, Race's theological pluralism clearly bears a commitment to the mutual belonging of humans across religious (and, as should be clear at this point, religious/secular) divides. In light of this, another way of framing my interrogation of this typology and of theological pluralism is to say that my concern has been *on what terms* this picture of belonging is fashioned and, relatedly, the ensuing account of the means of accomplishing it. The theology of religions is, at root, a discourse that explores the theological terms of belonging. We will no doubt disagree about these "terms," but this shared interest and hope for belonging is the sine qua non of the theology of religions in whatever form it takes.

This affirmation of shared purpose, however, does shed additional critical light on the logic of Race's typology. For in important respects, this shared horizon of belonging might be affirmed even within the types he fashions in supposed contradiction to the affirmation of belonging he detects in pluralism. Exclusivism and inclusivism are, by design, intended to demonstrate the sole viability of pluralism's picture of belonging. But exclusivism no less than pluralism holds out belonging as a hope or even a goal. It just views the terms of such belonging in a radically different way (i.e., evangelism vs dialogue). We may disagree with the terms of this account of belonging, as indeed I would. But that is a different matter than denying its existence altogether.

[2]   Willie James Jennings, *The Christian Imagination: Theology and the Origins of Race* (New Haven, Conn.: Yale University Press, 2010), 4.

But this denial is the inevitable fruit of the logic of Race's typology. For, however slight the offer and vision of belonging is in this intentionally malformed type, the apologetic logic of Race's typology makes it so that the possibility of belonging is yoked to the embrace of philosophy, the universal discourse, over and against the scandalously particular and historically contingent practices, beliefs, and resources of religious traditions and communities. "Applied to the critique of lived practices," this logic, which Ochs describes as a common logic of modern theologies more generally, "generates what we might call a hermeneutics of war . . . a mode of reparative argument that generates comparable sets of antagonistic postures regardless of the goal of one's argument."[3]

Ultimately, the problem of belonging that Race is most concerned with is that concerning the academy. For Race, the matter of interreligious community is subsidiary to and dependent upon the corralling of theological discourse within the confines of "modern thought." For Race, and his typology, interfaith belonging *requires* that religion be refashioned so that it might belong alongside the secular and academic.

The upshot of this approach, for me, was that the typology dissuaded me from exploring my own question about the theological relationship between my Jewish and Christian family members. In fact, Race's conception of theological pluralism as a response to philosophical criticisms is intentionally inhospitable to such concerns. In a chapter titled "The Jewish-Christian Filter," Race writes:

> Certainly, given the fact that Christian faith has its origins in the Jewish matrix of the first century of the Common Era, Christianity feels bound to Judaism as to no other religion . . . Yet could we not also argue that it is precisely this "intrinsic" attachment that Christianity feels towards Judaism which disqualifies the Jewish-Christian relationship from playing so determinative a role for the Christian response to other religions in the future? *How could a relationship so distinct be applicable to other relationships?* . . . If the hiatus in Jewish-Christian relations can be overcome by the sounder application of historical, biblical and theological critical principles, the door may be opened for a positive appreciation of the wider religious plurality.[4]

---

[3]   Ochs, *Another Reformation*, 7.

[4]   Alan Race, *Interfaith Encounter: The Twin Tracks of Theology and Dialogue* (London: SCM Press, 2001), 43f.

Race contends that, in demoting the significance of the Jewish-Christian relationship for Christianity's relationships with other traditions, he is not only establishing a sounder philosophical basis for these relationships, but also freeing Judaism from the threat of Christian supersessionism—a threat that endures so long as the universal significance of Jesus Christ is maintained. Once Christian theology adopts a pluralistic vision, Race concludes, "the Jewish-Christian filter itself [will have] been superseded!"[5] But the truth of this statement extends well beyond what Race intends. In fact, it perpetuates the very Jewish supersessionism it seeks to avoid.

As Ochs notes, "liberal Christian theologies seek a form of nonsupersessionist Christianity but tend to give rise to unintended forms of supersessionism."[6] What are these unintended forms? For Ochs, "the first sin of supersessionism is hermeneutical, since it veils the Gospels' ever-renewed relation to the Old Testament texts and thus, in effect, encourages strictly literal or one-leveled readings of the gospel message."[7] The contrast could not be more stark between this approach and Frei's, with its emphasis on a figural interpretation that takes the connection between New and Old Testaments with the utmost seriousness, as one that cannot simply be subject to a programmatic or systematic account. Indeed, Ochs suggests that a basic feature of "postliberal" theologies like Frei's is that "the reaffirmation of classical Christology after modernity is inseparably associated with the rejection of supersessionism."[8]

The point here is not to add another item to the list of shortcomings in Race's typological theology, but to ask whether or not this rejection of the central significance for Christian faith of Judaism—hermeneutically, historically, Christologically—might in fact be the foundation of all its shortcomings. This is not to say that this instinct is the overt cause of Race's apologetic appeal to philosophy, but that *this apologetic approach itself is only possible in light of his refusal to acknowledge the centrality of Judaism in the identity of Jesus* and, therein, in the scriptures that narrate his life and ministry and in the identity of those who, in reading and celebrating these narratives, come to understand their own identities in the light of his, as followers of Jesus.

If this is so, it makes sense that Frei's "postliberal" approach to Christian theology would provide both compelling criticisms of Race's theology

5   Race, *Interfaith Encounter*, 61.
6   Ochs, *Another Reformation*, 4.
7   Ochs, *Another Reformation*, 265.
8   Ochs, *Another Reformation*, 2.

and promising ways of reconceiving of the relationship between the particular and the universal in Christian faith. Frei's embrace of the plain sense of scripture, and the corresponding emphasis on the particularities of Jesus' life and teaching, can in this light be seen as acknowledgment that the depiction of Jesus in the Gospels as belonging to the God of Israel and with the people of Israel is an ineradicable and fundamental criterion of Jesus' identity, one that is at the heart of the questions concerning the relationship between Jews and gentiles raised across the rest of the New Testament and in the myriad of later ecumenical councils taking up the issue of the scriptural canon and beyond. Jesus does not belong to the academy, or to the church, or to Western civilization (or any other for that matter), but to the God of Israel and to the people called by this God. "Why were you searching for me?" the young Jesus asks his worried parents after he'd gone missing for three days. "Did you not know that I must be in my Father's house?" (Luke 2:49). There is an intrinsic connection between Jesus' Jewishness and his unsubstitutable particularity. This is also to say that Jesus' Jewishness, his belonging to the God of Israel and the people of Israel, is not a problem for the promise of his universal, salvific significance—the promise that creation, in all its complex and disparate diversity, belongs with the one God—but its premise. And the connection that Ochs discerns in the work of Frei and others between the reaffirmation of classical Christology, the hermeneutical embrace of the ongoing and "ever-renewed" relationship between the Old and New Testaments, and the rejection of supersessionism points to *two* interlocking insights for the Christian theology of religions moving forward.

First, the Christian theology of religions, like Christian theology in general, *must* pass through the question of Jewish/Christian relationship. Consequently, alongside the preceding critical analysis of the philosophical underpinnings of Race's theology, the issue with the typology might also be simply identified as its systematic repudiation of this principle. Any other approach inevitably embraces a supersessionist logic, wherein Jesus' significance is dislocated from his Jewish identity and Christian faith in him is conceived as intelligible apart from its indissoluble relationship to Israel.

But as Jennings powerfully points out, the avoidance of this question is at the heart of the corruption of the Christian imagination writ large, a corruption which has had devastating implications for Christian relationships to other religions, yes, but not only. For Jennings, the tragic history of Western Christianity's racial relations is itself a result of this atrophy of imagination under supersessionism, resulting in an idealistic Christology and a concomitant embrace of paradigms of mastery and control in Christian faith. From this, we can see that Jennings' work is oriented around Christological concerns very similar to Frei's—most notably, "the danger of claiming divine presence without its appropriate Christological mediation."[9]

The key difference might be in their framing of the source of the problem of presence in Christology. Jennings' focus on race as the most historically illuminating and presently urgent site to expose and explain the ongoing failure of Christianity to affirm and follow "the central trajectory of the incarnate life of the Son of God, who took on the life of the creature, a life of joining, belonging, connection, and intimacy," raises the possibility that Frei's Enlightenment-era focus obscures the possibility that these dangers manifested themselves prior to the Enlightenment and the defensive theological responses that started to recast Christian faith. Jennings' approach suggests the appeal to Christ's presence as a mechanism of theological mastery and control has a more ancient pedigree, stemming from the insidious logic of supersessionism itself. "Christian intellectual tradition in the New World," he writes, "denies its most fundamental starting point, that of the divine Word entering flesh in time and space to become Jewish flesh."[10]

The *second* point for the theology of religions to consider as it moves forward, which follows from the first, is captured in Jennings' insistence that a renewed appreciation of the centrality of the Jewish/Christian relationship for the theology of religions discourse calls for more attention to location, or place. To some extent, this has already been alluded to in the preceding analysis of and appeal to Frei's account of figural interpretation and its inherently historical character, as well as in his increasing emphasis on the community as context of discernment and consensus on the plain sense of scripture. But it is worth pausing for a moment to consider that Frei's focus on *identity* is one that he comes to in response to the mediating theologians' emphasis on presence and what he saw to be "the twin dangers of a mystification and of loss of morality to religion which result from making personal acquaintance or personal knowledge the model for what transpires between God and man in religion or Christian faith."[11]

While pluralistic theology reconfirms Frei's concerns, it might also be the case that Frei's construal of the problem of Christ's presence itself

---

[9]   Jennings, *Christian Imagination*, 113.
[10]   Jennings, *Christian Imagination*, 113.
[11]   Hans Frei, *The Identity of Jesus Christ* (Eugene, Ore.: Wipf & Stock, 1997), 53f.

obscures the significance of place and context in his own articulation of figural interpretation. Frei is responding to Enlightenment-influenced, apologetic, Christological-hermeneutical accounts, which is where he locates the source of contemporary theological mishandlings of the relationship between Jesus' identity and presence. But what if this second point is related to the first? What if the problem of Christ's presence is rooted not primarily in the logic of the Enlightenment, but in the older and more insidious logic of supersessionism?

Jennings, like Frei, does not focus on the theology of religions or theological pluralism. But in *The Christian Imagination*, he describes how the historical influence of supersessionism has entailed "the negation of a Christian intellectual posture reflective of the central trajectory of the incarnate life of the Son of God, who took on the life of the creature, a life of joining, belonging, connection, and intimacy," yielding what he describes as Western Christianity's "diseased social imagination."[12] This emphasis on the unsubstitutable particularity of the incarnate Jesus, an emphasis that cannot help but underscore the centrality of Jesus' Jewishness, pushes back against the anthropological idealism of theological pluralism, refusing to look past the particularities of people, communities, and religious traditions.

I noted in several places that Race's treatment of the empirical reality of religious pluralism and his theological response to it are strangely silent on the matter of indigenous or localized religious traditions. To raise the question of their omission is not to insinuate any intentionality behind it. The problem would rather seem to be simply that there are few resources in them for the theological imagination of pluralism to draw upon. As the LFMI puts it, theological pluralism is rooted in the conviction that "questions religion deals with are not questions which admit local or national answers."[13] If the underlying schema of theological pluralism rests on the availability of universalistic beliefs or horizons in religious traditions—whether expressed in a claim to monotheism, or in the anticipation of the eschatological consummation of all creation, or in metaphysical claims concerning the illusory nature of reality, the existence of karma or reincarnation, etc.—religions that are tied to particular peoples and particular places would seem to offer scant material. Their orientation around particular communities and places means that their "specific

[12]   Jennings, *Christian Imagination*, 6–7.
[13]   William Ernest Hocking, *Re-thinking Missions: A Laymen's Inquiry after One Hundred Years* (New York: Harper & Brothers, 1932), 7.

spatial reality is the hermeneutical horizon on which they see themselves and the world."[14] To interpret such traditions idealistically, mining them for universal truths, is necessarily to erode and obscure the centrality of the particular place and people from which they have emerged and toward which they are concerned.

In detailed accounts of horrific encounters between European Christians and the indigenous inhabitants of the Americas and Africa, Jennings suggests that the limitations of the Christian imagination that mark these meetings are tied to a "failure to recognize the complexity and majesty of life marked by place," which itself is the bitter fruit of supersessionist logic.[15] Jennings continues:

> This failure of recognition was far more than simply forgetting Israel by claiming that Christian *communitas* surpassed their common life. This failure was more than poor knowledge of history or memory loss. This historic failure of recognition brings Christians to the threshold of Israel's existence with a basic, life-altering question: How did we get here in the first place? Where is here? The here is outside Israel, outside the conversation between biblical Israel and its God, outside the continuing conversations living Israel has with that same God. Gentiles, the *goyim*, are outside Israel, lacking intimate knowledge of the ways and struggles of life inside. Yet to even know that we are outside, that we are Gentile, that we are not addressed in the conversations of biblical Israel with its God is already to admit an entrance. Someone allowed us to draw close enough to hear that there was a conversation going on between God and a people in the first place.[16]

The significance of place in Christian theology, for Jennings, takes into account its centrality in other traditions. But it draws its force from the recognition of Israel's prevenient and enduring covenant with God, a covenant which is both affirmed and intensified in Jesus, who is "defined by his people, yet determined by God. He is one with their story, but he has become the new storyteller."[17] And any approach to Christian theology that does not take seriously the significance of place in the unsubstitutable

---

[14]   Jennings, *Christian Imagination*, 54; cf. Keith Basso, *Wisdom Sits in Places: Landscape and Language among the Western Apache* (Albuquerque: University of New Mexico Press, 1996); Calvin Luther Martin, *The Way of the Human Being* (New Haven, Conn.: Yale University Press, 1999).

[15]   Jennings, *Christian Imagination*, 251.

[16]   Jennings, *Christian Imagination*, 251f.

[17]   Jennings, *Christian Imagination*, 263.

particularity of Jesus and in the account of his continued presence, is premised on and reproduces the sense of being *insiders*, rightful possessors and protectors of divine truth. "To weaken the connection of Jesus to Israel is also to miss the actual mode of connection he draws to us. The story itself gives us the clues to our presence," he writes. "We are the ones who believe the word of God to Israel. We were present in the story of Israel but we are also present in the Jesus story. *We are those outside of Israel who ask for a gift intended for Israel. We ask for Jesus' help.*"[18]

For Jennings, those outside of Israel remain outsiders, no matter their religion. They are receivers of the promise of salvation, the gift of eternal life with God, not because they deserve it but because they are *invited* by Jesus Christ to partake in it. From this angle, God's self-revelation in Jesus appears neither as a fulfillment that nullifies or renders obsolete God's covenant with Israel, nor a repudiation of its ethnic particularity, but a new foundation for the vision of kinship and intimate belonging at the heart of God's covenant with Israel. The patterns of belonging affirmed there are reconfigured around Jesus:

> Jesus did not seek to destroy kinship, to undermine its defining power rooted in story, memory and cultural practice. Rather, he drew it to a new orientation, a new determination. The family must follow him. The one family must follow from him—flow from his life as its new source . . . Those who under normal circumstances would never be together *must be together* to find Jesus of Nazareth, to hear him and gain from him their desires. Jesus, in forming a new Israel in the midst of Israel, positioned himself as the new source of desire.[19]

The very possibility of this perspective is excluded entirely in Race's typology. Each type is designed to identify who counts as a theological insider and the terms of this inclusion. Again, this approach is still an exploration of belonging, albeit one deformed by the implicit ideal of mastery and control that underpins it. This ideal is hardly unique to Race's typology, in fact it is one that Jennings discerns as (dis)orienting the entire project of academic theology and theological formation in academic contexts in the West.[20] For Race, the central theological problem is how to confer insider status on everyone *in spite* of their particular contexts and religious communities.

---

[18]   Jennings, *Christian Imagination*, 261f., emphasis added.
[19]   Jennings, *Christian Imagination*, 264.
[20]   Willie James Jennings, *After Whiteness: An Education in Belonging* (Grand Rapids: Eerdmans, 2020).

Jennings shows how this evacuation of cultural particularity, theological and otherwise—even if premised on the assumption that all are, behind the scenes, theological insiders—and the refusal to embrace being outsiders who are *invited in*, is the root of the problem, not just of racism and colonialism, but of the general disfigurement of Christianity into "a form of religious life that thwarts its deepest instincts of intimacy."[21]

In other words, Jennings shows that *universality and intimacy are not the same thing*. In fact, theological pluralism sacrifices its commitment to intimacy in the name of its commitment to universalism, imposing a purportedly universal hermeneutical horizon upon the particularities of all religious tradition and communities so as to rescue them from the limitations of their contexts. The parallels between this and the colonizing theological approaches Jennings outlines are striking, converging around a shared commitment in both to anticipating where and how God is present prior to any actual encounter between peoples. With this approach, there is no possibility of novelty or newness in our interreligious and intercultural encounters, no place for Christians to be reminded of and to embrace their status as gentiles and outsiders. We may be confronted with new phenomenological manifestations or expressions—new beliefs, in Smith's terms—but before we know anything about them, we know how to interpret their true meaning.

Similarly, Jennings observes that while an emphasis on the particularity of Jesus' life is not at odds with an emphasis on his universality, "universality . . . is a highly dangerous concept that, bound to the legacies of supersessionism and whiteness, did and continues to do strange things to the story of Jesus. I suggest a commitment not to an abstract idea of the universal or even of the universal applicability of Jesus, but to follow Jesus' own trajectory toward the many in Israel and through Israel to the many in the world . . . [into] a future . . . that would solidify the reconfiguration of kinship . . . the promise of the continuation of communion."[22]

Jennings shows that the approach of theological pluralism, concerned primarily with establishing universality, inevitably comes at the cost of intimacy, robbing our encounters and relationships of the chance to view not just the scriptures, traditions, and beliefs of others, but also the entirety of their lives, cultures, ecological contexts, and communities, as arising under the auspices of God's creation of the world and providential care of

---

[21]   Jennings, *Christian Imagination*, 9.
[22]   Jennings, *Christian Imagination*, 265.

it in anticipation of the future eschatological consummation of creation. "I yearn," Jennings writes, "for a vision of Christian intellectual identity that is compelling and attractive, embodying not simply the cunning of reason but the power of love that constantly gestures toward joining, toward the desire to hear, to know, and to embrace . . . Here theology elicits life patterns that mirror God's own seeking of the creation and of the creature turned away from the divine voice."[23]

The consequence of this is not necessarily that a new approach to the theology of religions and interreligious relationship needs to be designed. Indeed, certain already-existing approaches are obvious candidates for being commended and extended. Take Scriptural Reasoning, as an example. It envisions religious communities as houses and of interfaith encounters taking place in what Ochs and Ben Quash describe as a tent of meeting, "like Abraham's or Moses', but built of scriptural images rather than skins or cloth . . . a tent of imagination, that is, but a real tent nonetheless" wherein we invite others to deepen or enrich "one's identity in relation to one's own tradition, through the agency of a voice from outside" it.[24] Explicitly theological interfaith encounter, centered around reading scriptures of different traditions and a refusal to set aside the plain sense of scripture or to frame it in opposition to its *ongoing* significance in a constantly changing world, what Quash calls "the deep sense," is in many ways precisely the sort of stance that comes from taking the approach to Christian faith recommended by Frei and Jennings.

Indeed, as Frei presents it, the search for God's presence in the world is not primarily a matter for philosophy but for hermeneutics. Importantly, for Frei, affirming God's omnipresence need not come at the cost of historical particularity. For Frei believes that a historical realism emerging from faith in Jesus' resurrection need not subvert the search for Christ's presence in the world outside scripture and the church. To the contrary, faith in the resurrected life of the particular person Jesus is also a faith that implies Jesus' universal, if mysterious, presence. In other words, a nonmythological interpretation of the resurrection accounts in the Gospels does not limit God's presence within the confines of the Christian

---

[23]   Jennings, *Christian Imagination*, 291.

[24]   Daniel W. Hardy, Peter Ochs, and David F. Ford, "The Tent of Meeting" (unpublished paper, 2003), cited in Ben Quash, "Deep Calls to Deep: The Practice of Scriptural Reasoning," *Cambridge Inter-Faith Programme*, University of Cambridge, accessed May 10, 2021, https://www.interfaith.cam.ac.uk/resources/scripturalreasoningresources/deepcallstodeep.

tradition and community, it simply binds the search for Christ's universal presence to the description of his identity narrated in the Gospels. The relationship between Christ's identity and presence is addressed in the *analogia fidei*, affirming present experience and the world of history and sensation as a potential source of knowledge about God, while maintaining the ineradicable particularity of every historical occurrence and cautioning that any analogical discernment of Jesus' own unsubstitutable identity in other similarly particular events and persons is always accrued in a context of mystery, a result of the fundamental disparity between God and humanity:

> The past cannot be an absolute clue to the future, if the future is a genuinely open one. Not even the event of Jesus Christ can be such an absolute clue. The providential action of God over and in his creation is not that of a mechanical fate to be read off of one occasion. God's work is mysteriously, abidingly mysteriously, coexistent with the contingency of events. The history of his providence is one that must be narrated. There is no scientific rule to describe it . . . That is why Christians, precisely because they believe in providence, *know far less than certain ideological groups about the shape of the future* . . .[25]

Frei's theology, and his theological typology, show *the theology of religions discourse shaped by Race's typology itself to be a myth*: a now-traditional story, created to make sense of a phenomenon that is not easily explained, and advancing an explanation that carries an intuitive force which trumps alternative narratives that admit additional complexity. The real story, Frei suggests, is that the answers offered in determining the relationship between the particularity of Jesus Christ's identity and the universality of God's presence emerge from antecedent views of the relationship between *Glaube* and *Wissenschaft*. Until this is acknowledged, the Christian theology of religions will, ironically, serve only to demarcate different kinds of Christian theology itself. Only when Christian theology attends to the more fundamental question of its own distinct responsibilities to the competing authorities of faith and philosophy is it able to take seriously both the distinctness of Christian faith and other discourses *and* the possibility, held in hope, that this irreducible particularity is providentially ordered, and to a limited extent, figurally discernible, toward "a summing up of the history of the church together with the world . . . in which not only the events we find significant . . . but *all* events will find

[25]   Frei, *Identity of Jesus Christ*, 193.

their place . . . a summing up of the story of humanity within the vast world of nature. This is the Christian's hope in the future mode of the presence of Jesus Christ, of which the interaction of life in the church and the world is for him a token and a pledge."[26]

But for the theology of religions to truly take this hope to heart, it must take Jennings' call to consider the centrality of supersessionism in the attenuation of Christian theo-social imagination, which both affirms and extends Frei's, as well as critically recasting his concern with the Enlightenment. It must interest itself not simply in encounters limited to the explicitly scriptural or theological. Rather, the theology of religions has what might be called an "existential" horizon of concern, holding out hope for encounters with the risen Jesus in the everyday *lives* of non-Christians and the contexts (ecological, political, theological, etc.) in which these lives take shape. Again, this is undoubtedly implied in Frei's account of figural interpretation. But Jennings' insight that the problem plaguing Christianity in its encounters with *the other*—including but not limited to the religious other—has been the failure to embrace Jesus' belonging to the people of Israel and the God that calls them into this community as an intrinsic feature of his identity (and, therein, of his universal significance), and Jennings' emphasis on our reciprocal status as those outside of this intimacy yet who are invited to participate in it, frames the stakes of our encounters with non-Christians in ways that significantly sharpen and logically extend Frei's figural vision. Indeed, the fact that Jennings elaborates his argument as part of a theological genealogy of race, and that his argument there sheds so much light on the theology of religions, seems to suggest the questions of religious pluralism and race have more to do with one another than it might at first seem.

Reorienting the theology of religions discourse under this vision of Christian faith and theology is risky, rendering our encounters across lines of difference vulnerable to real disagreements, theological and otherwise. But if, as Jennings suggests, they are "the real risks of faith" in Jesus, risks "found only in the space of possible joining, and a destiny marked by love," then to avoid them is to evade them is to evade Jesus and his invitation to a new life together.[27] There is much we do not know about the shape of this new life together, and much we might believe wrongly and need to reconsider in light of new encounters, but this is as it must be if our life together is to be genuinely new.

---

[26]   Frei, *Identity of Jesus Christ*, 193.
[27]   Jennings, *Christian Imagination*, 286, 294.

Bibliography

Almond, Philip C. "W.C. Smith as Theologian of Religions." *Harvard Theological Review* 76, no. 3 (1983): 335–44.

Alston, William. *Perceiving God.* Ithaca, N.Y.: Cornell University Press, 1991.

Anderson, Gerald H. "American Protestants in Pursuit of Mission: 1886–1986." *International Bulletin of Missionary Research* 12, no. 3 (1988): 98–118.

Auerbach, Erich. "Figura." In *Scenes from the Drama of European Literature*, edited by Wlad Godzich and Jochen Schulte-Sasse, translated by Ralph Manheim, 11–78. Theory and History of Literature 9. Manchester: Manchester University Press, 1984.

———. *Mimesis: The Representation of Reality in Western Literature.* Translated by Willard R. Trask. Princeton, N.J.: Princeton University Press, 2013.

Badham, Paul. "John Hick's *An Interpretation of Religion.*" In *Problems in the Philosophy of Religion*, edited by Harold Hewitt Jr., 86–107. London: Macmillan, 1991.

Barth, Karl. *Church Dogmatics.* Vol. 1, *The Doctrine of the Word of God.* Part 1. Translated by G. T. Thomson. Edinburgh: T&T Clark, 1936.

———. *Church Dogmatics.* Vol. 2, *The Doctrine of God.* Part 2. Translated by G. W. Bromiley et al. Edinburgh: T&T Clark, 1957.

———. *Church Dogmatics.* Vol. 4, *The Doctrine of Reconciliation.* Part 1. Translated by G. W. Bromiley et al. Edinburgh: T&T Clark, 1956.

———. *The Epistle to the Romans.* Translated by E. C. Hoskyens. Oxford: Oxford University Press, 1968.

———. *Anselm: Fides Quaerens Intellectum.* Eugene, Ore.: Pickwick, 1960.

Bassham, Rodger C. *Mission Theology 1948–1975: Years of Worldwide Creative Tension.* Eugene, Ore.: Wipf & Stock, 2002.

———. "Seeking a Deeper Theological Basis for Mission." *International Review of Mission* 67, no. 267 (1978): 329–37.

Basso, Keith. *Wisdom Sits in Places: Landscape and Language among the Western Apache*. Albuquerque: University of New Mexico Press, 1996.

Berthrong, John, and Francis X. Clooney. Editors' Introduction to "European Perspectives on the New Comparative Theology." Edited by John Berthrong and Francis X. Clooney. *Religions* 3, no. 4 (2012): 1195–97.

Blocher, Henri. "Biblical Narrative and Historical Reference." In *Issues in Faith and History: Papers Presented at the Second Edinburgh Conference on Dogmatics*, edited by Nigel M. de S. Cameron, 102–22. Edinburgh: Rutherford House, 1989.

Bosch, David. *Transforming Mission: Paradigm Shifts in Theology of Mission*. Maryknoll, N.Y.: Orbis, 2011.

———. *Witness to the World: The Christian Mission in Theological Perspective*. Atlanta: John Knox, 1980.

Boublik, V. *Teologia delle religioni*. Rome: Studium, 1973.

Byrne, Peter. *Prolegomena to Religious Pluralism: Reference and Realism in Religion*. New York: St. Martin's Press, 1995.

Carino, Feliciano V. "Whitby: Partnership in Obedience." *International Review of Mission* 67, no. 267 (1978): 316–28.

Chapman, Mark D. *Ernst Troeltsch and Liberal Theology*. Oxford: Oxford University Press, 2001.

Clooney, Francis X, S.J. "Reading the World in Christ." In *Christian Uniqueness Reconsidered: The Myth of a Pluralistic Theology of Religions*, edited by Gavin D'Costa, 63–80. Maryknoll, N.Y.: Orbis, 1990.

Coakley, Sarah. *Christ without Absolutes: A Study of the Christology of Ernst Troeltsch*. Oxford: Clarendon, 1988.

Cobb, John B., Jr. "Beyond 'Pluralism.'" In *Christian Uniqueness Reconsidered: The Myth of a Pluralistic Theology of Religions*, edited by Gavin D'Costa, 81–95. Maryknoll, N.Y.: Orbis, 1990.

Comstock, Gary. "Truth or Meaning: Ricoeur versus Frei on Biblical Narrative." *HTS Teologiese Studies / Theological Studies* 45, no. 4 (1989): 741–66.

Copeland, E. L. "Christian Theology and World Religions." *Review and Expositor* 94 (1997): 423–35.

Cox, James L. *A Guide to the Phenomenology of Religion*. London: T&T Clark, 2006.

Cracknell, Kenneth. *Justice, Courtesy and Love: Theologians and Missionaries Encountering World Religions, 1846–1914*. London: Epworth Press, 1995.

Cramer, David C. "John Hick." *The Internet Encyclopedia of Philosophy*, February 27, 2015. https://iep.utm.edu/hick/.

Dawes, Gregory W. *The Historical Jesus Question: The Challenge of History to Religious Authority*. Louisville, Ky.: Westminster John Knox, 2001.

D'Costa, Gavin. "Christ, the Trinity, and Religious Plurality." In *Christian Uniqueness Reconsidered: The Myth of a Pluralistic Theology of Religions*, edited by Gavin D'Costa, 16–29. Maryknoll, N.Y.: Orbis, 1990.

———. *Christianity and World Religions: Disputed Questions in the Theology of Religions*. Oxford: Wiley-Blackwell, 2009.

———. "The Impossibility of a Pluralist View of Religions." *Religious Studies* 32, no. 2 (1996): 223–32.

———. *The Meeting of Religions and the Trinity*. Edinburgh: T&T Clark, 2000.

———. "Theology of Religions." In *The Modern Theologians*, edited by David Ford, 627–48. Oxford: Wiley-Blackwell, 1998.

DeHart, Paul. *The Trial of the Witnesses*. Oxford: Wiley-Blackwell, 2006.

Devanandan, Paul David. "The Christian Attitude and Approach to Non-Christian Religions." *International Review of Mission* 151, no. 162 (1952): 177–84.

DiNoia, Joseph A. *The Diversity of Religions: A Christian Perspective*. Washington, D.C.: Catholic University of America Press, 1992.

———. "Pluralist Theology of Religions." In *Christian Uniqueness Reconsidered: The Myth of a Pluralistic Theology of Religions*, edited by Gavin D'Costa, 119–34. Maryknoll, N.Y.: Orbis, 1990.

———. "Varieties of Religious Aims: Beyond Exclusivism, Inclusivism and Pluralism." In *Theology and Dialogue*, edited by Bruce D. Marshall, 249–74. Notre Dame, Ind.: University of Notre Dame Press, 1990.

Driver, Tom F. "The Case for Pluralism." In *The Myth of Christian Uniqueness*, edited by John Hick and Paul Knitter, 203–18. Eugene, Ore.: Wipf & Stock, 1987.

Dupuis, Jacques. *Toward a Christian Theology of Religious Pluralism*. Maryknoll, N.Y.: Orbis, 1997.

Eddy, Paul R. *John Hick's Pluralist Philosophy of World Religions*. Eugene, Ore.: Wipf & Stock, 2002.

———. "Religious Pluralism and the Divine: Another Look at John Hick's Neo-Kantian Proposal." *Religious Studies* 30, no. 4 (1994): 467–78.

Engelsviken, Tormod. "*Missio Dei*: The Understanding and Misunderstanding of a Theological Concept in European Churches and Missiology." *International Review of Mission* 92, no. 367 (2003): 481–97.

Evans, C. Stephen. "Kierkegaard and Plantinga on Belief in God: Subjectivity as the Ground of Properly Basic Religious Beliefs." *Faith and Philosophy* 5, no. 1 (1988): 25–39.

Flett, John G. *The Witness of God: The Trinity, Missio Dei, Karl Barth, and the Nature of Christian Community*. Grand Rapids: Eerdmans, 2010.

Ford, David F. "On Being Theologically Hospitable to Jesus Christ: Hans Frei's Achievement." *Journal of Theological Studies* 46, no. 2 (1995): 532–46.

Ford, David F., ed. *The Modern Theologians*. 2nd ed. Oxford: Wiley-Blackwell, 1998.

Frei, Hans. "David Friedrich Strauss." In vol. 1 of *Nineteenth Century Religious Thought in the West*, edited by Ninian Smart et al. Cambridge: Cambridge University Press, 1985.

———. "The Doctrine of Revelation in the Thought of Karl Barth, 1909–1922: The Nature of Barth's Break with Liberalism." Ph.D. diss., Yale University, 1956.

———. *The Eclipse of Biblical Narrative: A Study in Eighteenth and Nineteenth Century Hermeneutics*. New Haven, Conn.: Yale University Press, 1974.

———. "Epilogue: George Lindbeck and *The Nature of Doctrine*." In *Theology and Dialogue*, edited by Bruce D. Marshall, 276–82. Notre Dame, Ind.: University of Notre Dame Press, 1990.

———. *The Identity of Jesus Christ*. Eugene, Ore.: Wipf & Stock, 1997.

———. "Niebuhr's Theological Background." In *Faith and Ethics: The Theology of H. Richard Niebuhr*, edited by Paul Ramsey, 9–64. New York: Harper & Row, 1957.

———. *Reading Faithfully: Writings from the Archives*. Edited by Mike Higton and Mark Alan Bowald. 2 vols. Eugene, Ore.: Cascade Books, 2015.

———. "Religion (Natural and Revealed)." In *A Handbook of Christian Theology: Essential Information for Every Christian*, edited by Marvin Halverson and Arthur Cohen, 313–23. London: Fontana Books, 1962.

———. *Theology and Narrative: Selected Essays*. Edited by George Hunsinger and William C. Placher. Oxford: Oxford University Press, 1993.

———. "The Theology of H. Richard Niebuhr." In *Faith and Ethics: The Theology of H. Richard Niebuhr*, edited by Paul Ramsey, 65–116. New York: Harper & Row, 1957.

———. *Types of Christian Theology*. Edited by George Hunsinger and William C. Placher. New Haven, Conn.: Yale University Press, 1992.

Gairdner, William H. Temple. *The Reproach of Islam*. London: CMS, 1909.

Gillis, Chester. *A Question of Final Belief: John Hick's Pluralistic Theory of Salvation*. New York: St. Martin's Press, 1989.

Gort, Jerald D. "Jerusalem 1928: Mission, Kingdom and Church." *International Review of Mission* 67, no. 267 (1978): 273–98.

Grebe, Matthias. *Election, Atonement, and the Holy Spirit*. Cambridge: James Clarke, 2015.

Griffin, David Ray. "John Cobb's Whiteheadian Complementary Pluralism." In *Deep Religious Pluralism*, edited by David Ray Griffin, 39–66. Louisville, Ky.: Westminster John Knox, 2005.

Hallencreutz, Carl F. *Kraemer towards Tambaram: A Study in Hendrik Kraemer's Missionary Approach*. Lund: Gleerup, 1966.

————. "A Long-Standing Concern: Dialogue in Ecumenical History 1910–1971." In *Living Faiths and the Ecumenical Movement*, edited by S. J. Samartha, 57–71. Geneva: World Council of Churches, 1971.

Hancock, Angela Dienhart. *Karl Barth's Emergency Homiletic, 1932–1933: A Summons to Prophetic Witness at the Dawn of the Third Reich*. Grand Rapids: Eerdmans, 2013.

Hebblethwaite, Brian. Review of *Christians and Religious Pluralism: Patterns in the Christian Theology of Religions* by Alan Race. *Religious Studies* 20, no. 3 (1984): 515–16.

Hedges, Paul. "The Inter-relationship of Religions: A Critical Examination of the Concept of Particularity." *World Faiths Encounter* 32 (2002): 3–13.

————. "Particularities: Tradition-Specific Post-modern Perspectives." In *Christian Approaches to Other Faiths*, edited by Alan Race and Paul M. Hedges, 112–35. London: SCM Press, 2008.

————. "A Reflection on Typologies." In *Christian Approaches to Other Faiths*, edited by Alan Race and Paul M. Hedges, 17–33. London: SCM Press, 2008.

Heim, S. Mark. *The Depth of Riches: A Trinitarian Theology of Religious Ends*. Grand Rapids: Eerdmans, 2001.

————. *Salvations: Truth and Difference in Religion*. Maryknoll, N.Y.: Orbis, 1995.

Henry, Carl. "Narrative Theology: An Evangelical Appraisal." *Trinity Journal* 8, no. 1 (1987): 3–19.

Hick, John. *Arguments for the Existence of God*. London: Macmillan, 1970.

————. *An Autobiography*. Oxford: Oneworld, 2005.

————. "The Buddha's Doctrine of the 'Undetermined Questions.'" In *Disputed Questions in Theology and the Philosophy of Religion*, 105–18. Basingstoke, UK: Macmillan, 1997.

————. *Death and Eternal Life*. Louisville, Ky.: Westminster John Knox, 1994.

————. *Faith and Knowledge*. London: Macmillan, 1967.

————. *The Fifth Dimension*. Oxford: Oneworld, 2004.

————. *God Has Many Names*. Philadelphia: Westminster, 1982.

————. *An Interpretation of Religion: Human Responses to the Transcendent*. 2nd ed. New Haven, Conn.: Yale University Press, 2004.

————. "Jesus and the World Religions." In *The Myth of God Incarnate*, edited by John Hick, 167–85. London: SCM Press, 1977.

————. *The New Frontier of Religion and Science*. Basingstoke, UK: Palgrave Macmillan, 2010.

————. "The Next Step beyond Dialogue." In *The Myth of Religious Superiority*, edited by Paul Knitter, 3–12. Maryknoll, N.Y.: Orbis, 2005.

————. "The Non-absoluteness of Christianity." In *The Myth of Christian Uniqueness*, edited by John Hick and Paul Knitter, 16–36. Eugene, Ore.: Wipf & Stock, 1987.

———. "On Wilfred Cantwell Smith—His Place in the Study of Religion." *Method and Theory in the Study of Religion* 4, nos. 1–2 (1992): 5–20.

———. "The Outcome: Dialogue into Truth." In *Truth and Dialogue: The Relationship between Christianity and World Religions*, 140–55. London: Sheldon, 1974.

———. "Reincarnation and the Meaning of Life." Speech given to the Open End, Birmingham, UK, December 2002. http://www.johnhick.org.uk/article7.html.

Higton, Mike. *Christ, Providence and History: Hans Frei's Public Theology.* London: T&T Clark International, 2004.

———. "Frei's Christology and Lindbeck's Cultural-Linguistic Theory." *Scottish Journal of Theology* 50, no. 1 (1997): 83–95.

———. "Hans Frei and David Tracy on the Ordinary and Extraordinary in Christianity." *Journal of Religion* 79, no. 4 (1999): 566–91.

Hocking, William Ernest. *Re-thinking Missions: A Laymen's Inquiry after One Hundred Years.* New York: Harper & Brothers, 1932.

Hoekendijk, Johannes. "The Call to Evangelism." *International Review of Mission* 39, no. 154 (1950): 162–75.

———. "The Church in Missionary Thinking." *International Review of Mission* 41, no. 2 (1952): 324–36.

Hogg, William Richey. *Ecumenical Foundations: A History of the International Missionary Council and Its Nineteenth Century Background.* New York: Harper, 1952.

Hunsinger, George. "Afterword: Hans Frei as Theologian." In *Theology and Narrative: Selected Essays* by Hans Frei, edited by George Hunsinger and William C. Placher, 223–70. Oxford: Oxford University Press, 1993.

Hunsinger, George, and William Placher. Introduction to *Types of Christian Theology* by Hans Frei, edited by George Hunsinger and William C. Placher, ix–xi. New Haven, Conn.: Yale University Press, 1992.

Hurley, Robert J. *Hermeneutics and Catechesis: Biblical Interpretation in the Come to the Father Catechetical Series.* Lanham, Md.: University Press of America, 1997.

Hutchinson, P. "Jerusalem 1928." *Christian Century*, December 6, 1928, 1490–91.

Insole, Christopher J. *The Realist Hope.* New York: Routledge, 2016.

International Missionary Council.
  Edinburgh 1910
      Report of Commission IV: The Missionary Message in Relation to Non-Christian Religions. Edinburgh: Oliphant, Anderson & Ferrier, 1910.
  Jerusalem 1928
      The Jerusalem Meeting of the IMC. Printed statement. February 1927. WCC archives.

Report of the Jerusalem Meeting of the International Missionary Council, March 24–April 8, 1928. Vol. 1, *The Christian Life and Message in Relation to Non-Christian Systems of Thought and Life.* London: IMC, 1928.

Tambaram 1938
The Tambaram Series: The Authority of the Faith. Vol 1. Edited by William Patton. London: Oxford University Press, 1939.

Whitby 1947
Renewal and Advance: Christian Witness in a Revolutionary World. Edited by C. W. Ranson. London: Edinburgh House Press, 1948.

Willingen 1952
Goodall, Norman, ed. *Missions under the Cross.* London: Edinburgh House Press, 1953.

Jathanna, Origen Vasantha. *The Decisiveness of the Christ Event and the Universality of Christianity in a World of Religious Plurality.* Berne: Peter Lang, 1981.

Jennings, Willie James. *After Whiteness: An Education in Belonging.* Grand Rapids: Eerdmans, 2020.

———. *The Christian Imagination: Theology and the Origins of Race.* New Haven, Conn.: Yale University Press, 2010.

Johnson, John J. "Hans Frei as Unlikely Apologist for the Historicity of the Resurrection." *Evangelical Quarterly* 76, no. 2 (2004): 135–51.

Kärkkäinen, Veli-Matti. *A Constructive Christian Theology for the Pluralistic World.* Vol. 1. *Christ and Reconciliation.* Grand Rapids: Eerdmans, 2013.

———. *A Constructive Christian Theology for the Pluralistic World.* Vol. 2. *Trinity and Revelation.* Grand Rapids: Eerdmans, 2013.

———. *An Introduction to the Theology of Religions: Biblical, Historical, and Contemporary Perspectives.* Downers Grove, Ill.: IVP, 2003.

———. *The Trinity: Global Perspectives.* Louisville, Ky.: Westminster John Knox, 2007.

Kelsey, David. *Eccentric Existence: A Theological Anthropology.* Louisville, Ky.: Westminster John Knox, 2009.

Keum, Jooseop, ed. *Together towards Life: Mission and Evangelism in Changing Landscapes.* Geneva: WCC Publications, 2013.

Knitter, Paul. "Comparative Theology Is Not 'Business-as-Usual Theology': Personal Witness from a Buddhist Christian." *Buddhist-Christian Studies* 35 (2015): 181–92.

———. *Introducing Theologies of Religions.* Maryknoll, N.Y.: Orbis, 2002.

———. *No Other Name? A Critical Survey of Christian Attitudes toward the World Religions.* London: SCM Press, 1977.

———. *One Earth, Many Religions.* Maryknoll, N.Y.: Orbis, 1995.

———. Preface to *The Myth of Christian Uniqueness,* edited by John Hick and Paul Knitter, vii–xii. Eugene, Ore.: Wipf & Stock, 1987.

Kraemer, Hendrik. *The Christian Message in a Non-Christian World*. London: Edinburgh House Press, 1938.

Kwan, Kai-man. "Is the Critical Trust Approach to Religion Incompatible with Religious Particularism? A Reply to Michael Martin and John Hick." *Faith and Philosophy* 20, no. 2 (2003): 152–69.

Laing, Mark T. B. *From Crisis to Creation: Lesslie Newbigin and the Reinvention of Christian Mission*. Eugene, Ore.: Pickwick, 2012.

Latourette, Kenneth Scott. "Ecumenical Bearings of the Missionary Movement and the International Missionary Council." In *A History of the Ecumenical Movement, 1517–1948*, edited by Ruth Rouse and Stephen C. Neill, 4th ed., vol. 1, 351–402. Geneva: World Council of Churches, 1993.

———. "The Laymen's Foreign Missions Inquiry: The Report of Its Commission of Appraisal." *International Review of Mission* 22, no. 2 (1933): 153–73.

———. "Re-thinking Missions after Twenty-Five Years." *International Review of Mission* 46, no. 182 (1957): 164–70.

Latourette, Kenneth Scott, and William Richey Hogg. *Tomorrow Is Here: The Mission and Work of the Church as Seen from the Meeting of the International Missionary Council at Whitby, Ontario, July 5–24, 1947*. New York: Friendship Press, 1948.

Lehmann, Paul. "Willingen and Lund: The Church on the Way to Unity." *Theology Today* 9, no. 4 (1953): 431–41.

Lessing, Gotthold Ephraim. *Lessing: Philosophical and Theological Writings*. Edited and translated by H. B. Nisbet. Cambridge: Cambridge University Press, 2005.

Lindsell, Harold, ed. *The Church's Worldwide Mission: Proceedings of the Congress on the Church's Worldwide Mission, 9–16 April 1966 at Wheaton College, Wheaton, Illinois*. Waco, Tex.: Word, 1966.

Livingston, James C. "Religious Pluralism and the Question of Religious Truth in Wilfred C. Smith." *Journal of Religious and Cultural Theory* 4, no. 3 (2003): 58–65.

Mackay, John A. "The Theology of the Laymen's Foreign Missions Inquiry." *International Review of Mission* 22, no. 2 (1933): 174–88.

Markham, Ian. "Creating Options: Shattering the 'Exclusivist, Inclusivist, and Pluralist' Paradigm." *New Blackfriars* 74, no. 867 (1993): 33–41.

Martin, Calvin Luther. *The Way of the Human Being*. New Haven, Conn.: Yale University Press, 1999.

Martinson, Paul Varo. *A Theology of World Religions: Interpreting God, Self, and World in Semitic, Indian and Chinese Thought*. Minneapolis: Augsburg, 1987.

Masci, David. "Christianity Poised to Continue Its Shift from Europe to Africa." Pew Research Center, April 7, 2015. https://www.pewresearch.org/

fact-tank/2015/04/07/christianity-is-poised-to-continue-its-southward -march/.

Matthey, Jacques "God's Mission Today: Summary and Conclusions." *International Review of Mission* 92, no. 367 (2003): 579–87.

McCormack, Bruce. *Orthodox and Modern: Studies in the Theology of Karl Barth.* Grand Rapids: Baker Academic, 2008.

McDermott, Gerald R., and Harold A. Netland. *A Trinitarian Theology of Religions: An Evangelical Proposal.* Oxford: Oxford University Press, 2014.

Moyaert, Marianne. "Recent Developments in the Theology of Interreligious Dialogue: From Soteriological Openness to Hermeneutical Openness." *Modern Theology* 28, no. 1 (2012): 25–52.

Muck, Terry C. "Instrumentality, Complexity, and Reason: A Christian Approach to Religions." *Buddhist-Christian Studies* 22 (2002): 115–21.

———. "Theology of Religions after Knitter and Hick: Beyond the Paradigm." *Interpretation* 61, no. 1 (2001): 7–22.

Nah, David S. *Christian Theology and Religious Pluralism: A Critical Evaluation of John Hick.* Cambridge: James Clarke, 2013.

Neill, Stephen C. *The Unfinished Task.* London: Edinburgh House, 1957.

Netland, Harold. *Dissonant Voices.* Vancouver: Regent, 1991.

———. *Encountering Religious Pluralism: The Challenge to Christian Faith and Mission.* Downers Grove, Ill.: IVP, 2001.

Newbigin, Lesslie. *The Gospel in a Pluralist Society.* Grand Rapids: Eerdmans, 1989.

———. *Proper Confidence.* Grand Rapids: Eerdmans, 1995.

———. Review of *The Meaning and End of Religion* by W. C. Smith. *Theology* 82, no. 688 (1979): 294–96.

———. *Unfinished Agenda.* Edinburgh: St Andrew Press, 1993.

Niebuhr, H. Richard. "Types of Christian Ethics." In *Authentic Transformation: A New Vision of Christ and Culture,* edited by Glen H. Stassen, D. M. Yeager, and John Howard Yoder, 15–29. Nashville: Abingdon, 1996.

Nottingham, William J. Review of *Toward a Christian Theology of Religious Pluralism* by Jacques Dupuis. *International Review of Mission* 90, nos. 356–57 (2001): 197–98.

Ochs, Peter. *Another Reformation: Postliberal Christianity and the Jews.* Grand Rapids: Baker Academic, 2011.

Ogden, Schubert M. *Is There Only One True Religion or Are There Many?* Dallas: Southern Methodist University Press, 1992.

Pachuau, Lalsangkima. "Missiology in a Pluralistic World: The Place of Mission Study in Theological Education." *International Review of Mission* 89, no. 355 (2000): 539–55.

Panikkar, Raimondo. "The Jordan, the Tiber, and the Ganges." In *The Myth of Christian Uniqueness*, edited by John Hick and Paul Knitter, 89–116. Eugene, Ore.: Wipf & Stock, 1987.

Pecknold, C. C. *Transforming Postliberal Theology: George Lindbeck, Pragmatism and Scripture*. London: T&T Clark, 2005.

Perry, Tim S. *Radical Difference*. Waterloo, Ont.: Wilfrid Laurier University Press, 2001.

Peters, Ted. *God—The World's Future: Systematic Theology for a Postmodern Era*. Minneapolis: Fortress, 1992.

Phillips, D. Z. *Faith and Philosophical Enquiry*. New York: Schocken Books, 1979.

Pitman, David. *Twentieth Century Christian Responses to Religious Pluralism*. Farnham, UK: Ashgate, 2014.

Placher, William C. Introduction to *Theology and Narrative: Selected Essays* by Hans Frei, edited by George Hunsinger and William C. Placher, 3–25. Oxford: Oxford University Press, 1993.

———. *Narratives of a Vulnerable God: Christ, Theology, and Scripture*. Louisville, Ky.: Westminster John Knox, 1994.

———. Review of *The Trial of the Witnesses: The Rise and Fall of Postliberal Theology* by Paul DeHart. *Conversations in Religion and Theology* 5, no. 2 (2007): 136–45.

Plantinga, Alvin. "Pluralism: A Defense of Religious Exclusivism." In *The Rationality of Belief and the Plurality of Faith*, edited by Thomas D. Senor, 191–215. Ithaca, N.Y.: Cornell University Press, 1995.

———. "Reason and Belief in God." In *Faith and Rationality*, edited by Alvin Plantinga and Nicholas Wolterstorff, 16–93. South Bend, Ind.: University of Notre Dame Press, 1983.

———. *Warranted Christian Belief*. New York: Oxford University Press, 2000.

Quash, Ben. "Deep Calls to Deep: The Practice of Scriptural Reasoning." *Cambridge Inter-Faith Programme*, University of Cambridge. Accessed May 10, 2021. https://www.interfaith.cam.ac.uk/resources/scripturalreasoningresources/deepcallstodeep.

Quinn, Frederick. "Toward 'Generous Love': Recent Anglican Approaches to World Religions." *Journal of Anglican Studies* 10, no. 2 (2012): 161–82.

Quinn, Philip L. "Towards Thinner Theologies: Hick and Alston on Religious Diversity." *International Journal for Philosophy of Religion* 38, no. 1 (1995): 145–64.

Race, Alan. *Christians and Religious Pluralism: Patterns in the Christian Theology of Religions*. London: SCM Press, 1993.

———. *Interfaith Encounter: The Twin Tracks of Theology and Dialogue*. London: SCM Press, 2001.

———. *Making Sense of Religious Pluralism: Shaping Theology of Religions for Our Times.* London: SPCK, 2013.

———. "An Original Mind in Religious History." *Times Literary Supplement* 4707 (1993): 31.

———. "Theology of Religions in Change." In *Christian Approaches to Other Faiths*, edited by Alan Race and Paul M. Hedges, 4–16. London: SCM Press, 2008.

Raiser, Konrad. *Ecumenism in Transition: A Paradigm Shift in the Ecumenical Movement?* Geneva: WCC, 1991.

Ramachandra, Vinoth. "Response 3." In *A Trinitarian Theology of Religions*, edited by Gerald R. McDermott and Harold A. Netland, 305–12. Oxford: Oxford University Press, 2014.

Ratzinger, Joseph. "Relativism: The Central Problem for Faith Today." *Origins* 26 (1996): 309–17.

Richards, Glyn. Review of *Towards a World Theology* by Wilfred Cantwell Smith. *Religious Studies* 18, no. 4 (1982): 515–18.

Rosin, H. H. *Missio Dei: An Examination of the Origin, Contents and Function of the Term in Protestant Missiological Discussion.* Leiden: Inter-University Institute for Missiological and Ecumenical Research, 1972.

Ryle, Gilbert. *The Concept of Mind.* Whitefish, Mont.: Kessinger Legacy Reprints, 2010.

Samartha, Stanley J. "The Cross and the Rainbow." In *The Myth of Christian Uniqueness*, edited by John Hick and Paul Knitter, 69–88. Eugene, Ore.: Wipf & Stock, 1987.

———. "Mission in a Religiously Plural World: Looking beyond Tambaram 1938." *International Review of Mission* 77, no. 306 (1988): 311–24.

———. *One Christ—Many Religions.* Maryknoll, N.Y.: Orbis, 1991.

Schleiermacher, Friedrich. *The Christian Faith.* Translated by H. R. Mackintosh and J. S. Stewart. London: T&T Clark, 1999.

Schmidt-Leukal, Perry. "Exclusivism, Inclusivism, Pluralism." In *The Myth of Religious Superiority*, edited by Paul F. Knitter, 13–27. Maryknoll, N.Y.: Orbis, 2003.

Schoonhoven, Evert Jansen. "Tambaram 1938." *International Review of Mission* 67, no. 267 (1978): 299–315.

Schüssler Fiorenza, Francis. "Religion—A Contested Site in Theology and the Study of Religion." *Harvard Theological Review* 93, no. 1 (2000): 7–34.

Schwöbel, Christoph. "Particularity, Universality, and the Religions." In *Christian Uniqueness Reconsidered: The Myth of a Pluralistic Theology of Religions*, edited by Gavin D'Costa, 30–46. Maryknoll, N.Y.: Orbis, 1990.

Sheppard, G. W. *Comments upon the Jerusalem Conference, Topic I. The Christian Life and Message in Relation to Non-Christian Systems.* WCC Archives.

Smart, Ninian. "W.C. Smith and Complementarity." *Method and Theory in the Study of Religion* 4, nos. 1–2 (1992): 21–26.

Smith, Eugene L. "The Wheaton Congress in the Eyes of an Ecumenical Observer." *International Review of Mission* 55, no. 220 (1966): 480–82.

Smith, Wilfred Cantwell. *Belief and History*. Charlottesville: University of Virginia Press, 1977.

———. "Comparative Religion: Whither—and Why?" In *The History of Religions: Essays in Methodology*, edited by Mircea Eliade and Joseph M. Kitagawa, 31–58. Chicago: University of Chicago Press, 1959.

———. *Faith and Belief*. Princeton, N.J.: Princeton University Press, 1979.

———. *The Faith of Other Men*. New York: Harper Torchbooks, 1972.

———. "Idolatry: In Comparative Perspective." In *The Myth of Christian Uniqueness*, edited by John Hick and Paul Knitter, 53–68. Eugene, Ore.: Wipf & Stock, 1987.

———. *Islam in Modern History: The Tension between Faith and History in the Islamic World*. Princeton, N.J.: Princeton University Press, 1957.

———. *The Meaning and End of Religion*. Minneapolis: Fortress, 1991.

———. *Modern Islam in India: A Social Analysis*. Lahore: Minerva, 1946.

———. *Questions of Religious Truth*. New York: Charles Scribner's Sons, 1967.

———. *Towards a World Theology*. Basingstoke, UK: Macmillan, 1981.

———. *What Is Scripture?* Minneapolis: Fortress, 1994.

Sockness, Brent W. *Against False Apologetics: Wilhelm Herrmann and Ernst Troeltsch in Conflict*. Tübingen: Mohr Siebeck, 1998.

Sperber, Jutta. *Christians and Muslims: The Dialogue Activities of the World Council of Churches*. Berlin: de Gruyter, 1996.

Springs, Jason. *Toward a Generous Orthodoxy: Prospects for Hans Frei's Postliberal Theology*. Oxford: Oxford University Press, 2010.

Stanley, Brian. "Edinburgh 1910 and the Genesis of the *IRM*." *International Review of Mission* 100, no. 2 (2011): 149–59.

———. *The World Missionary Conference, Edinburgh 1910*. Grand Rapids: Eerdmans, 2009.

Stott, John. *Christian Mission in the Modern World*. Downers Grove, Ill.: IVP, 2008.

Strauss, David Friedrich. *The Christ of Faith and the Jesus of History*. Translated by Leander E. Keck. Philadelphia: Fortress, 1977.

———. *The Life of Jesus, Critically Examined*. Translated by George Eliot. London: Continuum International, 2005.

Surin, Kenneth. "'A Politics of Speech: Religious Pluralism in the Age of the McDonald's Hamburger." In *Christian Uniqueness Reconsidered: The Myth of a Pluralistic Theology of Religions*, edited by Gavin D'Costa, 192–212. Maryknoll, N.Y.: Orbis, 1990.

Swearer, Donald K. "The Moral Imagination of Wilfred Cantwell Smith: Religious Truth Lies Not in Systems but in Persons." *Harvard Divinity Bulletin* 39, nos. 1–2 (2011). https://bulletin-archive.hds.harvard.edu/articles/winterspring2011/moral-imagination-wilfred-cantwell-smith.

Swinburne, Richard. *Faith and Reason.* New York: Oxford University Press, 1984.

"Theology of Religions." In *The Concise Oxford Dictionary of the Christian Church*, 3rd ed., edited by E. A. Livingstone et al., 559–60. Oxford: Oxford University Press, 2014.

Thomas, Owen. "Religious Plurality and Contemporary Philosophy: A Critical Survey." *Harvard Theological Review* 87, no. 2 (1994): 197–213.

Thomas, Owen C., ed. *Attitudes toward Other Religions: Some Christian Interpretations.* London: SCM Press, 1969.

Tracy, David. *Blessed Rage for Order.* New York: Seabury, 1976.

Troeltsch, Ernst. *The Absoluteness of Christianity and the History of Religions.* Richmond, Va.: John Knox, 1971.

———. "Empiricism and Platonism in the Philosophy of Religion—to the Memory of William James." *Harvard Theological Review* 5 (1912): 401–22.

———. *Religion in History.* Edited and translated by James Luther Adams and Walter F. Bense. Edinburgh: T&T Clark, 1991.

———. *Writings on Theology and Religion.* Edited and translated by Robert Morgan and Michael Pye. London: Duckworth, 1977.

Vanhoozer, Kevin. *The Drama of Doctrine.* Louisville, Ky.: Westminster John Knox, 2005.

Van Lin, Jan. *Shaking the Fundamentals: Religious Plurality and the Ecumenical Movement.* Amsterdam: Rodopi, 2002.

Veitch, J. A. "The Case for a Theology of Religions." *Scottish Journal of Theology* 24, no. 4 (1971): 407–22.

Vicedom, Georg F. *The Mission of God: An Introduction to a Theology of Mission.* St. Louis, Mo.: Concordia, 1965.

Wainwright, Geoffrey. *Lesslie Newbigin: A Theological Life.* Oxford: Oxford University Press, 2000.

Wainwright, William J. "Wilfred Cantwell Smith on Faith and Belief." *Religious Studies* 20, no. 3 (1984): 353–66.

"Wheaton Declaration." *International Review of Mission* 55, no. 220 (1966): 458–76.

Wiebe, Donald. "On the Transformation of 'Belief' and the Domestication of 'Faith' in the Academic Study of Religion." *Method and Theory in the Study of Religion* 4, nos. 1–2 (1992): 47–67.

Wolterstorff, Nicholas. "Is It Possible and Desirable for Theologians to Recover from Kant?" *Modern Theology* 14, no. 1 (1998): 1–18.

———. "Will Narrativity Work as Linchpin? Reflections on the Hermeneutic of Hans Frei." In *Relativism and Religion*, edited by Charles M. Lewis, 71–107. London: Palgrave Macmillan, 1995.

World Council of Churches:

Amsterdam Assembly 1948

Visser t' Hooft, W. A. ed. *Man's Disorder and God's Design: The Christian Witness of God's Design*. Vol. 2. London: SCM Press, 1948.

Kandy Consultation 1967

"Christians in Dialogue with Men of Other Faiths." *International Review of Mission* 56, no. 223 (1967): 338–43.

Western European and North American Working Group of the Department on Studies in Evangelism 1967

The Church for Others and the Church for the World: A Quest for Structures for Missionary Congregations. Final Report of the Western European Working Group and North American Working Group of the Department on Studies in Evangelism. Geneva: WCC, 1967.

Uppsala Assembly 1968

Uppsala Report 1968: Official Report of the Fourth Assembly of the World Council of Churches, Uppsala, July 4–20, 1968. Edited by Norman Goodall. Geneva: WCC, 1968.

Bangkok Assembly 1973

Bangkok Assembly, 1973: Minutes and Report of the Assembly of the Commission on World Mission and Evangelism of the World Council of Churches, December 31, 1972 and January 9–12, 1973. Geneva: WCC, 1973.

1980–2005

Matthey, Jacques, ed. *You Are the Light of the World: Statements on Mission by the World Council of Churches 1980–2005*. Geneva: WCC Publications, 2005.

Wright, N. T. *The Resurrection of the Son of God*. London: SPCK, 2003.

Yates, Timothy. *Christian Mission in the Twentieth Century*. Cambridge: Cambridge University Press, 1996.

Yong, Amos. "'Not Knowing Where the Wind Blows . . .': On Envisioning A Pentecostal-Charismatic Theology of Religions." *Journal of Pentecostal Theology* 14 (1999): 81–112.

Index